A Selection of African Poetry

Revised and enlarged edition

Introduced and annotated by
K. E. Senanu and T. Vincent

CW00733177

Pearson Education Limited,
Edinburgh Gate, Harlow,
Essex CM20 2JE, England
and Associated Companies throughout the
world

© Longman Group Limited 1976
This edition © Longamn Group UK
Limited 1988

First edition 1976
Revised and enlarged edition 1988
Fifteenth impression 2013

Set in Linotron Erhardt
Printed in China   EPC/15

British Library Cataloguing in Publication
Data
A selection of African poetry. – Rev. and
    enl. ed.
    1. Poetry. African writers, to 1975.
    Anthologies – For schools – English
    texts
    I. Senanu, K. E.   II. Vincent, T.
    808.81'0096

ISBN 978-0-582-01683-5

Acknowledgments

We are grateful to the following copyright holders for permission to reproduce
poems:

Authors' Agents for 'The cathedral', 'Rediscovery', 'We have found a new land',
'More messages', 'My uncle the diviner' & 'Harlem on a winter night' by Kofi
Awooner from *Kick Mem Memory* (Greenfield Press); the author, Professor
Adeboye Babalola for 'Salute to the elephant'; the author, Professor Ulli Beier
for his translation of 'Pomegranate'; the author, Kwesi Brew for 'The mesh',
'The dry season', 'The executioner's dream', 'Lest we should be the last', 'A
sandal on the head' & 'The sea eats our lands'; the author, Professor J.P. Clark
Bekederemo for 'Streamside exchange', 'Fulani cattle', 'Song', 'The casualties',
'Night rain', 'Abiku' & 'Olokun'; Andre Deutsch Ltd for 'Thought on June 26'
by Mazisi Kunene from *Zulu Poems*; Author's Agents for 'Lullaby' & 'Threnody'
by Michael Echeruo; the author, E.Y. Egblewogbe for 'The wizard's pride' &
'Coming of day' ('Diary Entries') from *The Wizard's Pride & Other Poems* (Ghana
Pubg. Corp. 1974) © E.Y. Egblewogbe; Ghana Publishing Corporation for
'Sunset sonata' & 'Elavanyo concerto' by A. Okai from *Lorgorligi Logarithms*;
Greenfield Review Press for 'Fear' & 'earth to earth' by Kalu Uka from *Earth to
Earth*; Heinemann Educational Books Ltd for 'Heaven's gate' & 'Come thunder'
by Christopher Okigbo from *Labyrinths*, 'It is time for reckoning' & 'The fence'
by Lenrie Peters from *Katchikala* & 'We have come home' by Lenrie Peters
from *Satellites*, 'A troubadour I traverse', 'This sun on this rubble', selections
from 'After exile', 'Night song city', 'A common hate' & 'It is the constant image
of your face' all by Dennis Brutus from *A Simple Lust*, 'Poem of alienation' by
Jacinto from *Poems from Angola* trans. Michael Wolfers, 'The long-distance
runner' by Kofi Anyidoho from *Harvest of our Dreams* & 'Freetown' & 'Peasants'

2

by Syl Cheney Coker from *Concerto for an Exile*; the author, J. Kariuki for 'Come away my love'; the author, Mazisi Kunene for 'In praise of the ancestors' from *The Ancestors and the Sacred Mountain* (Heinemann Edl.); the author, Taban Lo Liyong for 'With purity hath nothing been won' & 'Language is a figure of speech' from *Another Nigger Dead* (Heinemann Edl.): Methuen London for 'Abiku', 'To my first white hairs' & 'Post mortem' by Wole Soyinka from *Idandre & Other Poems* (1967); Author's Agents for sections from 'Viatcum' by U Tam'si, trans. Gerald Moore; Author's Agents for 'The meaning of Africa' by Abioseh Nicol from *The Book of African Verse* ed. Reed & Wake (Heinemann Edl.) & 'Words of wisdom and love' by Abioseh Nicol from *African Voices* (Heinemann Edl.); the author, Professor J.H. Kwabena Nketia for 'Owusu' from *Funeral Dirges of the Akan People* (1955); the author, T.C. Nwosu for 'The call', 'Combat' & 'Star dust'; the author, Gabriel Okara for 'The call of the river man', 'New Year's Eve midnight', 'The snowflakes fall gently down', 'The fisherman's invocation', 'Moon in a bucket', 'Suddenly the air cracks' & 'Piano & drums'; the author, Dr. Niyi Osundare for 'A song for Ajegunle'; Oxford University Press for 'Amagoduka at Glencoe Station', 'An abandoned bundle', 'The birth of Shaka', 'Nightfall in Soweto', 'Just a passerby', & 'If you should know me' by Mbuyiseni Oswald Mtshali from *Sounds of a Cowhide Drum* (1971), part 'The black bagre' from *Myth of the Bagre* (1972) ed. Jack Goody, 'In memorium, 'Nuit de Sine', 'I will pronounce your name' & 'Be not annoyed' by Leopold Sedar Senghor from *Selected Poems* (1964) trans. John Reed & Clive Wake, 'Death of Liyongo' from *Swahili Poetry* (1962) ed. Lyndon Harries & 'Chaka' & 'Long, long have you held' by Leopold Senghor from *Prose and Poetry* (1965) trans. John Reed and Clive Wake, © OUP 1965; the author, Dr. Lenrie Peters for 'Lost friends' from *MBARI Collection*; Presence Africaine for 'Your presence', 'Africa', 'The vultures' & 'Certitude' by David Diop from *Coups de Pilon* (Paris, 1956) & 'Vatique' ('Vaticum') & 'Vanite' ('Vanity') by Birago Diop from *Leurres et Lueurs* (Paris, 1967); the author, David Rubadiri for 'An African thunderstorm' & 'Stanley meets Metusa'; School of Oriental & African Studies for 'Sunjata' by Prof. G. Innes from *Sunjata: Three Mandinka Versions* © Prof. G. Innes; Martin Secker & Warburg Ltd for 'Evening' by Bonny Lubega from *Poems of Black Africa* ed. Wole Soyinka; Author's Agents for 'Telephone conversation', 'Night', 'I think it rains' & 'Procession I – hanging day' by Wole Soyinka; John Reed & Clive Wake for their translations of 'Forest' by Tchicaya U Tam'si from *French African Verse* (Heinemann, 1972) & 'Daybreak' from 'Three daybreaks' in J.J. Rabearivelo *Translations from the Night* ed. John Reed & Clive Wake (Heinemann Edl. 1975) and Woeli Publishing Services for 'Hero & Thief' by Kofi Anyidoho from *Earthchild*.

We have unfortunately been unable to trace the copyright holders of 'Masked' & 'No coffin, no grave' by J. Angira, 'And so it came to pass' by Funso Ayejina, 'Song of Malphi' & 'Cattle egret' by Okot p'Bitek, 'The poem of Jao' by De Sousa, 'Love poem' & 'Letter to a contract worker' by A. Jacinto, 'Our man in Broad Street' by Khona Khasu, 'Harvest moon' & 'Dimeh in transition' by Bai T. Moore, 'Night', 'African poetry' & 'Hoisting the stag' by A. Neto and 'Cactus' by S. Rabearivelo and would appreciate any information which would enable us to do so.

Contents

5

Preface to the second edition

Twelve years after the first edition of *A Selection of African Poetry*, this enlarged second edition reflects the state and development of African poetry and takes into consideration reactions to the first edition. Some poems from the first edition have been dropped but many more new poems from different parts of the continent have been included. The immediate gain is a more representative, more varied and livelier collection, which promises a more exciting time in the classroom and a more rewarding experience for the general reader. Particular highlights include the representation of Liberian and Lusophone poetry.

For too long the impression has been given that there is little or no literary activity worthy of attention happening in Liberia. Part of the reason for this is Liberia's history and what has seemed, until recently, to be Liberia's preoccupation with its American connections, a cultural state that has also influenced its literary output. However, the situation is changing fast and there are quite a few active young writers (even if the economics of publishing have prevented their being known outside their country) who take literature seriously and whose works speak of the agony of Africa and the African and show evidence of the literary renaissance that has been running its course for the past few decades in Africa. The works of Bai T. Moore and Kona Khasu (pronounced Kaisu) are featured here to give some idea of new writing from Liberia.

Following successful liberation struggles, Lusophone literature (ie literature from Portuguese-speaking Africa) has become accessible to other parts of the continent. Much of this is what is known as "literature of resistance". The poetry of such writers as Noemia de Sousa, Agostino Neto and Antonio Jacinto represent this type of poetry, narrating in graphic imagery the people's travails and the triumphs of their new selves. Their poetry represents an essential dimension of the African experience.

This edition also contains selections from Christopher Okigbo's sequences. Time has made Okigbo's poetry more accessible to many readers, his unique style is better understood and it is now realised that in spite of the seeming foreignness and the acclaimed difficulty of his poetry, he is one of the most African of African poets and no anthology of African poetry can be complete that does not include his works.

Finally, this edition contains a glossary which explains some of the terms and techniques used either in describing features that exist in these poems or terms that can be regarded as part of the standard repertoire of critical writing. The intention is that students should understand these terms in the contexts of the poems assembled here, and that they should also be able to apply them meaningfully in their appreciation of any poetry or even in their own writing.

About the anthology

This anthology attempts to give students, and the general reader interested in poetry written in Africa, some idea of the variety and quality of African poetry, through representative samples. One of the problems that face students and teachers of African poetry is the absence of an anthology that serves both as an introduction to the variety of African poetry and as a help to experiencing that poetry as an essential part of their mental, aesthetic and cultural education. We have therefore tried to put together poems from the different regions of Africa (with the exception of North Africa) and provided notes, questions and commentaries that should reward study with pleasure.

When we prepared the first edition of *A Selection of African Poetry*, more than a decade ago, we took a simple chronological approach to arranging the material. We began with a few traditional poems, followed by a selection from poets according to their age. Thus, Leopold Sedar Senghor figured as the first modern poet in the anthology, since we had decided not to include the poetry of "pioneers" like Dennis Osadebay, Raphael Armattoe, Michael Dei-Anag, Gladys Casely-Hayford and R. R. Dhlomo. Although our chronological approach enabled us to concentrate on individual poets, we deprived ourselves of the opportunity of taking an overview of modern African poetry, even though some remarks in our introduction to the anthology would lead our readers to expect such guidance. We quote the relevant portion of our earlier remarks here, since it partially explains why we have adopted a new structure of the material in this new edition of *A Selection of African Poetry*:

> Beginning from older poets like Leopold Senghor and Birago Diop, we provide a historical perspective in which the protest movement of the 1930s and 1940s gave way to the crisis of identity which accompanied the attainment of political independence by African States in the late 1950s and early 1960s. If the earlier period was characterised by elaborate gestures of affirmation and self-assertion against hostile outside influences, the second period is noted for the satiric and deflationary tone of the writers anxious to debunk false positions taken by their immediate predecessors. And we can see that a third phase of African writing began to emerge in the mid-1960s: during which the writers turn more and more inward towards personal exploration and the rediscovery of their roots in the traditions of their ancestors. During this phase the writers have begun to think of themselves more as artists rather than as politicians and the forging of links with the artistic traditions of Africa is being steadily undertaken.

Although we would still stand by that tentative overview of modern

7

African poetry, it is obvious to us now that it needs both refining and exemplifying in the structure of the material of this new edition.

The close link between politics and the beginning of modern African poetry, implied above, has since been stressed by critics like Abiola Irele and Lewis Nkosi. But that link involves a more complex and subtle conception of politics than the critics have so far suggested. For us, politics does not consist only in the organisation and exercise of power in society. In essence, it involves a people's appropriation of their material, as well as their cultural and spiritual heritage as these react upon one another in history, because this is what in the final analysis gives them the authentic voice to express their identity. And the achievement of modern African poetry is precisely this mental and emotional appropriation of this concrete and spiritual heritage.

This appropriation has had to be done, to a large extent, in European languages. The modern African poet receives these languages which have their own historic features, modes and styles of expression. Faced with the task of adapting the inbuilt features of the received languages to serve their own purposes, the poets have increasingly exploited their awareness of indigenous traditions of poetry-making. Perhaps the best summary of the process that we believe has been taking place is in the words of the Irish poet, W. B. Yeats, who himself was engaged in a similar transformation of English poetry during the early part of this century:

How but in custom and in ceremony
Are innocence and beauty born?
Ceremony's a name for the rich horn,
And custom for the spreading laurel tree.

The most interesting and authentic modern African poetry seems to us to come from this process of subjecting the European languages to the traditions of poetry-making in Africa. But this has not been a linear achievement. The rediscovery of the traditions of poetry-making and the conscious attempt to exploit the verbal arts have grown as the poets have continued writing.

We observe four phases in this development, always, in the presence of the indigenous traditions. 1) The *pioneering* phase of the 1930s and 1940s, 2) the *transitional* phase of the 1950s and early 1960s, 3) the *modernist* phase of the mid-1960s and early 1970s, and 4) the *contemporary* phase which we are now experiencing.

Although we speak of phases, we would emphasise that these are not four periods rigidly separated either by exclusive styles and modes of writing or works of different poets. Most of the poets anthologised here have continued writing. In some cases their poetry does belong to a particular phase. For example, the poems of Abioseh Nicol, two of which we include here for the first time, seem to us to belong exclusively to the transitional phase, although he continues to respond to the changing socio-political situation of Africa right up to date.

8

In other cases, the poetry straddles a number of phases. For instance, it is obvious that some of the early poems of Awoonor and Soyinka belong to the phase that we refer to as *transitional* although much of their maturer poetry belongs to phases 3 and 4 as we define these below. Indeed, within each of the four phases we have identified, we observe differences of achievement between the regional and linguistic groupings of the poets, as well as differences among the individual poets within the groups.

The pioneering phase

We have called the first phase that of the *pioneers*. But since the phrase "pioneer poets" has often been used of writers of English expression like Osadebay, Casely-Hayford and Dei-Anag, we should point out that our "pioneer phase" also includes *Negritude* poets of French expression. The poetry of this phase is that of writers in "exile" keenly aware of being colonials, whose identity was under siege. It is a poetry of protest against exploitation and racial discrimination, of agitation for political independence, of nostalgic evocation of Africa's past and visions of her future.

However, although these were themes common to poets of both English and French expression, the obvious differences between the Francophone poets and the Anglophone writers of the 1930s and 1940s have been generally noted. Because of the intensity with which they felt their physical exile from Africa, coupled with their exposure to the experimental contemporary modes of writing in France, the style of the Francophone writers was more vigorous. Furthermore, because they felt the need to be authentic in their writing they had to go back to their indigenous tradition of poetry-making. The result in Senghor's case, as shown by "Nuit de Sine" for example, is a poetry that through its imagery and structured rhythms reveals a finer poetic sensibility.

The Anglophone pioneer poets on the other hand did not feel the same compulsion to explore their own artistic background and seemed satisfied with poorly imitating the English Victorian poets and the tradition of hymn writing. Hidebound by the essentially Edwardian and Georgian conventional forms of regular metre, standard rhymes and hymnal rhythms, writers like Osadebay, Casely-Hayford, Dei-Anag and, occasionally, Armattoe now sound patently archaic. There is no mistaking their pride in Africa, their desire to use the medium of poetry to express the virtues of Africanness, and their historical relevance. But they were so hampered by the forms of poetry they chose for expression that we do not believe their poetry worth close study. A representative poem of Casely-Hayford illustrates these points:

Rejoice and shout with laughter,
Throw all your burdens down,

If God has been so gracious
As to make you black or brown.
For you are a great nation,
A people of great birth.
For where would spring the flowers
If God took away the earth?
Rejoice and shout with laughter,
Throw all your burdens down,
Yours is a glorious heritage,
If you are black or brown.

This is a typical poetry of statement, prosaic and only redeemed by being presented in verse form. Although there is some attempt at the use of rhyme and there is a regular rhythm, there is no controlling imagery and the general impact is unsatisfactory. This type of poetry certainly does not possess the richness of Senghor's poetry.

On the other hand, the poetry written by ex-Portuguese colonials, (Lusophone poetry), although written much later, bears some relationship with the poetry of this pioneering phase. Firstly it is a poetry of protest, made more radical by the direct involvement of the poets in the guerilla warfare through which political independence was achieved. And as has often been remarked, there is some surface resemblance between the careers of Senghor and Neto as poet-politicians. But the circumstances of Senghor's activities leading to Senegal's independence are different from Neto's relationship with the political struggle, as the texture of their poems bears testimony to. Neto's poetry, with its simple direct language and its firm grasp of the realities of colonial exploitation and anguish, reads quite differently from the exuberant dreams of Senghor when he evokes the values of *Negritude*. Above all, the vivid images of the urban ghetto life, which Portuguese colonialism imposed on its victims, became the hallmark of Lusophone poetry. Nothing of this nature is present in Francophone poetry, except perhaps in that of David Diop.

Secondly, there was the strong desire among the Lusophone poets to repossess their land, not only literally and politically, but also culturally. There was a comparable kind of experimentation with poetry in Portuguese, strongly influenced by the rhythms of popular songs in the vernaculars of Angola and Mozambique. For all these reasons, in spite of the actual dates of the composition of the poems of Neto, Jacinto and de Sousa, it makes sense to see them as pioneers.

The transitional phase

The second phase, which we have chosen to call *transitional*, is represented by the poetry of writers like Abioseh Nicol, Gabriel Okara, Kwesi Brew, Dennis Brutus, Lenrie Peters and Joseph Kariuki. This is poetry which is written by people we normally refer to as modern and who may be thought of as belonging to the third phase. The characteristics of this poetry are its competent and articulate use of the received European language, its unforced grasp of Africa's physical, cultural and socio-political environment and often its lyricism. To distinguish this type of poetry we have to refer back to the concept of appropriation we introduced earlier. At the simplest and basic level, the cultural mandate of possessing a people's piece of the earth involves a mental and emotional homecoming within the physical environment. Poems like Brew's "Dry season", Okara's "Call of the River Nun", Nicol's "The meaning of Africa" and Soyinka's "Season", to give a few examples, achieve this level of appropriation. No longer does the school-going African have to find his piece of the earth in the green lands of Europe. What distinguishes this phase of modern African poetry from the next phase which we have called *modernist*, is the significant absence of experimentation with the European medium of expression. The writers were not unaware of the existence of traditions of poetry-making available in Africa, but the full impact of these traditions is not apparent in their verse making. The African environment is there in the lexical items and the themes, but we have to look to the modernists and their successors for the full harvest to come home.

The modernist phase

We have already said that the achievement of modern African poetry in the presence of indigenous traditions of poetry-making has not been linear. Thus the kind of experimentation under the influence of metropolitan writers like Eliot and Pound that we observe in the poetry of Okigbo can be compared to the experimentation already evident in the pioneering work of Senghor. The elaborate verse line that Senghor had borrowed from people like Claudel had enabled him to incorporate into his poetry the rhythms of the music of the Khalam. By the *modernist* phase, therefore, we are referring to the awareness, under the impact of early twentieth-century metropolitan practices, that poetry need not come in the conventional nineteenth-century garb of regular metre and rhyme.

This awareness led to the experimentation with oral material, such as the translation from Ewe dirges which abound in Kofi Awoonor's poetry in the 1960s. A similar sense of liberation and experimentation can be seen behind the work of Okigbo, although he was strongly influenced by the imagist practices of Pound and Eliot. But even before the remarkable evidence of poems like "Path of Thunder", it is clear that his familiarity with the myths, ceremonies and rituals of his people was transforming his idiom, if not his rhythms. In East Africa, experimentation took a more deliberate form very early in the work of someone like Okot p'Bitek, who started by collecting folk tales and songs in the vernacular.

Following these examples of songs, he composed his first original poetry in Acholi before translating them into English. Perhaps the outstanding characteristic of this phase of modern African poetry is in the poets' self-conscious search for techniques from native traditions as a means of extending and authenticating their sensibility. The result of this search can be seen with varying degrees of success in the works of people like Soyinka, Awoonor, Kunene, Okigbo and Okai.

The contemporary phase

There is no absolute distinction between this third phase that we have just been considering and the fourth phase which we have called *contemporary* poetry writing. But at the same time, it is clear from such a poem as Kofi Anyidoho's "Hero and thief" that some of the new poetry is, indeed, attaining the appropriation of Africa's spiritual heritage. For in them "custom" has, indeed, become "the spreading laurel tree". We do not claim that this is the only way in which the younger contemporary poets are writing or should write. In fact, some of Anyidoho's poetry remains impenetrable as a result of the intensity of the traditional idiom. But what we see happening in people like Muckhtarr or Niyi Osundare or Funso Ayejina is that the intensity of their understanding of the traditional aesthetic has made their exploration and their grasp of the contemporary situation firmer and their poetry more expressive and more resonant. It is because of this close link between traditional African poetry and what we describe as modern African poetry that we have chosen to begin this anthology with a representative sample of the traditional poetry.

Traditional poems

So far we have consistently referred to the oral traditional poetry of the African peoples and its importance in their assertion of their cultural identity. We have, indeed, gone ahead to make the degree to which modern African poets approach these traditional forms of poetry a cardinal point in the categorisation we attempt here. All this points to two significant facts. The first is the unfortunate situation whereby traditional poetry as serious art worthy of attention was ignored for a long time and has only recently commanded the attention it deserves from African scholars. This attitude was fostered by early colonial interpreters of African culture who did not see any merit in the "tribal songs".

The second significant fact is the unequivocal recognition that poetry in one form or another is a cultural heritage of all peoples who all have rational conceptions of what it is. The true origin and nature of poetry tends to become blurred by the overly conscious and highly artistic written forms of modern poetry. Poetry is meant to be recited or sung

orally. The written forms and attendant theories that have been formu-
lated about poetry represent developments in the medium in response
to the growth and the complexity of human societies and the problem
of communication. Recent studies of the traditional literature of many
societies have revealed that African communities have always had their
own ideas of the nature and function of poetry. Among the Somali the
poet is revered and poetry has been long recognised as a serious and
functional form of art. The Swahili *Utenzi* shows clearly that poetry is
known and appreciated as a special form of art practised by the gifted.
Among the Yoruba the *Ewi* describes this art form, while Awoonor has
shown in *Guardians of the Sacred Word* that poetry is a well-known art
in traditional Ghanaian society.

Traditional poems are a serious art form dealing with the range of
human experiences: they conjure up whole worlds, are rich in figurative
language and present beautiful pictures in words. They contain deep
reflections about the world and man's place in it, and treat the relation
between man and his environment and nature. These themes are found
in oral poetry composed as religious poetry, songs and lyrics, dirges,
praise-poetry, occupational poetry, the poetry of abuse, satires and
celebratory poetry. Although we refer to them as traditional poems, they
continue to be composed in the various contemporary indigenous African
languages, illustrating the dynamism of the forms.

In this anthology we have included a few samples of traditional oral
poetry to show something of this variety and the intrinsic beauty of the
poems themselves. Furthermore, a sensitive reading of these poems and
the later poems in this anthology does show something of the debt which
modern African poetry owes the traditional forms, in terms of both
themes and technique. A poem like "Salute to the elephant" is a typical
occupational poem in the mode known as the *Ijala* among the Yoruba.
This is heroic poetry sung by hunters, ostensibly dedicated to the
animals they hunt for food and money. The form is also used for poetry
on a variety of other themes. "Breaking kola nut" is a poem that goes
to the heart of African values. It is what goes with the distinct ritual
act of pouring libation and gives some idea of the complexity and
relevance of "simple cultural acts". The dynamic and contemporary
nature of traditional poetry is shown by "It all started with the conver-
sion", while "Sunjata" is a good example of epic poetry.

One of the problems associated with the study and propagation of
traditional poetry is the question of translation. This is a problem which
also arises with the Francophone and Lusophone poems respresented
in this anthology. The major objection to translation by purists is that
they are not valid representations of their originals in their entirety.
However good they are, translations do violence to the originals, and
literary works are best studied in the original language of their compo-
sition, they argue. While admitting that bad translations distort a great
deal of the original and that even in good translations something of the
artistry is lost, we must emphasise that good translations are in them-

selves creative works and that they often succeed in conveying the essential qualities and meanings of the original. The specific case of oral poetry raises two issues. The difference between the mode of expression of oral poetry – the performance dimension of it, the context of the performance, the modulations of tone which often make nonsense of what look like ordinary repetitions in print, the facial expressions and sometimes extempore orchestral accompaniment and the audience participation – and the cold print of translations is vast. But even so the pale text often displays qualities that repay close study, betraying compositions of great imaginative depth and beauty. Finally, because of the plethora of indigenous languages in which the oral poetry of Africa is expressed and the fact that it is impossible for us to know these several languages sufficiently well to appreciate their literatures, translations have become very useful and recognised means of introducing readers to new areas of experience that would otherwise remain closed to them.

Approaching the poems

In preparing the supporting material for the poems we have included in this anthology, our concern has been to help make poetry meaningful to our readers, especially our student readers. We are aware that the appreciation of poetry is a difficult undertaking in our schools. Not because poetry is a foreign importation with which students come into contact only in the classroom, but because although there has always been a living tradition of oral poetry in Africa – consisting of work songs, riddles, proverbs, praise songs, epic narratives, dirges, etc – not many people going through formal education get introduced early enough to acquire the skills of poetry appreciation. And poetry appreciation is, indeed, a skill which can only be gradually acquired. Students' attention needs to be drawn to the strategies and devices which poets use and the effects they achieve by these means.

A basic assumption when we approach a poem is that the poem as a whole does mean something and that the voice we hear in the poem is anxious to say something to us. Our initial difficulty in understanding what the poem means may come from our being unfamiliar with some of the words that the poet uses. An obvious way of dealing with this difficulty is to use a good dictionary. But in anticipation of this difficulty we have provided notes on the words, phrases, names, which we think might create a problem for the understanding of the poems we have included here. However, our notes by no means exhaust the possible list of unfamiliar words. On the other hand, it may not always be necessary to know the precise meaning of each unfamiliar word in the poem in order to begin appreciating the poem. Let us, for example, take a brief look at a short traditional poem translated from Ewe:

My song bursts in the name of Toti with vosa
Taking a regal step.

Dare the hyena howl, let him howl.
Let the watchdog thunder endlessly.
The God of Song has descended on Ahosuglo.
War has begun, says So-kple-So.
We shall ourselves adorn.
Master Singers, Choric Leaders,
To you we kneel in homage,
Announcing nor death nor sickness.

Obviously, some of the words in this poem on which a reader needs notes are: *Toti, vosa, Ahosuglo* and *So-kple-So*. But even with these the reader may need help with only *vosa* for he can guess that the other words are names of people about whom he does not need to know a great deal to be able to proceed to appreciation. Aware, then, that *vosa* means a sacrificial offering, we note that the poet or singer begins by invoking and paying homage to a predecessor whom he names. This is a familiar practice all over the world, whether it is a call by the ancient Greek and Roman writers on the muses as the source of their inspiration, or, as at the beginning of Milton's "Paradise Lost", a prayer to the Holy Spirit for illumination. In our poem, after the invocation, there follows a series of images which *suggest*, rather than state, the momentous nature of the singer's undertaking. The descent of the *God of Song* is signalled by these heralds of danger – the howling hyena, the thundering watchdog. The meaning of this portion of the poem is summed up by the line, *War has begun, says So-kple-So*.

The next line is curious, almost a paradox and certainly illogical. Surely, what is required when war has begun is an armour not ornamental dress! As readers, we take mental note of this "problem" for meaning, to see whether the rest of the poem does provide an answer. The singer proceeds on his cheerful way, apparently oblivious of our problem. Or is he? Whatever he has in mind when he adorns himself while war is on, the last line of the poem suggests that he does not consider the incidence of this war a disaster. It is neither death nor sickness that he announces, that he sees and speaks about to his predecessors. In fact, adorning himself now seems to suggest that the singer feels equal, if not superior, to the forces of danger that herald the descent of the *God of Song*. He is after all *Ahosuglo*. And so the last portion of the poem reflects back on the "problem" which we noticed earlier.

A basic principle of organising or structuring meaning in poetry (demonstrated here) is that it is the *entire* poem which means something. In a successful poem, therefore, there is a unity and coherence, whereby the parts throw light on one another and the poem as a whole.

Of course, this poem is a translation from Ewe, a language in which personal names invariably have a meaning. So that, although Toti is the name of a famous singer from south-eastern Ghana who died in the 1940s, the word also means a pestle. In a similar manner, Ahosuglo (literally Aho   tsu   glo) means someone who triumphs over a surprise attack made upon him by his enemies. Therefore, the names carry allusions that are important for structuring the meaning of the poem.

Again the phrase 'Toti with vosa' has the stress pattern: ' – – ' – , a combination of a dactylic and trochaic feet, which not only enacts the rhythmic pounding of pestle in a mortar, but a stately movement. This is what the second line of the poem refers to. This stately movement, however, is not as evident in the translation as the original. For in the original there are devices for line ending – predominantly long open vowels some of which we notice in *vosa*, *Ahosuglo* and *So-kple-So*.

We will not go into any further detail with this poem. But we need to point out some of the strategies and devices used by the poet to achieve meaning. By strategies we mean the steps by means of which the unity or coherence of the poem is achieved: the units of the putting together of the poem. These units or sense groups are sometimes indicated by the punctuation or the sentence structure, or by a recurrent line. For example, it is clear from our poem that the first unit of meaning consists of the first two lines. The next unit also consists of lines 3 and 4, while line 5 alone makes up the next sense group. In an elaborate poem like Kofi Awoonor's "More messages", an important means of making up the sense groups in the poem is the repeated question *Will they let me go*. We could say then that the sense groups make up the framework, or the skeleton of each poem. Relying on the sense groups in our poem we could, for instance, say that the basic thought in this traditional Ewe poem is a struggle that is involved in artistic creation and that inspiration is seen as a sudden assault on the poet's personality which he must triumph over since he is Ahosuglo. But, when we have said this, we would have offered only a bare summary of what the poem means. For the poet-singer also employs various devices which enrich this basic meaning. He uses images, pictorial language, paradox, allusions, markers of the endings of lines, which have the effect of imposing a measured movement to balance the swift and wide ranging imagery. These are devices which we discover not only in traditional poetry but in the poetry which continues to be written by our contemporaries. It is important, therefore, that in our approach to every poem we endeavour to discover the framework, the skeleton as well as the flesh put on it, by the poet. We can take another brief look at a modern poem, "I think it rains" by Soyinka to illustrate the points we are making.

Wole Soyinka's "I think it rains" is a good example of a short and subtle modern poem which needs to be experienced whole to be fully appreciated. On our first reading of the poem we notice that the word and the idea of rain plays a significant part in the ordering and meaning of the poem. Secondly, we notice that the poet seems to feel some oppression. He is burdened by a feeling of unease. He feels restricted and it is as if he were suffocating under some weight. Next we realise that we need to know the contextual meanings of such words and expressions as *uncleave, closures of the mind, purity of sadness, skeined trans-*

parencies, searing dark longing, cruel baptisms and *conjugation*. Now we can begin to formulate some tentative interpretation. To give him some comfort, the poet imagines it is raining heavily, a thought which he pursues with some excitement. He observes the rain very carefully from stanza to stanza, the smoke-like dust which it raises from the thatches of houses in the village, how it falls in straight shafts and how the rain dissolves and washes away debris, freeing many dark corners. To relate the idea of the rain to the poet's conditions, we can now say that the poet imagines that the rain will wash off those things that inhibit and cage him and make him feel as if he were enclosed in a tiny space made of mud or material that can be easily dissolved by rain.

Finally, apart from the dominant image of the rain, the poet uses some other images to show the delicate nature of the idea he is working out; his *skeined transparencies, purity of sadness* and *cruel baptism* indicate the process through which he arrives at some reconciliation with himself. Besides, the poet's organisation of the sense units of this poem are also seen in his sentence patterns and the contemplative tone of the poem. Thus we can make a final statement by saying that in this poem Soyinka uses rain as a symbolic image to explore the state of his mind and emphasise a theme of freedom of expression which runs through his writing and activities.

What has happened in our approach to the poem is that we have discovered that a single word, both in its literal and symbolic meaning, is the main structural device that the poet uses to impose a unified and coherent meaning on his thoughts. An appreciation of what happens in a poem can come as we try to discover both the strategies and the devices of organisation in each poem.

To help meet the demands on the student readers anxious to acquire some skills in the appreciation of poetry, we have provided supporting material in three forms: 1) notes on words, phrases, devices which may not be immediately understood, 2) questions which we hope will enable readers to discover the structure of the poems for themselves and to appreciate them more deeply and 3) commentaries on each poem which include a general description of what the poem may be said to be about and also a context for the poem.

We would like to emphasise that our commentaries do not exhaust the meaning of the poems and we certainly do not wish to establish an orthodoxy in the interpretation of these poems. We hope that with the notes and the questions, our readers will discover other meanings, sometimes even contradictory to those we have found in reading and enjoying these poems.

Kojo Senanu
University of Ghana
Legon.

Theo Vincent
University of Lagos
Lagos.

Traditional Poetry

Salute to the elephant

O elephant, possessor of a savings-basket full of money
O elephant, huge as a hill, even in a crouching posture.
O elephant, enfolded by honour; demon, flapping *fans of war.*
Demon who snaps tree branches into many pieces and moves on to the
    forest farm.
5 O elephant, who ignores "I have fled to my father for refuge",
Let alone "to my mother".
Mountainous Animal, Huge Beast who tears a man like a garment
And hangs him up on a tree.
The sight of whom causes people to stampede towards a hill of safety.
10 My chant is a salute to the elephant.
Ajanaku who walks with a heavy tread.
Demon who swallows palm-fruit bunches whole, even with the spiky
    pistil-cells.
O elephant, praise named Laaye, massive animal, blackish-grey in
    complexion.
O elephant, who single-handed causes a tremor in a dense tropical
    forest.
15 O elephant, who stands sturdy and alert, who walks slowly as if
    reluctantly.
O elephant, whom one sees and points towards with all one's fingers.
The hunter's boast at home is not repeated when he really meets the
    elephant.
The hunter's boast at home is not repeated before the elephant.
Ajanaku looks back with difficulty like a person suffering from a sprained
    neck.
20 The elephant has a porter's-knot without having any load on his head.
The elephant's head is his burden which he balances.
O elephant, praise named Laaye, "O death, please stop following me"
    –
This is part and parcel of the elephant's appellation.
If you wish to know the elephant, the elephant who is a veritable ferry-
    man.
25 The elephant whom honour matches, the elephant who continually
    swings his trunk,
His upper fly-switch,
It's the elephant whose eyes are veritable water-jars.
O elephant, the vagrant par excellence,
Whose molar teeth are as wide as palm-oil pits in Ijesaland.

30 O elephant, lord of the forest, respectfully called Oríiríbobo
O elephant whose teeth are like shafts.
One tooth of his is a porter's load, O elephant fondly called Otíkó
Who has a beast-of-burden's proper neck.
O elephant, whom the hunter sometimes sees face to face.
35 O elephant, whom the hunter at other times sees from the rear.
Beast who carries mortars and yet walks with a swaggering gait.
Primeval leper, animal treading ponderously.

(*trans. A. Babalola*)

Notes

line 3   demon, flapping fans of war   The metaphors here refer to the
elephant's destructive nature and its huge ears that indeed look like
fans.

line 11   Ajanaku   (which literally means "killer of Ajana") is an attributive
name for the elephant. Legend has it that Ajana captured live animals
and kept a sample of each species. One day he was trampled to death by
the elephant which he had in his mini-zoo.

line 24   a veritable ferry-man   The idea being stressed here is the elephant's
association with death. In ancient legend (and in classical legend also)
the ferry-man conveyed bodies to the land of spirits.

line 30   Oríiríbobo (also Otíkó)   Both a play on words and sound
(onomatopaeia) referring to the size of the elephant.

line 37   Primeval leper   A reference to the phalanges of the elephant which
look like stumps, similar to limbs afflicted by leprosy. A mixture of awe
and disgust is implied in the image.

Questions

1 One technique which the poet adopts to keep our attention is variety.
Discuss the various forms of variety in this poem.
2 What qualities of a praise-song does this poem possess?

Commentary

Ijàlá, the hunter's chant, is one of the most popular sequences in Yoruba oral
literature. Apart from specific addresses to individual animals, these chants also
treat other situations that may not seem to have any direct bearing on the hunter
and his occupation. This poem is an *Ijàlá* chant addressed to the elephant. It
deals in a comprehensive way with aspects of the animal stretching from its econ-
omic and physical properties, to its enormous and destructive qualities, to
peoples' reactions to it and the admiration and dread it inspires. Understandably,
the emphasis is on the size of the animal and the amount of energy that is locked
up in its frame. To bring out all these features the poem uses hyperbole and
a series of similes, as well as personification and euphemism.

The myth of the Bagre

On the river bank
there was an old man
with a pipe.
Do you see the dogs?
5 When they see someone,
they try to bite him.
The old man
calls them to heel
and they make no noise.
10 See the younger one
starting to greet,
greeting softly.
The old man answers,
and when he has done so,
15 he then asks me
what I want.
And I tell him
that the affairs of God
trouble me greatly.
20 The old man
spoke again.
"What can I do?"
God's affairs
bring great suffering.
25 What shall I do?
I was going out
but I saw something
in the dark wood.
Then I saw a being child
30 and began to run.
They started to call,
they called out to me
and when they'd done so,
they spoke and asked me
35 what I wanted.
And I told them
that the affairs of God
began to trouble me;
they troubled me greatly,
40 me and the elder one.
They overpowered me,
put me on the path
and I entered the woods.
For many days

45 I hurried here.
They overpowered me
and I came here.
He finished speaking
and the being children
50 turned and caught him.
They held him gently
and made him sit.
When they'd done so
they took some guinea corn
55 and showed it him,
"Do you know this?"
"No, I don't."
And they told him
it was food.
60 Do you see the being child
begin to eat it?
He did eat it
and found it pleasing.
Do you see the man
65 dipping his hand in,
beginning to eat,
putting the food in his mouth,
starting to chew?
Does it please you?
70 He said it does so.
So he spoke
and when he'd done so,
the being child
told him
75 to stop
and they'd bring some flour.
They brought some
and he asked them,
"What's that?
80 Is it ashes?"
He was told
to sit and watch.
He sat there
while the being child
85 fetched some water,
poured it on the flour,
and began to mix it.
When he'd done so,
he took out his hand,
90 **began** to lick it,
and it tasted good.

Then the being child
said to him,
"Eat and see".
95 He began to eat
and when he'd done so,
he said,
"It's true."
[The being] asked him
100 if he knew about guinea corn.
He answered, "No",
and asked
"What made guinea corn?"
and they replied,
105 "God created guinea corn."

Notes

line 1   This extract starts from line 105 of "The Black Bagre". In the preceding
100 lines we are told of the existence of the gods, especially those who
troubled the tribe's two original ancestors, the elder and younger
brothers.

line 2   The *old man* is in fact God, who reappears later in the narration in
Heaven.

line 4   A swift change to the direct mode of address, emphasising the
involvement of the initiate audience.

lines 10–14   Formulary description of action in three phases (see
commentary).

line 15   Suddenly, the narrator has become the protagonist, the younger one.

lines 23–24   Can also be rendered: *God's doings bring great burdens.*

line 25   Spoken by the narrator-protagonist.

line 28   The *dark wood* is often the beginning of man's journey towards the
understanding of the ways of God.

line 29   a being child   Beings of the wild; spiritual beings between God and
man, and capable of both good and evil.

line 31   The singular being has suddenly become plural.

lines 31–35   Formulary description of action.

lines 36–46   The narrator protagonist restates the motive of the journey,
underlining its compulsion.

line 40   elder one   Elder brother (see commentary).

line 50   Since the *being children* are spirits of the wild, the word *caught* has a
metaphorical meaning, i.e. to be possessed and therefore compelled to go
through the rites of initiation into the spirits' cult. The rest of the
narration exists on this double level: it is a realistic story, as well as a
symbolic initiation into the knowledge of how things came into being.

line 60   Another switch to a direct address mode, since this is a significant
moment in the narration, demanding initiates' involvement.

line 80   The younger one's ignorance is disarming and the line is meant to
be humorous. At the same time the ritual value of the occasion is to
demonstrate man's dependence upon supernatural agencies for his basic
needs.

Questions

1 What features of this narration make you want to read it to the end?
2 In view of the answers given by the speaker when he is questioned, what meaning would you attach to the word *want* in this narration?
3 Comment on lines 36 to 46, giving reasons why some lines are repeated and what effect this has.

Commentary

"The myth of the Bagre" is a long narration of nearly 12,000 'lines' which unfolds and accompanies the ritual processes of the initiation of young men and women of the LoDagaa tribe of the North Western region of Ghana. Their initiation ceremonies are designed to lift the ban or taboos which prohibit the young from eating the new fruits and crops of the land before they have been ritually born into the tribe and before the crops have been ritually harvested. But the myth is also a creation story, an unfolding of the tribes' wisdom concerning the origin of things.

About half of the narration, called "The White Bagre", outlines the procedure of the ceremonies, the announcement of the ban, the initiation ceremony, the gathering of the crops and the preparation of the beer from the grains. The beer becomes the ritual poison from which the initiates die, to be later reborn into the tribe.

The other half of the myth, called "The Black Bagre", embodies creation stories, such as the meeting of the first ancestors, called the elder and the younger brothers, with God and with the beings of the wild. It tells of the knowledge which man acquired from these beings.

The recitation of the myth to the new initiates in the Bagre room is done by an elder or a senior member of the Bagre Association. The short lines of the narration are chanted by this single reciter to a rhythm of two sticks beaten upon a trough, or to the shaking of a rattle.

Each line has two beats or stressed syllables accompanied by a varying number of unstressed syllables. The reciter chants a line, which is then repeated by the audience of initiates and their guides. The oral features of the myth are underlined by the flexible narrative and the dramatic devices employed by the reciter. These include (i) rapid changes from indirect to direct modes of speech, (ii) swift and frequent changes of person i.e. narrator into protagonist and then back again to narrator, (iii) the flexible use of pronouns, both singular and plural, (iv) the repetition of the central theme which motivates the narration and the drama, and (v) the description of all action in a formula which indicates that the action is about to take place, is taking place and has taken place.

These characteristics encourage a re-enactment by the initiates of ancestral events by destroying the distinction between past and the present time, between narrator and narrated event and between the individual and the group. The wisdom of the tribe is thus not simply committed to memory, but chanted, danced and acted out during the month-long ceremony of initiation.

The Fulani creation story

At the beginning there was a huge drop of milk.
Then Doondari came and he created the stone.
Then the stone created iron;
And iron created fire;
5 And fire created water;
And water created air.
Then Doondari descended the second time.
And he took the five elements
And he shaped them into man.
10 But man was proud.
Then Doondari created blindness, and blindness defeated man.
But when blindness became too proud,
Doondari created sleep, and sleep defeated blindness;
But when sleep became too proud,
15 Doondari created worry, and worry defeated sleep;
But when worry became too proud,
Doondari created death, and death defeated worry.
But then death became too proud,
Doondari descended for the third time,
20 And he came as Gueno, the eternal one.
And Gueno defeated death.

Notes

Title The Fulani are mostly a nomadic cattle-rearing people who are found
in the Savannah belt across West Africa from Senegal to Mali, Niger
and northern Nigeria. However, there are also town-dwelling Fulanis.

line 1 Most creation myths or stories start with some positive assertion which
either contributes directly to or prepares the ground for the creation of
man. In this case, it is *milk*. Milk is probably the most symbolic and
significant item among the Fulani. It is a means of sustaining life, but
the economy and social organisation of the group also revolves around
milk and the cattle that produce it.

line 2 In Fulani myth, *Doondari* is an ancestral figure and source of creation.
The stone is also important for grinding millet or corn which mixed with
milk is the staple food of the people.

line 9 According to this myth, man was created out of five elements: stone,
iron, fire, water and air. There is an interesting correlation between this
account and what occurs in Western medieval metaphysics. According to
the latter, all living matter, including man, is made up of four elements:
earth, water, fire and air. These have to be present in defined
proportions in a good even-tempered man.

line 10 Compare the consequences of man's pride here with the result of
man's disobedience in the Bible and the loss of paradise.

line 18   cf. John Donne's Holy Sonnet, "Death be not proud".

line 20   *Gueno*   Supreme and divine God of life and death. The eternal life, which he is, gives man hope and confidence in the world – important aspects of Christian and Muslim beliefs.

Questions

1 Give an account of the creation myth of your people. In what ways is it similar or different from the one under study? How are the features of the myth reflected in your people's culture – their beliefs and attitudes to life and death?
2 What is poetic about this account?

Commentary

Creation myths or tales are common among all peoples and all cultures. They are part of the rich oral lore of traditional societies handed down from generation to generation by word of mouth.

These tales, which are the fruits of the people's poetic imagination seek to account for the origin of the world and man, the process of creation, how social values and evil originated, man's attempts to grapple with the material and spiritual world around him and understand qualities, values and mysteries that define man and his fate. One of the best known creation myths is that recorded in the Book of Genesis in the Holy Bible.

This poem gives us the Fulani version of the creation myth. It is a straightforward account which is divided into two parts. The first part gives the different stages that led to the creation of man – when *Doondari descended the second time*. The second part of the poem deals with how evil in the form of the difficult experiences of man in the world came into life through man's pride (which led to loss of paradise) and was manifested in deformity, worry and death. Notice the careful gradation of the afflictions. The climax is death. But there is a twist in the end which gives hope of eternal life and the continuation of life. Connecting words like *And, Then, But* are carefully deployed to ensure that continuity which is a crucial aspect of creation is maintained. What looks like monotonous repetition of form is indeed careful arrangement of cause and effect in images or ideas that succeed in the end in presenting us with the picture of man's fortune in life.

A particularly fascinating aspect of the structure of this simple poem is the way in which the first half of it is balanced against the second half. The five elements in the first half are balanced against the five stages of man's defeat and victory. What we have is a splendid story that describes a cycle of creation and defeat caused by pride. Doondari's third and last descent established the almighty power of God before which all manner of pride is nothing.

Breaking kola nut

God the Creator
Who lives on high
And his eyes cover the whole ground
Who lives under the ground
5 And no dirt soils him;
Who lives in the waters
And is dry;
Who moves with the winds –
The wind is never seen by eyes –
10 And yet air is everywhere,
I come with greeetings
And with pleadings!

GOD THE TRYST MAKER,
Who makes tryst with men,
15 Makes appointments with them
Where and when he pleases,
And they cannot escape!
God who creates and who destroys,
Who beats up human beings
20 And consoles them;
Crushes them and remains their friend;
Who brings and who takes away,
And who creates
Before the created knows,
25 At dawn we open our doors and our mouths,
At night we close our doors
But not our minds!

It is KOLA I bring!
It's all I can offer!
30 A little baby
Can only hold its mother
As far as its hands can go!
KOLA is small
And yet is big!
35 Like the sacrificial food,
It is more important that it goes round
Than that it fills the stomach.
Our fathers' fathers
And their fathers before them –
40 All our ancestors –
Saw all the fruits of the land
But they chose kola

As the prime substance for hospitality
And for offerings:
45 What an old man lying down has seen,
Has the young man ever seen better
Though he perches on the highest tree?

Of all food on earth,
Only kola
50 Is not cooked by water and fire
But by spoken word!
The rich can afford it! and the poor can afford it;
And kola is the biggest offering
Men bring to you GREAT GOD,
55 To whom the swallower of what swallows an elephant
And with an hippopotamus tucked into its mouth
And palmyra as chewing stick,
Whistles freely,
Is smaller than spittle!

60 It is not that kola
Is the sweetest food on earth,
Or that it fills the stomach fastest;
But it's only with kola
That we pray for life.
65 And whoever brings kola
Brings life,
And brings health,
And brings prosperity,
And brings peace,
70 And children,
And what we shall feed them with!
For it's YOU, God
Who brings kola
And ordains its manner of breaking.
75 This KOLA
Is like a mound in the middle of the arena,
On which we stand and speak in the assembly
Of people, and of spirits,
And our ancestors,
80 And YOU Great God
The TRYST MAKER,
And the words reach the ears they're made for!
So our fathers' fathers' fathers
Hear my voice!
85 God hear my voice!

I am a little innocent child who washes his stomach only!
But your eyes see me

And you can judge;
If I've ever touched the wife of a relation
90 Or seen the nakedness of a sister;
If I've ever stolen what belongs to any human being
Or oppressed a widow or cheated an orphan;
Or borne false witness, or spoken calumny;
If I've killed any human being
95 With knife or spear,
Or arrow or rope,
Or poison or witch-craft,
If I've done any of these things,
May this our land
100 And the Mother Earth EAT ME!

But if none of these is my guilt
And my fellow-man would afflict me
Because of anger of the heart or anger of the eye,
Then let whoever comes to kill me
105 KILL HIMSELF!

Anybody who says he must see me and my household
With evil eyes
Let his eyes perish in the seeing!
Any person who says an innocent house-hold
110 May not sleep
Make him roost with the chicken.
I pray for the good of the people in the bush,
And the good of those at home;
For the good of those in the hills
115 And the good of those in the valleys;
For the good of those at work
And for the good of those at play,
But if a man I can stand by does not stand by me
Let what kills traitors kill him.
120 If a spirit I can vouch for does not vouch for me
Let what kills spirits kill it.

If anybody would bring poison into this house
Let his polluted hand enter his mouth!
Let no guest bring evil to his host;
125 On his departure
May no hunch grow on his back.
Let a rat not dare to eat the bag of a medicine-man
And let the medicine-man not dare curse the rat.

It is said that an innocent man,
130 Guiltless of any sin big or small

28

Crosses the waters on a piece of calabash;
That it's with a snail's good tongue
That the snail moves over thorns.
So I'll keep clean my hands;
135 You will defend me from cows:
A man can not wrestle with a cow.

If I must suffer for my offences
It is just;
If for the guilt of my children
140 I'll bear it –
The mouth speaks what earns the jaw a slap.
A man's head shakes the ant's nest.
His trunk suffers for it.
What is good is what we want.
145 I have not asked you to give that to me only:
Eating everything alone is bad eating!
If the kite perches,
Let the eagle perch.
Whichever denies the other the right to perch.
150 May its wings break.

GOD
May we never be in need and find no helper.
A man who has friends is greater than a wealthy man!
Give our wives fruitfulness –
155 One blow, one fall.
Give us children
And give us the means to feed them.
Let any of us or our children
Who goes out to work
160 Come back
With plenty of money,
And come back safe.
Let any weed that brushes us
On our departure
165 Brush against us on our return –
It is not an evil weed.
When we are at the back,
Let evil be in front;
And when we are in front
170 Let evil be behind
Let no illness come
And let no doctor cure.
Let no one be ill
And let no one heal.
175 But I have not spoken and it is final

You have the yam;
And YOU have the knife.
To whomsoever you give
And in whatever measure, he will eat! . . .
180 I break the KOLA NUT.

(translated from the Igbo by Lawrence Emeka)

Notes

line 14 Tryst Lovers' meeting at a secret place or time; the meeting place
itself. Here, the providential power of God who orders man's life,
determines his fortunes and his death as and when He wills.

line 35 Food prepared as part of sacrifice (ritual), shared out to audience or
witnesses or all for whom sacrifice has been performed. Cf the Christian
Holy Communion.

lines 45–47 The young man by reason of his advantage of height should
have a greater prospect, but the elder because of his age, experience
and developed powers has more insight.

lines 49–54 The process of cooking here consists of the incantations and
libations offered. The kola nut is ready to be eaten after it has been
used to ask for blessings and hallowed as a vehicle for showering
blessings on recipients.

lines 55–59 All these are large animals and it must be something of an
inconceivably enormous size to which these can appear as spittle (saliva).

lines 60–71 The symbolic significance of kola nut clearly spelt out.

line 89 A taboo in traditional society. There follows a string of other
forbidden acts, both immoral and antisocial.

line 100 Mother Earth The earth goddess which many recognise as
representing the female principle in African cosmology is a powerful
goddess. While acting as the guardian of a people and place and the
goddess of fertility, she can also be fiercely destructive and vengeful.

line 103 anger of the heart or anger of the eye Hatred or envy.

lines 106–111 "Live and let live" is an important dictum of the communal
nature of traditional African society. No one goes out to deliberately
frustrate another.

lines 127–128 A figurative expression which goes to the very heart of
African culture. The medicine-man is an important and influential man in
traditional society. Apart from his ability to cure physical wounds, he is
also a religious figure who has spiritual powers. He acts as intermediary
between the world of the living and the dead. He is endowed with
mysterious and supernatural powers which he must not misuse or the
consequences on him would be grave.

lines 135–136 A cow Symbol of strength and destruction.

line 143 Cf "stirring a nest of hornets". The ants will climb all over the
man and sting him in several places.

lines 145–150 Altruism, lack of greed and gregariousness are cardinal
aspects of traditional African society. See note on lines 106–111.

line 155 An euphemism expressing the wish that women should conceive
easily.

line 175 But I have not spoken and it is final Recognition of God, the
creator, as the final arbiter.

Questions

1 Examine the structure of this poem and trace the progress of the poet's ideas.
2 Suggest ways in which the omnipotence of God is constantly stressed in this poem.
3 Explain the simile used in lines 75–85 and comment on how adequately it relates to the character of kola so far delineated.
4 Identify some of the poetic devices used in this poem and comment on how effective they are.
5 This poem tells us much about traditional African society. Isolate and discuss some of this information.

Commentary

The kola nut – *cola nitida* (two lobes) and *cola acuminata* (four lobes) – is an important fruit among Africans for many reasons. It is commonly eaten. Furthermore, it is not only a significant economic fruit, it is also one that has great cultural value, fulfilling crucial socio-religious functions. It is also generally offered as a mark of hospitality, and offering kola is a great gesture of friendship and comradeship. But for the true essence of kola as a cultural symbol to be appreciated, the simple act of offering and breaking the kola nut is a ritual enactment. Breaking kola nut is a solemn ritual, a piece of drama during which a whole society lights up, reflecting the spiritual and social realities of the people, their mores and relationships.

This poem, which is a dramatic monologue, is a complex offering. It is a serious poem, a rhetorical *tour de force* which contains a lot of variety in tone and attitude. It moves from the invocation in which, the omnipotence, purity and mystery of God are stressed, to prayerful supplication, some social admonition, general reflection about life and finally submission to the power of almighty God, the only dispenser. It uses many of the techniques of rhetoric in Africa: aphorisms, proverbs, idioms and witticisms. In addition the poem employs subtle repetitions of words and phrasing and parallelism as techniques to intensify the ideas expressed.

This is a rather long and comprehensive version of the utterance during this ritual. There are much shorter versions. However, the important ritual of breaking the kola generally provides the opportunity for this type of reflection and prayer.

Sundjata

Foretelling the Defeat of Sumanguru

The leader of the Jaanes
Prescribed these two white rams
For Susu Sumanguru Baamangana. . .
Sumanguru kept the two white rams in his compound.
5 He fashioned pure silver

And attached it to the leg of the one named after himself;
He intended to change matters.
He fashioned pure gold
And attached it to the one he had named after Sundjata.
10 Since he did not know Sundjata's name,
He said, "The person whom God is to create,
Is he not yet born?
Is he in this town?
Is he in his mother's womb?
15 Is he a spirit?
If it be God's will
It is that child who will destroy my reign;
It is after him that I name this sheep."
He put the pure gold on that one.

20 Those two white rams were together for some time
Then came a day, –
Susu Sumanguru Baamangana
It was the evening before Friday;
Thursday was nearly over and the evening before Friday had begun
25 When dawn broke it would be Friday –
Susu Sumanguru Baamangana and his attendants were sitting;
The sheep appeared
With the two white rams among them;
The one named after Sundjata mounted a ewe
30 And was about to tup it;
The one named after Sumanguru took a few steps backwards
And butted the one named after Sundjata.
Sundjata left the ewe
And faced the other ram.
35 They butted each other
And butted each other
And butted each other.
Susu Sumanguru Baamangana was sitting
With his griots
40 And his attendants.
The ram named after Susu Sumanguru Baamangana
Pushed back a little way
Sundjata's namesake did likewise;
As they crashed into each other
45 One of the horns of Susu Sumanguru Baamangana's namesake
    snapped.
Sundjata went back a little way
Then came crashing into the other ram,
Which fell to the ground.
The attendants fell upon it and slaughtered it.
50 Sumanguru was perplexed:

32

He went to the leader of the Jaanes,
And told him what happened.
The leader of the Jaanes said to him
"I am not God
55 But since I began serving God
Since I first knew my right hand from my left,
On any occasion when someone gave me work to do,
I went into retreat,
And what I saw, I saw;
60 That is what I have seen in this instance
That is what the Lord has revealed to me.
He declares that he is God and that no-one can know him.
He has ordained this kingship and it cannot be altered.
Therefore enjoy such luck as you are going to enjoy
65 Before this child appears."

Notes

For the name Susu Sumanguru Baamangana, some versions of this epic have
Sosso Soumaoro Kanté, a sorcerer ruler of Sosso, a town north-east of the
capital of Mali. Sosso Soumaoro had conquered Mali from Dankaran
Touman, a half-brother of Sundjata, who had usurped the throne of Mali
against the expressed will of their father Naré Maghan.

line 1 Jaanes Also called Cissés in some versions, were divine priests who
could see into the future and prescribe ritual sacrifices that might avert
disaster.

line 9 Sundjata Again there are variant versions of this name, e.g. Sogolon
Djata, Maghan Djata, Maghan Sundjata. But a constant element in all
these variations is Djata or Diata, which means lion in a number of
contemporary West African languages. Part of the legend of Sundjata is
that he was born by a buffalo mother – an ugly hunchback called
Sogolon – after fourteen years of pregnancy. For seven years after his
birth he did not walk. But one day, he uprooted a huge baobab tree and
raised himself up from the ground by lifting the trunk of the tree and
bringing it, root and leaves, to Sogolon's door. His praise singer or griot
immediately cried:

> "Room, room, make room
> The lion has walked;
> Hide antelopes
> Get out of his way."

Questions

1 By what various means does the narrator convey a sense of the
supernatural in this extract?
2 What effect does the narrator achieve by repeating the full name of
Sumanguru?

3 In view of what happens later, why do you think Sumanguru fashions pure gold for the ram named after Sundjata?

4 Does the fact that the quarrel between the two rams is over a ewe have any significance?

5 In line 2 we are told that the leader of the Jaanes *prescribed two white rams for Sumanguru*. In view of his later remarks, what do you consider as the meaning of his prescription?

Commentary

"Sundjata" is an extract from one version of the epic of old Mali, the thirteenth century kingdom of West Africa, founded by the powerful ruler, Sundiata (*c.* 1230–55). An epic is a form of long narrative in prose or verse, based on oral traditions of history and legends, preserved and recited by court praise-singers or griots and passed on from generation to generation in the family. Usually, the epic presents a world of extraordinary events centred round a heroic and superhuman figure, his achievement (particularly his conquests over rivals) and his establishment of a just rule. The praise-singers or griots attached to the courts of such rulers preserve the memory of the achievements, interpreting them and keeping them "as free and pure of all untruth" as humanly possible, because through them they teach succeeding rulers the art of governing according to the principles of their ancestors.

The presentation of the pattern of events surrounding the epic hero, varies from griot to griot. But the world of the epic is generally characterised by the following: (i) a correspondence between the different levels of life i.e. the natural and the supernatural, the human and the animal; (ii) an orderliness, deriving from the power and the control of the gods and invisible forces, which is made manifest through prophecies and oracles that are eventually fulfilled; (iii) a clear distinction between good and evil, between those who are wicked, greedy, arrogant, ambitious, treacherous and those who are just, kind, generous, loyal, sympathetic; and (iv) the great passions of courage, determination, endurance even sorrow which move the extraordinary human figures of the epic world.

Because of the relationship and correspondence between the various levels of existence in the epic world, men have their guardian spirits or jinns and totem animals. On the other hand, they are vulnerable to powers embodied in certain objects. For example, Sumanguru, the sorcerer ruler of Mali, who is eventually defeated by Sundjata, could only be overcome by the scratch of an arrow tipped with the spur of a white cock. Similarly, the powerful Liyongo, in the next epic extract, was only vulnerable to a dagger made of copper.

Events on one level of existence become symbolic or expressive of other levels: for example, although the thunder and lightning which heralded the birth of Sundjata point to his ascendancy, in the first extract this ascendancy is simply presented as the natural fight between two rams over a ewe, as if it were only the desire for procreation and survival. In view of these characteristics, the world of the epic poem at first seems remote from our everyday experience. But on closer examination, because the powerful emotions both experienced and aroused by the inhabitants of the epic world stand out so stark, naked and striking, they succeed in showing us what basically we human beings are like.

The death of Liyongo

1   And thus upon his way he thought   with fear in his heart   and on
       the second day in the evening   he came as far as Shaka and
       entered the city.
    He went into his father's house   and his father was glad for him
       and welcomed him with joy   giving him a place to rest his limbs.
    Massaging his limbs   together with his whole body   because of the
       weariness of the journey   with the idea of soothing him.
    The youth took rest   and then came out into the street   talking and
       laughing   with his friends as he walked about.
5   Yet in the folds of his attire   he had hidden the dagger   but no man
       saw it   as he sought a way of killing his father.
    Each day as he went to him   Liyongo was asleep   he could by no
       means find a way   and the youth was worried.
    Then when he saw his father asleep   he would call him loudly   so
       that his father would be startled   and if not so then he would
       kill him.
    But he would always quickly wake   and rise up for whatever reason
       and the youth would say, Give me food   for I am hungry, he
       would say.
    The youth was worried   and overwhelmed with terror   but he kept
       his purpose   and the days were consumed up as with fire.
10 As the days sped by   the Lord of Pate sent him news   saying here
       we are ready   to prepare for your wedding-day.
    On the day that he received the letter   his father was tired   and lay
       stretched out in sleep   understand, he was flat out.
    His breathing sounded loudly   like thunder in the rain   the youth
       understood   that indeed he was wrapt in sleep.
    He knew that his father was unconscious   the youth intended evil
       for the yearning that he had   to go and seek out a wife.
    He pierced him in the navel   as he lay flat on his back   when
       Liyongo awoke he did not see him   for the youth had fled.
15 His father waking up,   and seizing arrows and bow   he went outside
       going into the town.
    And he sank on one knee   and drew an arrow to its aim   as was his
       custom during life   he put an arrow in the bow-string.
    And that place, I will say   was near to a well   but people did not
       stand about   for all had fled.
    No one drew water there   man or woman   the news through all the
       land   had spread.
    That Liyongo is standing   he is there by the well   now people have
       stopped drawing water   they have no way to get water.
20 There is no one to get it   no person to draw water   everyone stays
       at home   there is no one who appears.

35

The people of the town   for water for the mosque   take it in a jug
   until it is all finished up.
Soon all the water came to an end   and none in the jugs remained
   but Liyongo does not leave off   for he has placed the arrow in
   the bow-string.
From hunger they buried people   and all were distressed   they
   arranged a council-meeting   to arrive at a decision.
The decision was unanimous   We had better go to his mother   if his
   mother comes   she will calm him with her sympathy.
25 They went to his mother   and his mother agreed   and they all left
   together   and came outside the city wall.
And his mother besought him   singing songs of lament   on purpose
   to lead him   but Liyongo did not hear.
And his mother to approach him   feared in trembling   from afar she
   regarded him   with countless beseechings.
And they did not understand   that Liyongo even then had already
   died   for the fear that overcame them   they did not go near him.
So each day, going to him   his mother cried   but he did not get up
   even for a single hour   and it was thought he was angry.
30 When she returned from her pleading   his mother explained   I do
   not know what he blames   but anger has taken hold of him.
My son is angered   it is not his custom not to hear   he has refused
   to get up   and I do not know what is our misdeed.
This is not his usual way   for if I go to him with a request   he
   listens at once   but now he is gravely vexed.
His mother nearer to him crept   laying aside her danger   and anger
   swept over her   at all she then so clearly saw.
It is not possible now for him to slay   if he is angry he does not
   speak   it is the throes of death   and the groaning.
35 His mother marvelled   saying, It is cruel shame   all in this hour my
   son has died   he has refused to hear my voice.
And so within the span of day   to earth he fell a corpse   and the
   throng of people realised   Liyongo has passed away.
They all drew near   his mother and the people as well   they all
   looked at him intently   It is a dagger, he has been stabbed.
He has been stabbed in the navel   a copper dagger, know ye   they
   bore him to the town   and he was buried without delay.
The news spread   until it reached Pate   and when the Sultan was
   told   he was filled with joy . . .

Notes

line 1   he   Refers to the son of Liyongo.
Shaka   The capital of Liyongo's kingdom on the mainland facing the islands
   of Pate, Pemba and Zanzibar.
line 5   the dagger   A copper dagger to which Liyongo is vulnerable (see line
   37).

line 8   *Give me food for I am hungry*   An indirect confession of the
    uncontrollable greed which pushes the youth on to patricide.
line 9   *the days were consumed up as with fire*   A significant metaphor which
    draws together the nervous laughter, (line 4) the ravenous hunger (line
    8) and the intense fright of the youth.

Questions

1 Write a character sketch of the main protagonists in this extract.
2 Identify some examples of tragic irony in the narrative.
3 In what ways is the heroic stature of Liyongo conveyed to us?
4 Comment on the significance of the Lord of Pate's message to the youth.
5 We are told of the stabbing of Liyongo in line 14, but we do not learn of
   his death until line 28. What does this suspense achieve?
6 "The epic presents a world that is unified at various levels." Do you find
   this true of the incidents connected with the death of Liyongo?
7 It is reported that, at the end of each public recitation of the above portion
   of the legends connected with Liyongo, the audience often breaks into
   tears. Can you give any reasons why this might happen?

Commentary

The stories centred round the legendary hero, Liyongo, had existed as songs
in Swahili for a considerable length of time before they were reduced to writing
by the eminent Swahili scholar and poet, Muhammad bin Abubakar bin Umar
al-Bakari (also known as Muhammad Kijuma) in 1913. Some of the songs which
circulated among the Swahili-speaking Africans of the mainland have been
attributed to Liyongo himself.

The central theme of these stories is the conflict between Daud Mringwari,
the ruler or lord of Pate, and his cousin Liyongo: a conflict seen as expressing
the clash between the Arab and African strands in Swahili culture.

Daud Mringwari was the son of the paternal aunt of Liyongo i.e. his mwana
wa shangazi. Daud rightly succeeds his uncle Mringwari I, according to the
predominantly African matrilineal system of inheritance. But, aware of the
Arabian patrilineal law of succession, by which Liyongo the eldest son of Mring-
wari I, could lay claim to his throne, he sets about systematically persecuting
Liyongo and finally succeeds in having him murdered.

Two of the stories which illustrate Liyongo's bravery and ingenuity are worth
referring to briefly as a background to our extract. In the first of these stories,
Liyongo had escaped from the island of Pate and set up his own rule at Shaka
on the mainland. His cousin, Daud, suborned the leaders of neighbouring tribes
on the mainland to invite Liyongo to a round of feasts at which each ruler played
host in turn. Each host climbs and plucks the fruit of the dum-tree to entertain
his guests. When it comes to Liyongo's turn, his guests have agreed among them-
selves to shoot him down with arrows when he climbs the dum-tree. But so clever
was Liyongo that he shoots down the top-most and ripest bunch of the dum-
fruit for his guests without having to climb the tall tree to his doom.

In the second story, Daud succeeds in enticing Liyongo to a festival of dances
and tournaments, where a hundred soldiers overcome Liyongo, arrest and
imprison him. Liyongo sends a secret message (rendered in song) through a
maid-servant to his mother from the prison. His guards, who have consistently

confiscated any meal sent to Liyongo, disregard the huge loaf made of coarse bran which the maid delivers, smuggling a file to Liyongo. And so while a final dance is being performed at the request of Liyongo, he himself suddenly appears among the crowd to the dismay of his cousin Daud. After this Liyongo repairs to his kingdom, on the mainland.

And so we come to our extract, in which Daud employs the services of Liyongo's own son, seducing him by an offer of his daughter's hand in marriage. The psychological truth of the callow youth's motivation and behaviour, the filial tenderness and heroic endurance of Liyongo, the tragic pathos of the mother's pleas contrasted with the cynicism of the Sultan of Pate are only part of the powerful effect of this final episode of Liyongo's legend. The majestic rhythm of the elaborate Swahili verse-line, divided into four parts (three of which are marked by rhyme ending) but linked to succeeding lines by the recurrent rhyme, -ya or -wa, can hardly be guessed from Kijuma's English version, excellent though his translation is. These qualities illustrate the sophisticated and complex art of oral narration represented by this epic.

Owusu

Valiant Owusu,
The stranger on whom the citizen of the town depends,
Father, allow my children and me to depend on you
So that we may all of us get something to eat,
5 Father on whom I wholly depend.

When father sees me now, he will hardly recognise me.
He will meet me carrying an old torn mat and a horde of flies.
Father with whom I confer
My children and I will look to you.
10 Father on whom I wholly depend.

Killer of hunger,
My saviour,
Father the slender arm full of kindness
Father the rover whose footprints are on all paths.

Notes

Title Owusu A common Akan name.
line 3 Father Not literally meant, but applied to someone who has become a protector and the breadwinner for a widowed wife and her children.
line 7 Image of a homeless destitute forced to sleep in the open and to go unwashed.
line 8 The tense of this verb *confer* is present, and this implies an ongoing process of consultation through prayers offered and fulfilled.

line 11   *Killer of hunger*   Refers back to quality of valour attributed to the
   dead in the opening line.
line 14   *the rover*   A variation on the stranger-citizen antithesis; but here the
   emphasis is on the pioneering courage of the man who has left his
   footprints on hitherto unexplored paths for others to follow.

Questions

1 In what way is the belief that the dead are not entirely separated from the
  living expressed in this dirge?
2 Pick out the devices by which the speaker conveys her sense of deep loss.
3 What is the effect of the repetition of some lines in this dirge?

Commentary

A dirge, among the Akan-speaking people of Ghana, is not only a song of
mourning for the dead. It usually involves recalling and celebrating the ancestors
and the achievement of the lineage group to which the dead person and the
living mourners belong. The typical Akan dirge, therefore, follows a formula in
which the dead man's name is coupled with the names of his ancestors, whose
achievements are enumerated in a series of praise adjectives. The line formula
is usually name followed by attributes placed in figurative language. This device
is illustrated in lines 2, 13 and 14.

   This particular dirge has peculiarities of its own. It was entirely improvised
by a woman on the death of a school teacher, a non-native of the village, who
had adopted her and her children when she had lost her husband. She could
therefore not speak of the dead man's lineage and string together the names of
his ancestors. What she does in this dirge is to spontaneously devise praise-
names extolling the personal qualities of the dead. Her great admiration for the
dead is also expressed when she calls him *father*. Another feature of the dirge
worth noticing is the repetition of lines, sometimes exact, sometimes with slight
variations.

It all started with the conversion

It all started with the conversion,
We accepted the conversion in the belief that we were accepting
God,
Yet this God we said we would accept,
This Bible is pregnant with abomination.
5 It is held by a man whose collar faces westward.
In the front is the part that is folded over,
At the back is an opening where butterflies stay,
And that is where a cannon is lodged
Which appears below the ear and comes out at the chin,
10 And it shatters the sinews of those in front.

And when the country was in a plight,
The cannon penetrated deeply,
It penetrated and calmed things down.
The great dog, the child of Grey,
15 Who is called big George,
The son of Grey,
Said he was rearranging the land,
Yet in this time of abhorrence and shame
He stood apart and shaded his eyes,
20 Watching the result of the piling of corpses.
People lay stark without any shots fired
Because they knew how to crawl on their bellies,
Avoiding the cannon as they made towards the killer.

Notes

line 4   The two main agents of colonialism were education and Christianity. The conversion was from belief in African traditional religion and the culture that it manifested to the new religion of the Christian God and its tenets. But because of what Africans considered deceitful attitudes of the preachers of the Bible and the fact that the Europeans often times justified their actions by some peculiar interpretations of the Bible, the Africans came to look upon the Book as an ally in a wicked and destructive campaign; it became a decoy.

abomination   Something loathsome and obscene.

line 5   collar   Here refers to the clerical collar worn by clergymen.

westward   Refers to the fact that these missionaries came from the West.

lines 6–10   The reference is to the attire of the clergy. The collar and front piece are fastened at the back and they are open. They easily pull out their hidden bullets from these openings and do their targets in. The impression given is that they shoot people from the back, which is a treacherous act. There is the popular remark that the colonial exploiters came with the Bible in one hand and the gun in the other.

line 11   The Xhosa fought many wars of resistance with the white colonialists, in 1850–1851 and 1877–1878. They were eventually defeated, but they were protesting the seizure of their land and the destruction of their economy. In a seminal form this is the apartheid situation the blacks are protesting in South Africa today.

in a plight   Refers to the wars.

lines 12–13   Effective use of euphemism and understatement to convey the great havoc and loss which the whites caused with their guns and the eventual subjugation of the protesting Xhosa.

lines 14–16   Sir George Grey was Governor of the Cape Province, 1854–1861.

lines 17–19   The conquest of the Xhosa was assured when missionaries allied with Sir George Grey who had political and administrative power.

line 21   stark   Stiff, rigid, stubborn. The Xhosa were a brave and warlike people, quite familiar with the arts of war.

1 Discuss the use of irony in this poem.
2 What elements of this extract make us believe that this is part of a praise-
poem?

Commentary

There are two interesting facts about this poem. Firstly it is "an extract from
a Xhosa praise-poem addressed to Kaiser Mantanzima by Phakamile Yali-
Manisi". Secondly it was composed extempore on a topic suggested to the poet.
The result says something for the ability of the poet and also tells the readers
something about the nature of oral poetry. The oral style is evident but the poem
does not contain the type of eulogies and epithets that characterise praise-poetry
and seems more interested in narrating significant historical experience.
However, there is implied, a tribute to the courage of the Xhosa who resisted
the perfidy of the British administration and demonstrated a good sense of
military tactics. The quality of the poem is its subdued style with telling
undertones.

As camels who have become thirsty

As camels who have become thirsty after they have been grazing in
the Haud for a long time
And who are stopped in front of the well, while a youth sings to them
And while the word "hoobay" is chanted and voices interchanged,
So I grow wild with impatience when you say "Hodan".
5 What seems to you so simple, to me brings grief and woe.
Until people tread earth into her grave, I shall not give her up.
Rapt in a deceitful trance I thought I was sleeping with her
But it was only that a jinn counterfeited the image of her sister.
I aimed to snatch her by her hand – the place beside me was empty.
10 When I discovered that I was striving but that no one was there
I woke up abruptly, having tossed from side to side.
I rumpled my bed, like a prowling lion
I attacked and pounded the bedclothes as if it were they who had
caused my deprivation.
I lowered my face, like a hero against whom men have combined.
15 I was humbled like a boy from whom a herd of camels, which
belonged to the clan, were looted.
I felt disgraced like a woman to whom the words "I divorce you" had
been spoken.
It is degrading to yearn for what you cannot have.
Alas, alas, what a disaster has come upon me!

Notes

line 2 *stopped in front of the well* Refers to the action of camels being made to wait by the well while the herders draw the water for them. The camels know that the songs which the herders sing refer to water and so they become more eager to slake their thirst.

line 3 *"hoobay"* Refrain used in the watering songs.

line 4 *"Hodan"* Name of the lady for whom the poet has deep love. The songs which the herders sing excite the thirst of the camels just as the mention of his lady–love's name makes him mad with passion.

line 6 Until she dies and is buried.

line 8 *jinn* (also genie or djinn) A magical spirit in Arabian fairy tales.

line 16 In Islamic culture a man can terminate his marriage by repeating *"I divorce you"* four times. This open declaration has the force of law.

Questions

1 Discuss the use of similes in this poem.
2 How does the poet dramatise his love for Hodan?
3 Explain line 5.

Commentary

The question of the authorship or anonymity of oral poetry is one of the interesting critical points in any discussion of oral poetry. However, in some cases we are able to identify specific oral composers, Ilmi Boundheri in this case.

The culture of poetry among the Somali has a long and popular heritage. Indeed, Somalia has been described as "a nation of poets" and even now poetry composition and recitation is a very familiar art, almost a national pastime. Oral poetry is composed on a variety of topics – especially love, politics, nature – and often functions as a means of communication. Oral poetic art has become highly developed in Somalia and acquired much sophistication.

Somali poetry takes much of its colour and imagery from the occupation, the topography and religion of the people. This love poem manifests all these qualities. Boundheri was a remarkable oral poet. He is known to have died of love, and in his poetry he applied the classical alliterative style of Somali poetry (not evident in this translation) to the theme of love.

In this poem Boundheri has discovered that the woman he loves has married another and he is overwhelmed by grief. The poem then is a lament for lost love. He uses effectively the image of thirsty camels and the whole poem is a texture of similes showing the futility of his longing and rage. The last two lines contain a moral and a recognition of the psychological havoc that he has suffered. Notice the clarity of this poem. Also notice that it has a well-defined structure presenting well-marked, logical stages in the development of the theme of the poem, stages marked by the exploration of different images.

Slowly the muddy pool

Slowly the muddy pool becomes a river.
Slowly my mother's illness becomes her death.
When wood breaks, it can be mended.
But ivory breaks for ever.
5 An egg falls to reveal a messy secret.
My mother went and carried her secret along.
She has gone far –
We look for her in vain.
But when you see the kob antelope on the way to the farm,
10 When you see the kob antelope on the way to the river –
Leave your arrows in the quiver,
And let the dead depart in peace.

Notes

lines 1–2 The two parallel lines which begin this poem state concisely and through imagery the theme of the poem. They also set the pattern for the exploration of the subject of death. *The muddy pool* represents or is the counterpart of *mother's illness* just as *river* is death. There is the implication of a change from a state of disease (a muddy pool is contaminated and stagnant) to one of cleanliness since the river purifies through its dynamic flow. There is the sense of release from some restriction. The meaning would then seem to be that death which has "afflicted" the poet's mother is a continuity which transports her into a finer state where life continues in a more refined state.

line 4 Ivory is a hard white substance of which elephant tusks are made. It is precious and expensive. The metaphor here conveys the idea of the final and irreparable nature of death.

line 5 A wholesome egg contains the seed of life and mortality in its embryo. This is the "secret" spilled when the egg is broken, and an accident which cannot be repaired. *Messy* refers to the look of the spilled embryo and albumen. The broken egg no longer holds life nor can a live chick come out of it because the fall has destroyed or is the cause of the destruction of the life in it.

line 6 In traditional society death is not an end brought about by natural causes. It is always the result of the malevolence of some enemies. The mother did not reveal the secret of the cause of her death.

lines 7–8 Refers to the custom among some traditional African societies of searching for the spirit of the dead at cross roads.

lines 9–12 In traditional mythology the spirits of the dead can assume the form of animals as they journey from this world into the other world. The *kob antelope* embodies the spirit of the poet's dead mother on her way into the world beyond. In some traditional beliefs human beings are said to have animal counterparts (totems). Once these animals are killed the human beings they represent also die. In European thought this phenomenon is known as metempsychosis or transmigration.

Questions

1 Attempt a detailed analysis of the style of this poem, paying particular attention to its form and imagery.
2 Compare the ideas expressed here with your people's ideas on death.

Commentary

The dirge is one of the main poetic types of African oral traditional literature. Death for the African is more than the clinical cessation of the human mechanism. It is a transformation, and a mystery which is constantly contemplated and impossible to unravel. The dead, especially elders, join a galaxy of ancestors who have very strong influence on the living. The beliefs which surround death help to define the African attitude to life.

This brief lamentation contains a great deal of the cultural beliefs of the African about death. The lament is done through a series of logically connected metaphors, similes and allusions. The form is dominated by parallel and antithetical lines and repetitions. Structurally, the poem of twelve lines can be divided into three parts with each quatrain providing a definite development in the revelation of the ideas about death, ending with the dead spirit departing this world into the next via the body of a *kob antelope*.

Jean-Joseph Rabearivelo

Jean-Joseph Rabearivelo was born in Antananarivo, Madagascar, in March 1901. The only child of a devoted, but unmarried, mother, Joseph-Casimir, as he was first called, received his only formal education in first cycle Catholic mission schools. Nevertheless, he subsequently improved his knowledge of the French language through enormous and disciplined reading on his own.

Madagascar had become a French colony in 1905 and, although there were a few enlightened and sympathetic French writers, like Jean Paulhan and Pierre Camo who spent some time in Madagascar working for the colonial administration and who encouraged the young Malagasy aspiring to be a writer, Rabearivelo felt very much isolated from the metropolitan culture of France which greatly attracted him the more he read about it. Herein lay one of the tragic ironies of his short life: for whereas, by his self-acquired culture, he would have been acceptable company for any of the metropolitan French men of letters he read and imitated, in Madagascar, Rabearivelo was the victim of the stuffy colonial administration. He felt isolated in his own country. From 1924 his work as a proof-reader for the local publishing house in Antananarivo brought him in touch with the local intelligentsia and visitors like Paulhan and Camo. His early poetry under the encouragement of Pierre Camo was published in the local literary magazines. Yet his unfulfilled aspirations for recognition increasingly led to a life of dissipation. In 1937, he saw what he regarded as a perfect opportunity to quit the island and go to France as the representative of his country at the Paris Exhibition Universelle. At the last minute, however, the colonial administration decided to send a group of Malagasy basket-weavers to represent the colony. Shattered by this loss of an opportunity to fulfill his life's ambition, Rabearivelo committed suicide on 22 June 1937.

Rabearivelo's poetic career stands in ironic contrast to that of the generation of francophone poets, like Senghor and David Diop, who were to form the vanguard of the *Negritude* movement that emerged barely a decade after his death: for while they were colonial evolués in France, struggling against the white man's culture and hankering after their roots in Africa, Rabearivelo felt an exile on his African soil, yearning to belong to the metropolitan culture of France. And yet, it is in Rabearivelo's mature poetry that we encounter some of the most vivid impressions of the continent's physical reality and the specific nature of its colonized subject's experience of frustration and alienation.

Rabearivelo brought out five volumes of his poetry before his death. The last two volumes published before his death – *Near Dreams* (*Presques-Songes*) 1934, and *Translations from the Night* (*Traduit de la Nuit*) 1935, contain some of his mature and most beautiful poems.

His early poetry was very much influenced by the French poets of the late nineteenth and the early twentieth century, i.e. the symbolists and the surrealists. The result of this is the powerful role of the imagination and fantasy in his poetry. Of an early poem like "Pomegranate", we can truly say that in it what the imagination sees becomes absolutely true. But his mature poetry owed its clarity of imagery and its spare but effective language to the verbal techniques and the proverbs of the indigenous oral poetry called the hain tenys. Of the poems included in this anthology, "Cactus" and the "Three daybreaks", which come from *Presques-Songes*, are examples of his mature work.

Cactus

That multitude of fused hands
that offer flowers to the sky –
that multitude of fingerless hands
unshaked by the wind,
5 they say a hidden spring
wells in their unbroken palms
they say that inner spring
refreshes myriad herds
and many wandering tribes
10 in the borders of the South.

Fingerless hands spurt from a spring
Fused hands wreathe the sky.

Here,
when the flanks of the city were made as green
15 as moonbeams glancing through the forests,
when still they cooled the hillsides of Iarive
crouched like bulls after food,
upon these rocks, too steep for goats,
they drew apart to guard their springs.
20 Lepers in finery of flowers.

Fathom the cave from which they came
to find the cause of their ravaging sickness –
source cloudier than evening
and more distant than the dawn –
25 you will know no more than I.
Blood of the earth, sweat of the stone
seed of the wind
flowing together in these palms
have dissolved their fingers

30 and replaced them with golden flowers.

I know a child,
still a prince in the kingdom of God
who would go on:
"And Fate took pity on the lepers,
35 and told them to plant their flowers
and to guard their springs
far from cruel men."

Notes

line 2   flowers   The poet sees the cluster of pin-like prickles that cover the palms of the cactus plant, as flowers.

line 3   fingerless hands   A vivid description of the palms of the plant. This is taken up later, in line 20, where they are indirectly compared to the palms of lepers who have lost their fingers.

line 5   they   That is, people generally. The poet is recounting folk explanation of the survival of the cactus in the desert conditions of its environment.

line 10   borders of the South   The southern part of the island of Madagascar, which is drier and supports only nomadic life.

lines 5–10   It is not clear whether the *hidden spring* refers to an underground source of water which nourishes the plants on the outskirts of Antananarivo, but flows unseen until it reaches the southern part of the island of Madagascar, where it then comes to the surface to refresh nomadic life. Or whether the spring remains hidden throughout, and its refreshing effect, even in the south, is indirect and only felt when the nomadic tribes and their herds suck the fleshy palms of the cactus plant.

line 13   Here   The outskirts of Antananarivo, in the northern part of the island, in contrast to the south.

line 15   A surrealist image: the attempt is to convey the rare effect of the green palms of the cactus plant against the background of the grey desert all round; the effect is as magical as the moonbeams lighting up the surface of the green leaves in the darkness.

line 19   drew apart   Because the plant grows so high up the hills, it would seem as though it deliberately sought isolation from men. Hence the comparison with lepers in the next line.

line 22   ravaging sickness   Leprosy.

lines 26–30   A mysterious combination of elements which, for the poet, accounts for the change that has taken place in the palms of the plant as in the hands of the lepers.

line 31   a child   Someone (like the poet himself) who looks at the plant through innocent eyes and sees how adapted it is to its environment and its function.

Questions

1 The poem opens in a manner of someone pointing to an object which he proceeds to describe. How do we, as listeners, succeed in identifying this object with the cactus plant?

2 Lines 11 and 12 seem to summarise what has been said in the preceding ten lines. By paying attention to the verbs in these two lines, state what else they add to what has gone on before.
3 How effective is the comparison in line 17?
4 What does the poet achieve through the comparisons used in lines 23 and 24?
5 Some anthologies delete the last section (lines 31–37) of this poem. Would you say that this last section is essential to the total meaning of the poem?

Commentary

This is a poem which seems to proceed out of a child-like curiosity and wonder. Its strength lies in a careful observation of details and daring comparisons which give evidence of the pure fantasy and the powerful imagination of the poet. But what the imagination sees becomes absolutely true: for the imagination penetrates the surface reality and brings out the essential (surreal) truth about the cactus: the mystery of its peculiar form and its existence.

In a way, the poet is meditating on the ability of the cactus plant to survive in a harsh dry climate: it is green where everything else is brown. But the last seven lines suggest that Rabearivelo saw the plant as a symbol of his own life as an artist. A similar view of the life of the artist is seen in "Daybreak III".

Pomegranate

The rays of the new-born sun
    search under the branches
the breast of the ripe pomegranate
    and bite it till it bleeds.

5 Discreet and shuddering kiss
    hard and scalding embrace.
Soon the pure thrust
    will draw purple blood.

Its taste will be sweeter,
10   because it was pregnant with desire
And with fearful love
    and scented blossoms –
Pregnant by the lover sun.

Notes

Title *Pomegranate* Round thick-skinned reddish fruit containing seeds in a red juicy flesh. Native to Asia and North Africa.
line 1 *new-born sun* Early morning sun.
line 3 The fruits which are of the size of an orange or an apple look like breasts as they hang from the branches.

48

line 4 bite The effect of the sun shining on the fruit is conceived of in this way to bring out the idea of passion.

bleeds There is a lot of play on the colour red in this poem. The pomegranate is a red fruit and a ripe fruit will be even more strikingly so; normally, the process of ripening for fruits involves changing their colour to golden yellow or red. The leaves of a pomegranate tree are red, yellow and white and the scene created by the golden rays of the early morning sun playing on this environment will certainly be very attractive. Or it could mean that the fruit becomes redder as the intensity of the sun increases, which again has sexual connotation.

line 6 scalding To scald is to burn with hot water or steam. This is a very poetically conceived encounter. The poet takes into consideration the moisture which is in the atmosphere and settles on cold surfaces as dew.

lines 7–8 It is early morning and this metaphor conjures up the image of virginal purity. Reference here is to the bleeding that is supposed to accompany a virgin's first experience of the sexual act.

line 10 because it was pregnant with desire The fruit was mature enough and it was at the point of ripening. In line with the sexual image which the poet employs in this poem, the fruit itself was hungry for satisfaction and so the intercourse was satisfying and led to the fruit being impregnated (ripened). Once a fruit is ripe it can be propagated. Words like *bite, bleed, kiss, embrace, thrust, desire, lover* all build up the sexual atmosphere.

line 11 The fruit was looking forward to the love making with trepidation because it was the first time.

line 12 scented blossoms Sweet smelling flowers. The picture is that of a perfumed garden which acts as an aphrodisiac, an aid to love-making by providing an invigorating environment.

Questions

1 Pick out the words and phrases which suggest the sun's aggression against the fruit.
2 How does the poet suggest that the fruit is not merely a victim of the sun's aggression?
3 Explain in detail the imagery of this poem.
4 In what sense can you call Rabearivelo a nature poet?

Commentary

One of the common observations made by critics of African poetry who are familiar with European and English poetry is that there are no significant African nature poets in the great romantic tradition. However, a close look at African poetry shows that there are quite a few poets for whom nature is more than a decorative backcloth in their poetry or the source of one or two images. African poets may not have formulated comparable philosophical ideas about nature, but their poetry exhibits a sensitiveness and depth of penetration which is engaging. Rabearivelo was one such poet. He was, amongst other things, a nature poet and his nature poetry partakes of his feverish imagination which often approached mystic heights.

In this poem the poet envisages the early morning sun striking a pomegranate fruit as a process of courtship and an act of love-making with the sun as the male principle and the fruit as the female principle. The first stanza describes the contact between the two objects with the word *search* possibly connoting courting. This is the first stage. The second stanza describes the foreplay as the two expectant objects tenderly but passionately express their love. In the last stanza the conjugal act has taken place, the sun has inseminated the fruit and fertilized it. All this has taken place in an idyllic environment. There is a metaphysical (in the sense of the type of poetry written by John Donne and others) quality to this poem that makes it fine and beautiful.

Three daybreaks

I

Have you seen the dawn go poaching
in night's orchard?
See, she is coming back
down eastern pathways
5 overgrown with lilyblooms.
From head to foot she is splashed with milk
like those children the heifers suckled long ago.
She holds a torch in hands
stained black and blue like the lips of a girl
10 munching mulberries.

Escaping one by one there fly before her
the birds she has taken in her traps.

II

Is it from the East or from the West
the first call comes? We do not know.
But now
in their huts transfixed by stars
5 and other assegais of the dark,
the cocks enumerate themselves,
blowing into sea-shells,
answering on every side,
until the sleeper in the ocean comes again,
10 until the ascension of the lark
who goes to meet him and the songs she carries
are drenched in dew.

III

All the stars are melted together
in the crucible of time,
then cooled in the sea
and turned into a many-faceted stone-block.
5 A dying lapidist, the Night,

50

setting to work with all her heart
and all her grief to see her mills
crumbling, crumbling,
like ashes in the wind,
10 cuts with what loving care the prism.

The craftsman on her own unnoticed grave
sets up this monument of light.

Notes

Poem I
lines 3–4 cf. "But look, the dawn in russet mantle clad Walks o'er the dew
    of yon high eastward hill", Hamlet, Act 1 Sc. 1: 166–67.
line 5 The morning clouds (cumulus) touched by the rays of the sun.
line 7 Refers to a folk tale in which orphans nurtured by virgin cows on
    milk alone, look immaculately white.
line 9 A fanciful image suggested by the rays of the sun as it lights up
    patches of the dark clouds (black) and the clear sky (blue).
Poem II
lines 4–5 The attempt is to convey the impression of the cocks woken up
    and momentarily dazed by the stars that shine ever so brightly in the
    early hours of the morning.
line 9 the sleeper The sun.
Poem III
line 5 lapidist A craftsman who cuts precious stones to bring out their
    beauty, making them gems.

Questions

1 Three figures occur in the three poems: the female "vandal" in Poem I, the
  "sleeper" in Poem II, and the "dying craftsman" in Poem III. How does
  the mood of each poem depend on the activities associated with each
  figure?
2 Identify some of the trophies with which the female vandal in Poem I
  returns from her adventure. How are the birds related to these other
  trophies?
3 Comment on the effectiveness of the five lines beginning *But now* in Poem
  II.
4 Lines 5–10 of Poem III constitute one long sentence in which the main
  verb does not occur until the very last line. Paying attention to the long
  vowels and the words emphasized in the six lines, show how the rhythm re-
  inforces the meaning of this particular poem.
5 The first two poems begin with questions, the third with a statement. How
  far does this account for the difference in tone between Poem I and Poem
  III?
6 "There is a sense in which these three poems together suggest a
  progression from innocence, through experience, to maturity." Would you
  agree with this comment?

Commentary

These are three poems which present equally persuasive but different impressions of the coming of day. In the first poem, it is the dawn, personified as a female figure, that invades and overcomes the night. In the second poem, the arrival of the dawn is only indirectly suggested: awakening is conveyed through the marshalling of the ranks of the cocks, as if for battle. In contrast, in the third poem, it is the night that laboriously forms the dawn out of the ashes of its own disintegration.

The central metaphor (conceit) of Poem I, is the act of poaching which is attributed to the dawn. This adventure yields trophies with which the dawn emerges.

In Poem II, the picture of the battle-call evoked by the 'enumerating' of the cocks, is superseded by the ceremonious welcome to a dignitary, with all the attendant splendour of colour and music.

Poem III takes the dawn at an earlier stage than the first two poems. It virtually creates a myth of the sun formed by all the stars that drop into the sea and melt together, as the night fades. This globe of a star will emerge as the sun and mark the end of the night. Obversely, it is the night that calls forth the sun, and, like an artist, sacrifices his life in order to create a monument of light. Poem III throws some light on how Rabearivelo saw his frustrated life feeding his art and this reveals his essentially romantic vision of the artist.

Leopold Sedar Senghor

Leopold Sedar Senghor, poet, philosopher, scholar and statesman, is one of the oldest and most prominent living persons associated with African poetry and culture. He was born in 1906, of the Serere ethnic group in Joal, Senegal. A staunch Catholic, he was educated in Dakar, Senegal and Paris, France where he made history as the first West African to graduate from the Sorbonne and teach in a French University. Senghor became involved in French colonial politics, which prepared him for the leadership role he was to play among his people. He fought in the French army in the Second World War and was a prisoner of war in Germany, experiences recorded in *Hosties Noires*. After the war he became the Deputy for Senegal in the French Constituent Assembly, President of the Council of the Republic, and Counselling minister at the office of the president of the French Community. In 1960 he became the President of the Federal Assembly of Mali and later in the same year President of an Independent Republic of Senegal, retiring in 1980. Among his numerous publications including critical and philosophical essays are five volumes of poetry: *Chants d'Ombre, Hosties Noires, Chants pour Naett* (first published as *Chants pour Signare*), *Ethiopiques* and *Nocturnes*.

Senghor is the greatest African exponent of the philosophy of *Negritude*. *Negritude* as an ideology was first developed in reaction to the cultural deprivation and Western cultural decadence which Senghor and others experienced in Europe. It aims amongst other things to reassert and revive, through literature, the cultural values, identity and authenticity of Africans, and to extol the ancestral glories and the beauty of Africa, partly through a renunciation of what is Western and partly through a re-ordering of imagery. *Negritude* has passed through many phases, partly in response to the criticisms levelled against it, especially the charge of romanticism and racism. It is now seen as a humanistic creed, an ideology that emphasises the values of African civilisation and the black contribution to human civilization.

In literature, negritudian ideals are manifested in the use of traditional images, local references, and symbols, in the lyric impulse which harnesses the rhythm of traditional oral poetry, and in a bold declaration of those qualities that distinguish the African from the European, especially intuition and rhythm. Senghor's poems vindicate these and other points, which account for both the success and failure of his poetry. The poems possess lyrical beauty (they are meant to be recited to the accompaniment of local musical instruments), but some are tainted by emotional and oversentimental indulgences.

Senghor has won several international prizes for his contribution to African literature, and has instituted prizes to promote the arts in Africa.

In memoriam

Sunday.
The crowding stony faces of my fellows make me afraid.
Out of my tower of glass haunted by headaches and my restless
    Ancestors
I watch the roofs and hills wrapped in mist
5 Wrapped in peace . . . the chimneys are heavy and stark.
At their feet my dead are sleeping, all my dreams made dust
All my dreams, blood freely spilt along the streets, mingled with blood
    from butcheries.
And now, from this observatory, as if from the outskirts of the town
I watch my dreams listless along the streets, sleeping at the foot of the
    hills
10 Like the forerunners of my race on the banks of the Gambia and
    Salum
Now of the Seine, at the foot of the hills.
Let my mind turn to my dead!
Yesterday was All Saints, the solemn anniversary of the sun
In all the cemeteries, there was no one to remember.
15 O dead who have always refused to die, who have resisted death
From the Sine to the Seine, and in my fragile veins you my
    unyielding blood
Guard my dreams as you have guarded your sons, your slender-limbed
    wanderers
O dead, defend the roofs of Paris in this sabbath mist
Roofs that guard my dead
20 That from the dangerous safety of my tower, I may go down into the
    street
To my brothers whose eyes are blue
Whose hands are hard.

Notes

line 2   The crowding stony faces   Serious expressionless faces of religious
    devotees making their way to Sunday service.
line 3   Either the poet was unwell (and could not join the crowd) or too
    much reflection has given him a headache. He is anxious to pay homage
    to his ancestors to appease them.
line 6   Dreams are a strong image in this poem. They refer to his ambition,
    desire for excellence, the great hope he had about the transforming
    power of Europe, ideals for which blood had been spilt and sacrifice
    performed. These dreams have been thwarted, buried and no longer
    motivate him. One dream the poet had at the time of writing this poem
    must have had to do with his wish to honour his ancestors.
line 9   listless   Indifferent, uninterested. In this context, it can be seen as
    modifying either the poet (I) or dreams. It is a problem of translation;

but judging by the tenor of the poem, this feeling and sense of langour would seem to refer to the poet.

line 10 **Salum** A river in Senegal.

line 11 **Seine** One of the major rivers in France. It divides Paris into two just as the Thames does London.

lines 12–14 Two main thoughts occupy the poet's mind. First, the general reflection on the failing of his dreams. Second, the thought of his ancestors whom he would have loved to be able to remember in the way the French remember their ancestors. In France, November 1 is All Saints and it is observed as a public holiday. In the Christian calendar, the following day is All Souls on which people remember their ancestors with flowers and meditation. They visit their graves in the cemeteries. Senghor could not physically participate in this important ceremony since his ancestors were not buried in Paris.

lines 15–16 Here, Senghor stresses reverence for ancestors and the belief that although physically dead they are alive, guard their offspring and are influential in all their undertakings. This belief is held in his native Senegal and in France. Sine and Seine are used synecdochically.

line 16 **Sine** River in Senegal near where Senghor was born. Runs parallel to the Salum.

line 20 This is an example of oxymoron. *Dangerous safety* sounds paradoxical. But the explanation is that the poet is watching the worshippers from a high point which is dangerous because the poet can get dizzy and fall to his death. Yet, it is safe because it provides just about the right physical and psychological distance which the poet needs to analyze and meditate on the scene below him.

lines 21–22 The universal brotherhood and identification which are important aspects of Senghor's mental and philosophical attitude. *My brothers whose eyes are blue* can refer to the whites or the wealthy ones among them, while *Whose hands are hard* refer to the poor labouring ones, both white and black.

Questions

1 Describe the scene or situation which the poet is presenting.
2 Most of the lines of this poem are long and read like prose. Yet this piece is a poem. What qualities make you accept this classification?
3 What dreams does the poet refer to? What do these dreams signify in this poem and other poems by the same author which you have read?
4 Who is referred to in the last two lines and how do they fit into the general pattern of ideas in this poem?
5 Discuss the sound and rhythm of this poem.

Commentary

This is one of Senghor's earliest poems and it is taken from his first collection *Chants d'Ombre*. The poems in this collection, like "In memoriam" were inspired by the feeling of exile and alienation which he experienced during his studentship in Paris and by the consequent longing for return to his idealised home. This poem is written in memory of his dead ancestors who Senghor believes continue to exert strong influences on their offspring. The occasion was the Catholic Christian ceremony in which believers remember their dead by visiting their graves and adorning them with flowers.

The theme of ancestors is one which Senghor constantly celebrates in his poems. Indifferent now to, or in spite of the observance of the Christian Sunday, his salvation and refuge are his ancestors, who are always present. The poem appropriately ends with a prayer in which he consigns himself and his brothers (both white and black to show the universal brotherhood which he urged) to the care of their ancestors.

The poem manifests some characteristics of Senghor's style and ideas in the way he juxtaposes Africa and Europe, subtly insisting on antithesis, reconciliation and identification in his perception of their relationship. Senghor's attitude to France remains ambivalent. France, or Europe for that matter, has inspired many high hopes in him, hopes which have been dashed and have remained mere dreams.

Nuit de Sine

Woman, lay on my forehead your perfumed hands, hands softer than fur.
Above, the swaying palm trees rustle in the high night breeze
Hardly at all. No lullaby even.
The rhythmic silence cradles us.
5 Listen to its song, listen to our dark blood beat, listen
To the deep pulse of Africa beating in the mist of forgotten villages.

See the tired moon comes down to her bed on the slack sea
The laughter grows weary the story-tellers even
Are nodding their heads like a child on the back of its mother
10 The feet of the dancers grow heavy, and heavy the voice of the answering choirs.

It is the hour of stars, of Night that dreams
Leaning upon this hill of clouds, wrapped in its long milky cloth.
The roofs of the huts gleam tenderly. What do they say so secretly to the stars?
Inside the fire goes out among intimate smells that are acrid and sweet.

15 Woman, light the clear oil lamp, where the ancestors gathered around may talk as parents talk when the children are put to bed.
Listen to the voice of the ancients of Elissa. Exiled like us
They have never wanted to die, to let the torrent of their seed be lost in the sands.

Let me listen in the smoky hut where there comes a glimpse of the
    friendly spirits
My head on your bosom warm like a dang smoking from the fire,

20 Let me breathe the smell of our Dead, gather and speak out again
    their living voice, learn to
Live before I go down, deeper than diver, into the high profundities
    of sleep.

Notes

Title   Means "Night of Sine".
line 5   The qualification of blood by *dark* is deliberate. Senghor intends
    thereby to distinguish African blood from European blood. In view of his
    crusade and his perception as a poet, this line of thought may be
    accepted. But it can also be argued that it seems to carry his argument
    too far, since the blood of all human beings is the same colour.
line 16   Elissa   The name of a village in upper Portuguese Guinea, where
    Senghor's ancestors were buried.
line 19   dang   A Wolof word for a kind of granulated flour meal, known also
    as couscous.

Questions

1 How does the poet sustain the mood which he builds in this poem?
2 Do you find this type of poem satisfying? Give reasons for your reaction.
3 Describe the village scene in your own words.

Commentary

Night is one of the dominant symbols and images in Senghor's poetry and this
poem is a clear demonstration of this fact. "Nuit de Sine" is an evocation of
the mystery, beauty and fragrance of the African night – the stars, the moon,
the trees, the quiet villages and the familiar scenes associated with them.

Stanza one is a general evocation of the natural surroundings achieving an
atmosphere of deep calm and peace suitable for meditation. The second stanza
introduces human elements whose reactions underscore the power of night and
bring the world of man and nature closer. The third and fourth stanzas also
evoke the general natural surrounding but the all-important theme of ancestors
is introduced, stressing the eternal link between the ancestors, the living and
the unborn. By the time we get to the end of the poem, the worlds of man and
nature have been united under the power of night and there is clear reference
to the eternal cycle of life and death, of death and renewal in the last lines which
also have religious overtones.

The sheer exuberance and irresistible drowsiness induced by the poem come
through the modulated tone, the metaphors, the cumulative variation in ideas and
attitudes, the exploitation of sound patterns, the cadence and rhythm which sink
us *into the high profundities of sleep* by the time we get to the end of the poem.

I will pronounce your name

I will pronounce your name, Naett, I will declaim you, Naett!
Naett, your name is mild like cinnamon, it is the fragrance in which
    the lemon grove sleeps,
Naett, your name is the sugared clarity of blooming coffee trees
And it resembles the savannah, that blossoms forth under the
    masculine ardour of the midday sun.
5 Name of dew, fresher than shadows of tamarind,
Fresher even than the short dusk, when the heat of the day is
    silenced.
Naett, that is the dry tornado, the hard clap of lightning
Naett, coin of gold, shining coal, you my night, my sun!. . .
I am your hero, and now I have become your sorcerer, in order to
    pronounce your names.
10 Princess of Elissa, banished from Futa on the fateful day.

Notes

line 1   In the collection *Chants pour Naett*, Naett is the name of the young
African girl to whom the poems are dedicated and of whom they sing.
Sometimes Naett appears as a symbol of Africa also.

line 2   A *cinnamon* is an East Indian tree which produces aromatic inner bark
used as spice. The rest of the line completes this image of the sensuous.

line 5   A *tamarind* is a fruit-bearing tropical tree.

line 8   One of Senghor's innovations in African poetry is his inversion of
traditional images associated with black and anything dark. Rather than
see black and dark as outrageous and evil, Senghor portrays it as
beautiful and good. In this line he retains the traditional associations of
the sun as bright and regal, but adds his new view of night.

line 9   There are three points to note about this line. Firstly, it touches on
the private and public functions of Senghor, the poet. He often appears
in both roles. Secondly, the conflation of ideas in the symbol is hinted
at, and finally the poet's devotion to and enchantment with the object of
his admiration turns him into a praise-singer. The latter is the meaning
of *I have become your sorcerer*. There is also a literal sense in which
sorcerer here is linked with the evocative quality of this poem. Notice that
he now talks of *names*.

line 10   *Futa* was a kingdom in the eighteenth and nineteenth centuries
whose capital was Fouta Djallong. This line stresses the antiquity of the
theme of the poem.

Questions

1 Discuss the variety of similes and metaphors used in this poem and explain
their significance to the theme of the poem.
2 What do you think is the importance of line 9? Discuss fully.

Commentary

Although from its theme this poem should belong to the collection *Chants pour Naett*, one of Senghor's later works, it is, in fact, listed in *Chants d'Ombre*. A probable explanation would be that in Senghor's glorification of everything African, the continent and the human beings, especially the women, fuse into one. In effect then, love and concern for the one is the same as love and concern for the other.

"I will pronounce your name" is a love poem celebrating or declaiming the poet's love for Naett. There is something traditional about the form of this poem which reminds us of praise-singers. Besides the evocative repetition of Naett, the poem progresses by a cumulative use of similes and metaphors, sometimes a bit startling, like *the dry tornado, the hand clap of lightning*, but all agreeing with Senghor's vision by praising various aspects of Naett. The sensuous images that begin and run through this piece are characteristic of Senghor.

Notice the preponderance of nature imagery in this poem. Naett is as striking as the metaphors used to describe her. It is also important to note here that "night" has a positive connotation and is related to Senghor's praise of the black man and woman and everything black.

Chaka

A dramatic poem for several voices
To the Bantu martyrs of South Africa

(against a background of funeral drums)

WHITE VOICE

Chaka, there like the panther or the evil-mouthed hyena
Three assegais nail you to the ground. The void howls for you.
This is your passion then. May the stream of blood that bathes you,
    be as a penance for you.

CHAKA (calmly)

5 Yes I am here between two brothers, two traitors two thieves
Two fools . . . ah! not as the hyena, but as the Thiopic Lion with
    head erect.
Here returned to the earth. How bright it is, the Kingdom of
    Childhood!
10 And it is the end of my passion.

WHITE VOICE

Chaka you are trembling in the deep south and the sun at the zenith
    bursts into laughter,
Dark in the daytime O Chaka, you do not hear the flutings of the
    doves.
15 Nothing except the bright blade of my voice piercing through and
    through your seven hearts.

CHAKA

Voice, white voice from beyond the sea, my inner eye lights up the
    diamond night.
There is no need for your false daylight. My breast is the shield
20   against which your lightning breaks.
Morning dew on the tamarinds, and my sun arises at the horizon of
    glass.
I hear the noonday cooing of Noliwe, I exult in the marrow of my
    bones.

WHITE VOICE

25 Ha ha ha ha Chaka. It is very well for you to talk about Noliwe, the
    beautiful girl you were to marry
Her heart like butter her eyes the petals of the waterlily her words
    soft as a water spring.
You have killed her to escape from your conscience.

CHAKA

30 And you talk about conscience to me?
Yes, I killed her, while she was telling stories of the blue lands
I killed her yes! my hand did not tremble.
A flash of fine steel in the odorous thicket of her armpit.

WHITE VOICE

So you admit it Chaka! Will you admit to the millions of men you had
35   killed
Whole regiments of pregnant women and children still at the breast?
You, provider-in-chief for vultures and hyenas, poet of the Valley of
    Death.
We looked to find a warrior, All we found was a butcher.
40 The ravines are torrents of blood. The fountain runs blood
Wild dogs behowl death in the plains where the eagle of Death
    hovers
O Chaka Zulu, worse than plague than the rolling fire of the bush.

CHAKA

A cackling farmyard, millet-eaters in a muffled cage.
45 Yes a hundred glittering regiments, plush velvet silken plumes,
    gleaming with grease like red copper.
I have set the axe to the dead wood, lit the fire in the sterile bush
Like any careful farmer. When the rains came and the time for
    sowing, the ashes were ready.

WHITE VOICE

50 What? not a word of regret. . .

CHAKA

Evil is regretted.

WHITE VOICE

The greatest evil is to steal the sweetness of breath.

CHAKA

The greatest evil is the weakness of fear.

WHITE VOICE

The weakness of the heart is forgiven.

CHAKA

55 The weakness of the heart is holy. . .
Ah! you think that I never loved her
My Negress fair with palmoil, slender as a plume
Thighs of a startled otter, of Kilimanjaro snow
Breasts of mellow rice-fields, hills of acacias under the East Wind.
60 Noliwe with her arms of boas, lips of the adder
Noliwe, her eyes were constellations. . . there is no need of moon or
    drum
But her voice is my head and the feverous pulse of the night. . .
Ah! you think that I never loved her!
65 But these long years, this breaking on the wheel of the years, this
    carcan strangling every act
This long night without sleep. . . I wandered like a mare from the
    Zambezi, running and rushing at the stars
Gnawed by a nameless suffering, like the leopard's in the trap.
70 I would not have killed her if I had loved her less.
I had to escape from doubt
From the intoxication of the milk of her mouth, from the throbbing
    drum of the night of my blood
From my bowels of fervent lava, from the uranium mines of my heart
75   in the depths of my Blackness
From love of Noliwe
From the love of my black-skinned People.

THE VOICE OF THE WIZARD ISANUSSI (far off)

Think hard Chaka. I am not compelling you. I am only a wizard a
    technician.
80 There is no power gained without sacrifice. Absolute power demands
    the blood of the dearest of all.

A VOICE (as of Chaka, far off)

She must die then. . . there is no other way.
Tomorrow her blood will sprinkle your medicine like milk on the
    dryness of the couscous.
85 Wizard, out of my sight. Even the condemned man is given a few
    hours to forget.

CHAKA (suddenly awakening)

No no white voice. You know full well. .

WHITE VOICE

I know that your goal was power.

CHAKA

It was a means. . .

WHITE VOICE

90 Your pleasure. . .

CHAKA

My calvary.
I saw in a dream all the lands to the far corners of the horizon set
under the ruler, the setsquare, the compass
Forests mowed down hills levelled, valleys and rivers in chains.
95 I saw the lands to the four corners of the horizon under the grid
traced by the twofold iron ways
I saw the people of the South like an anthill of silence
At their work. Work is holy, but work is no longer gesture
Drum and voice no longer make rhythm for the gestures of the
100   seasons
Peoples of the South, in the shipyards, the ports and the mines and
the mills
And at evening segregated in the kraals of misery.
And the peoples heap up mountains of black gold and red gold. . .
105   and die of hunger.
I saw one morning, coming out of the mist of the dawn, a forest of
woolly heads
Arms drooping bellies hollow, immense eyes and lips calling to an
impossible god.
110 Could I stay deaf to such sufferings, such contempt?

WHITE VOICE

Your voice is red with hate Chaka.

CHAKA

I have hated nothing but oppression.

WHITE VOICE

Red with hate that burns the heart.
It is the weakness of the heart that is holy, not that whirl-wind of
115   fire.

CHAKA

It is not hate to love one's people.
I say there is no peace under arms, no peace under oppression
No brotherhood without equality. I wanted all men to be brothers.

WHITE VOICE

You raised the whole South against the white man. . .

CHAKA

20 There you are, White Voice, partial voice voice of imposture.
Voice of the strong against the weak, conscience of the possessors
    from across the seas.
I did not hate the Pink Ears. We welcomed them as messengers of the
    gods
25 With pleasant words and delicious drinks.
They wanted merchandise. We gave them everything: ivory, honey,
    rainbow pelts
Spices and gold, precious stones parrots and monkeys.
Shall I speak of their rusty presents, their tawdry beads?
30 Yes, in coming to know their guns, I became a mind
Suffering became my lot, suffering of the breast and of the spirit.

WHITE VOICE

To accept suffering with a dutiful heart is redemption. . .

CHAKA

And mine was accepted. . .

WHITE VOICE

With a contrite heart. . .

CHAKA

35 For the love of my black-skinned people.

WHITE VOICE

The love of Noliwe and the sleepers of the Valley of Death?

CHAKA

For the love of Noliwe. Must I say it again?
Each death was my death. There were the coming harvests to prepare
And the millstones to grind the white flour from the tenderness of
40   black hearts.

WHITE VOICE

Much will be forgiven to those who have suffered much. . .

Notes

line 1 *panther* Black leopard.
line 2 *Assegai* Throwing spear often with an iron tip used by some South
    African tribes for hunting and warfare.
line 3 *Passion* The suffering and death of Christ; here refers to Chaka.
line 4 *Penance* Punishment willingly imposed on oneself to show that one is
    sorry for doing some wrong.
line 5 Chaka was assassinated by his two brothers and some comrades who
    were jealous of his successes and reputation.
line 6 *Thiopic* Refers to Ethiopia. The elision here is for poetic reasons.
    The lion has always been associated with Ethiopia as a symbol of her
    might – more than in the ordinary sense in which the lion features in

the armorial bearing of many countries. Emperor Haile Selassie was
known as the Lion of Ethiopia.

line 16   Seven is a magical figure. Chaka's bravery was said to be
supernatural.

line 21   tamarind   A tropical plant cultivated for its edible fruit and sweet
smelling flowers.

line 33   odorous   Having a smell.

lines 34–43   Chaka's fierce rage and ruthlessness in war won him notoriety
in the eyes of some latter-day historians. What some see as bravery in
him others see as savagery. This type of controversy is part of the
complexity and greatness of the man.

line 61   constellations   Group of fixed stars, often having a name.

line 74   lava   Molten rock thrown out by an active volcano
Uranium   A radio-active element (metal) used in the production of
atomic power.

line 91   calvary   Very bad experience which causes great suffering; cross.

line 95   grid   A system of numbered squares printed on a map so that the
exact position of any place on it may be stated or found easily.

line 98   Work is now punishment and humiliation because the people are
being exploited.

line 99   There is no mirth either, only a dreary existence.

line 103   Kraal   Traditional fenced compound in South Africa; also enclosed
piece of ground for the safe-keeping of cattle at night.

Questions

1 What picture of Chaka emerges from this poem?
2 Comment on Chaka's description or praise of Noliwe in the light of
Senghor's known defence of the African woman.
3 How does Senghor succeed in making this dramatic poem contemporary?

Commentary

In our brief comment on Mtshali's "The birth of Shaka" (see page 256) we
observe that Chaka as an intrepid and imaginative soldier and symbol has
inspired many political fighters and writers throughout black Africa. This
dramatic poem by Senghor is one example. The poem is made up of two chants
and the interlocutors are Chaka, a white voice and the voice of the wizard
Isanussi. What is presented here is a substantial part of the first chant.

The poem focuses on the last moments of Chaka's life on earth and then
unfolds in a flashback to refer to many incidents in Chaka's life and career that
contribute to the popular image of the man. Many legends and myths grew
around Chaka in his life time. The use of the white voice serves not only to
present uncomplimentary aspects of the man according to accounts by his foes,
but also gives Chaka the opportunity to express his opposition to white subju-
gation and defend the nobility of his actions. The experience with Noliwe is
a sore point but Chaka defends his action admirably. The wizard is introduced
to embody the popular link of Chaka with the supernatural.

Although Senghor is treating a historical incident, he emphasises its relevance
for contemporary times by exploring the anti-apartheid dimensions of the poem.

Senghor also uses the opportunity to press home his negritude ideas. In the final analysis, this poem remains vintage Senghor with its mellifluous lines and their general romantic evocativeness.

Long, long have you held

Long, long have you held between your hands the black face of the
    warrior
Held as if already there fell on it a twilight of death.
From the hill I have seen the sun set in the bays of your eyes.
When shall I see again, my country, the pure horizon of your face?
When shall I sit down once more at the dark table of your breast?

Hidden in the half-darkness, the nest of gentle words.

I shall see other skies and other eyes
I shall drink at the spring of other mouths cooler than lemons
I shall sleep under the roof of other heads of hair in shelter from
    storms.

10 But every year, when the rum of springtime sets my memory ablaze,
I shall be full of regret for my homeland and the rain from your eyes
    on the thirsty savannahs.

Notes

line 1 Warrior Refers to the poet persona. The use of the word recalls the
    tendency in traditional society to see any young man as a potential
    soldier or warrior to defend his people and his fatherland. It was also a
    familiar epithet to describe Africans who were struggling to get some
    education and fighting for recognition in European countries. Cf Lenrie
    Peters' "We have come home."
line 2 Describes the deep affection with which the face was cuddled.
line 3 bays of your eyes This refers to the sockets in the face where the
    eyeballs are lodged. The contour of the face is referred to in terms of
    the physical features of the landscape.
line 10 rum A strong alcoholic drink made from the juice of the sugar
    cane. It is common in the West Indies. The reference here is to the
    excitement which spring brings in the temperate countries. In spring all
    the world is awake after the dreary months of winter when all nature
    seems dead.
line 11 full of regret Means full of longing for; he misses his home. There
    is also a suggestion of tears here (rain from your eyes). The poet weeps
    for his home land. There is also the possible reference to physical rain
    since springtime in Europe is the beginning of the rainy season in West
    Africa – Senegal is in the Savannah belt.

Questions

1 What insight does the fusion of the land and woman give into the poet's emotion in this poem?
2 Explain lines 4 and 5, and 7 to 9.
3 Compare this poem to any poem by Dennis Brutus in this collection on a similar theme.

Commentary

Literature written in exile, whether voluntary or forced exile, has a strong romantic streak. The same is also true of literature written to glorify one's country, race, etc. The context of much of Senghor's poetry shares these qualities.

In this poem, written while Senghor was away from his home, he expresses his love and fondness for his country in the metaphor of love for a woman. The language is deliberately sensuous and conveys a great deal of romantic evocation and suggestiveness – feelings enhanced by the tone and attitude in the poem and the relaxed rhythm of the piece. Here, country is personified as a woman, indeed both are fused together as that which provides succour and comfort. For the poet, his country represents his entire universe – the sky, nature, woman – and it is in these that he gets his greatest satisfaction. Speaking of his country in terms of his beloved woman enriches the poem and is responsible for the seeming complex syntax of the poem which is finally the essence of the beauty of the piece.

Birago Diop

Birago Diop was born in Ouakam, a suburb of Dakar in Senegal, in 1906. He showed a keen interest in literature early in life. He was not only born into a family of gifted people who did everything to promote literature, but he also himself read a great deal of European literature. Indeed his family had had a significant and formative influence on his literary output and style. His love of folklore and subtle characterisation of women he learned from his grandmother and aunts, and his partiality for genealogical poems he inherited from his brother Youssouffa. A family incident also provided the first immediate inspiration for writing poetry: the death of his brother Massyla.

While studying veterinary science in France, Diop struck up friendship with the early leading Francophone African writers in Paris, Senghor and Damas, and he collaborated with them in the founding of the literary movement that gave birth to the concept of *Negritude*. His consciousness of his race and culture became intensified and was to influence his subsequent works. He wrote two main types of literary works; short stories and poems. The predominant strain in his writings is the preoccupation with the theme of ancestors and historical legends.

Birago Diop's creative works were therefore influenced by his immediate environment and experiences. He was very realistic, and did not adopt the theoretical approach of his contemporaries to literature. He did not concern himself with any search for a new medium of expression, but was inspired by an earnest desire to recreate old tales and to write poems which speak not only of the ancestral heritage of the African, but also deal with ordinary human situations.

Vanity

If we tell, gently, gently
All that we shall one day have to tell,
Who then will hear our voices without laughter,
Sad complaining voices of beggars
5 Who indeed will hear them without laughter?

If we cry roughly of our torments
Ever increasing from the start of things,
What eyes will watch our large mouths
Shaped by the laughter of big children
10 What eyes will watch our large mouths?

What heart will listen to our clamouring?
What ear to our pitiful anger
Which grows in us like a tumour
In the black depth of our plaintive throats?

15 When our Dead come with their Dead
When they have spoken to us with their clumsy voices;
Just as our ears were deaf
To their cries, to their wild appeals
Just as our ears were deaf
20 They have left on the earth their cries,
In the air, on the water, where they have traced their signs
For us, blind deaf and unworthy Sons
Who see nothing of what they have made
In the air, on the water, where they have traced their signs.

25 And since we did not understand our dead
Since we have never listened to their cries
If we weep, gently, gently
If we cry roughly of our torments
What heart will listen to our clamouring,
30 What ear to our sobbing hearts?

Notes

line 9   Notice what the poet does with *laughter* in the first two stanzas. First
it is the derision with which more experienced and wiser people will
regard our complaints. Then secondly it is used with sarcastic humour to
describe the mouths of black people weeping unabashedly. The use of
big children has a particular sting. It implies immaturity.

line 11   To *clamour* is to complain, demand or appeal loudly in a noisy
manner for attention. Its use follows logically from the first two stanzas.

line 12   *Pitiful* is used in two senses here: firstly, in the sense of self-pity
which can earn the contempt of others; secondly, in the sense of a puny
feeling of anger which has an unpleasant effect on us and makes others
pity us. Whichever way we take it, the poet's point is that it is a futile
anger which we have brought upon ourselves.

line 13   A *tumour* is a malignant growth, like cancer, which can easily cause
death.

line 14   *Black* describes the passage of the gullet, which remains dark to us
since we cannot see through it. In this case the adjective would seem to
be superfluous. It could also be said to refer to the fact that the African
is black. This latter use could be seen as sentimental.
   Plaintive throats   Here means mournful voices.

line 16   *Clumsy* here means guttural or muffled. In traditional African beliefs,
ancestral voices are said to sound this way since they are spiritual voices
and their revelations have to be deciphered. Masqueraders who speak or
sing with guttural voices are supposed to be incarnations of our
ancestors.

Questions

1 How would you describe the poet's attitude in this poem? (Consider his overall tone.)
2 Do you think that the poet is biased in his interpretation of social history and his insistence on one solution? Give reasons for your answer.
3 What use does the poet make of repetition in this poem?

Commentary

This poem is typical of Birago Diop, who is preoccupied in many of his poems with that aspect of African culture which emphasises the importance of and the guiding spirit of our ancestors. Here the poet is concerned to promote the necessity for Africans to remember their roots, to maintain close relationships with and learn from the wisdom of our ancestors. It is because we have neglected the warnings, advice and values of our forbears that we have been left rudderless and defenceless. Because this has been a wilful act it is needless and inadvisable for us to bemoan our fate or indulge in self-pity. It is our vanity – typified by our empty pride in European ways which we do not quite understand and disregard for our ancestral voices – that has led to our misfortune.

Three qualities of this poem need special comment. The first is the poet's introspection and wry humour, which brings out the misery of those who forsake their ancestors. In this way the poet enables us to laugh at ourselves and express deep emotions without feeling sentimental. The other features to note are the lyricism of the poem aided by subtle use of repetitions, and the structure of the poem. The first three stanzas ask questions and the next two make assertions which by implication provide answers to these questions. The final stanza recapitulates the points made so far and seals the fact that however we intend to narrate our unpleasant experiences, we can expect no sympathy since we have neglected our ancestors.

Viaticum

In one of the three jugs
The three jugs where on certain evenings return
the tranquil souls,
the breaths of the ancestors,
5 the ancestors who were men,
the ancestors who were sages,
Mother has dipped three fingers
three fingers of her left hand:
thumb, forefinger and middle finger
10 I have dipped three fingers
three fingers of my right hand:
thumb, forefinger and middle finger.

With her three fingers red with blood,
with dog's blood,

69

15 with bull's blood,
with goat's blood,
Mother has touched me three times.
She touched my forehead with her thumb,
with her forefinger my left breast
20 and my navel with her middle finger.
I have held out my fingers red with blood,
with dog's blood,
with bull's blood,
with goat's blood,
25 I have held my three fingers to the winds
the north wind, the east wind,
the south wind, the west wind;
and I have raised my three fingers towards the Moon
towards the full Moon, the full, naked Moon
30 when she was at the bottom of the biggest jug.
I have thrust my three fingers into the sand,
into the sand which had grown cool.
Mother said: "Go through the World, go
in Life. They will follow thy traces."

35 Since then I go,
I go by the tracks and on the roads,
beyond the seas and further still
beyond the sea and further, further still,
beyond the sea and beyond the place beyond.
40 And when I come to the wicked men,
the black-hearted men,
when I come to the envious,
the black-hearted men,
before me advance the breaths of the forefathers.

Notes

line 1 The number *three* is symbolic. It is often used for invocations in magical and sacrificial performances. Notice how frequently it is used. The jugs, the animals whose blood is spilt, the fingers, even the elements are three in number.

line 3 tranquil souls They are serene and undisturbed, referring to the spirits of the ancestors whose presence is felt as a breeze.

lines 26–27 Refer to the four corners of the earth.

line 28 Sacrifices are often done at night when the moon is bright because mysterious powers over the fortunes of men are attributed to the moon. Fairies, for instance, in most folk cultures are believed to appear when the moon is full and bright.

line 30 It is usual to refer to the moon as *she*. By the same token the sun is referred to as *he*. This practice was started by St. Francis. The poet is here referring to the reflections of the moon in the jug.

line 31   This line describes a symbolic action of invocation or a sign of respect during sacrifice. The earth is seen as exerting a great deal of power in the philosophy and world-view of Africans.

line 35   The sacrifice is complete and accepted; the poet has been guaranteed the guidance of the spirit of his ancestors. Notice the original construction of the phrase.

Questions

1 Describe the relationship between the poet and his mother and his ancestors.
2 The poet uses many symbols in this poem. Identify them and explain their significances.
3 Examine how the poet achieves the incantatory rhythm of the poem.
4 Discuss whether the constructions of lines 5 and 6 have any special significance.

Commentary

Viaticum is a religious term used either to describe money or victuals given to an officer going on some official business, or the eucharist which the Roman Catholic priest administers to a dying man to prepare him for the journey to the other world. The *viaticum*, then, is a sacrificial ritual meant to prepare one for a journey. This poem not only enacts such a sacrifice but is itself a ritual. The trappings of ritual are there in the frequent use of the symbolic and magical number three, in the spilt blood of animals, and in the invocation of the moon and the earth. This ritual prepares the poet for the journey through life and assures him of the protection of the spirit of his ancestors against all ills. Notice that, in keeping with the basic idea of this poem, the rhythm is incantatory.

David Diop

David Diop, who was born in Bordeaux to a Senegalese father and a Cameroonean mother in 1927, belonged very much to the protest period of African writing. After a childhood and primary education in the Cameroons and Senegal he spent most of his short life in France. He was never a robust young man and, having to face the rigours of life in France of the Second World War, his longing for Africa grew. Especially seeing his compatriots fight and die for Europe, his criticism of European society and his denunciation of colonialism intensified.

As soon as possible after the war he visited Senegal and returned later to teach. In August 1960, he was killed with his wife in an aircrash off Dakar.

Most of David Diop's manuscripts were destroyed in the air crash and therefore his reputation rests in a total of twenty-two poems published before his death. The four poems in this anthology are full of Diop's nostalgia for Africa's past, his denunciation of the hypocrisy and arrogance of her colonial rulers, and his vision of an independent and sovereign Africa. But Diop was also aware of the global implication of Africa's struggle and his poem "Certitude", anthologised here in English for the first time, shows evidence of this wider vision.

Your presence

In your presence I have rediscovered my name
My name that was hidden so long under the pain of separation
I have rediscovered the eyes no longer veiled with fever
And your laughter like a flame piercing the shadows
5 Has revealed Africa to me beyond the snows of yesterday
Ten years my love
With days of illusions and abandoned ideas
And sleep restless with alcohol
Ten years of suffering poured on me from the world's breath
10 Suffering that burdens today with the taste of tomorrow
And turns love into a boundless river
In your presence I have rediscovered the memory of my blood
And the necklaces of laughter hung round our days
Days sparkling with ever new joys.

Notes

line 3 Eyes frank and open in their expression or import; not attempting to hide anything out of fear.

line 4 The *shadows* of the time that has passed since separation; experiences that, like darkness, have hidden Africa from the speaker's view.

line 5 Africa is eternal and permanent in contrast to the soon melted snows of Europe.

line 7 *abandoned ideas* Shattered views, thoughts that have proved futile.

line 8 Sleep induced by the stupor of drink, but which provides no rest.

line 10 Suffering that is gone through today, as well as anticipated for the days after; seen as liable to continue in the future.

line 11 The image is of a river, in flood, overflowing its bank and having no landmarks; therefore treacherous.

Questions

1 Why does the speaker concentrate on many details of his past life? What do the images of the past tell us about him?

2 What indications do we get as to whom the speaker is addressing in the poem?

3 By what means are we given the impression that the speaker is passionately involved in what he says in the poem?

Commentary

The essence of Diop's poetry lies quite often in the measured recurrence of words and rhythms, which convey the patterned flow of the speaking voice, often rising to a climax. In this poem there are several repeated phrases which provide the backbone to the structure of the poem. The most obvious is "I have rediscovered". The repeated words and phrases also indicate the passionate nature of the utterance we are faced with in this poem.

This is a poem in which the speaker affirms and cherishes a precious find which he had lost earlier and despaired of recovering. As in U Tam'si's "Viaticum", laughter in this poem defines Africa and the African. In contrast to this open gesture are the eyes, tormented by secrets they wish to hide and the nights in which oblivion is unsuccessfully sought through drink.

Africa

Africa my Africa
Africa of proud warriors in ancestral savannahs
Africa of whom my grandmother sings
On the banks of the distant river
5 I have never known you
But your blood flows in my veins
Your beautiful black blood that irrigates the fields
The blood of your sweat

The sweat of your work
10 The work of your slavery
The slavery of your children
Africa tell me Africa
Is this your back that is bent
This back that breaks under the weight of humiliation
15 This back trembling with red scars
And saying yes to the whip under the midday sun
But a grave voice answer me
Impetuous child that tree young and strong
That tree over there
20 Splendidly alone amidst white and faded flowers
That is your Africa springing up anew
Springing up patiently obstinately
Whose fruits bit by bit acquire
The bitter taste of liberty.

Notes

line 7 A conceit based on the fact that black loamy soil is generally fertile.
lines 8–12 A chain of inter-related aspects of colonial experience. The
parallel structure of the lines and the rhythmic build-up towards a climax,
which comes with the line *Africa tell me Africa*, are most effective. The
lines present a complex but unified picture of bitter exploitation and
suffering.
line 20 Black Africa's rebirth was often seen by people like Diop and
Senghor as taking place in the midst of the degeneration and collapse of
white civilisation.

Questions

1 Compare the speaker's tone and attitude in lines 8–11 with his tone in the
question which begins at line 13 and ends at line 17.
2 Why is Africa imagined speaking in *a grave voice*, and why does she refer to
the speaker in the poem as an *impetuous child*?
3 Comment on the last three lines of the poem and show how the speaker's
attitude to the new Africa differs from his attitude to the old evoked in the
first eight lines of the poem.

Commentary

By the power of his imagination, Diop here calls forth three stages in Africa's
history: the pre-colonial days of proud warrior tribes, the colonial experience
of subjugation and humiliation, and post-colonial freedom and sovereignty. The
first seven lines present an idealised image of Africa. Then follows a realistic
picture of Africa's experience of bitterness, despair and mockery under colonial
rule. The last eight lines present a future of hope built on some of the realistic
elements of colonial experience: Africa as a young tree patiently springing up
and gradually acquiring *the bitter taste of liberty*.

The vultures

In those days
When civilisation kicked us in the face
When holy water slapped our cringing brows
The vultures built in the shadow of their talons
5 The bloodstained monument of tutelage
In those days
There was painful laughter on the metallic hell of the roads
And the monotonous rhythm of the paternoster
Drowned the howling of the plantations
10 O the bitter memories of extorted kisses
Of promises broken at the point of a gun
Of foreigners who did not seem human
You who knew all the books but knew not love
Nor our hands which fertilise the womb of the earth
15 Hands instinct at the root with revolt
In spite of your songs of pride in the charnel-houses
In spite of the desolate villages of Africa torn apart
Hope lived in us like a citadel
And from Swaziland's mines to the sweltering sweat of Europe's
        factories
20 Spring will be reborn under our bright steps.

Notes

Title   As a description of European imperialists in Africa, this word alone
    powerfully conveys the poet's condemnation and loathing for colonial
    rule. The images of violence in the first five lines are exaggerated, but
    they express vividly what is involved when one group of race or people
    impose their will on others.

line 3   An image of the humble Christian kneeling to receive the sacrament of
    baptism and, by implication, a description of the cooperation between
    missionary and colonial ruler.

lines 4–5   A powerful image of the violence through which colonial peoples
    were "tutored towards self-rule", and through which the visible
    achievements of the rule were attained.

line 7   *metallic hell of the roads*   Tarred roads built with the enforced labour
    of workers for whom the suffering entailed was a living hell.

line 8   *paternoster*   Literally, Our father. The Lord's Prayer said with
    monotonous and meaningless repetition.

line 14   Compare with line 7 of the poem "Africa". There is an implicit
    reference to the blood of Africa, which nourishes and fertilises the
    earth.

line 15   The general meaning of the line is that the hands (which in the
    previous line fertilise the womb of the earth) are deeply rooted in revolt
    by the very fact that they nourish growth.

line 16   *charnel-houses*   Houses full of the skeletons of the murdered – the
implication is that the colonial rulers pride themselves on the number of
their dead victims.
line 19   *Swaziland's mines*   Used here as a symbol of enforced African
labour.

Questions

1 What does the speaker mean by lines 8 and 9?
2 What effect does the speaker achieve by changing from narration to direct
address in line 13?
3 Show how the rhythm of the poem is related to the tone of the speaking
voice. What do tone and rhythm contribute to the meaning of the poem?

Commentary

This poem embodies some of the most powerful images of Africa's colonial
experience. European control of Africa, under the pretext of a civilising mission,
is seen as closely allied to the work of the Christian missionaries in converting
Africa to a religion which demands humility.

As is usual with Diop, it is the speaking voice which begins this poem: first
narrating, rising gradually to a vehement denunciation and, finally, proclaiming
hope and release to the oppressed. The structure of the poem depends on the
changes in the tone of the voice we hear speaking to us. Generalised metaphors
of violence are followed by more specific images of oppression, indicating a more
intense involvement of the narrator, until narration yields place to a direct
address. The images of condemnation are strong, so that the more positive images
of hope held up at the end of the poem inevitably appear weak beside them.

Certitude

To those who fatten themselves on murder
And measure the stages of their reign by corpses
I say that days and men
That the sun and the stars
5 Are shaping out the rhythmic brotherhood of all peoples
I say that the heart and the head
Are joined together in the battle line
And that there is not a single day
When somewhere summer does not spring up
10 I say that manly tempests
Will crush those who barter other's patience
And the seasons allied with men's bodies
Will see the enactment of triumphant exploits.

Notes

line 5   The suggestion is that the sun and the stars are shaping men into an orderly relationship with one another.

line 6   the heart and the head   Representative of men's feelings and reasoning.

line 7   in the battle line   Fully committed and dedicated to the fight against oppression.

lines 8–9   Thinking in terms of the whole Earth, the poet sees hope in the fact that each day the revolution of the Earth ensures sunshine and growth somewhere.

Questions

1 In what ways does the poet communicate his anger in this poem?
2 How far does the imagery of this poem support the claim made by the speaker?

Commentary

This is a poem which embodies an affirmation of faith that the orderly revolution of the planets, the forces of nature and its changing seasons, and time itself are allies of the oppressed of the earth. To these forces the poet adds history as the purposeful activity of men directed towards the fulfilment of a hope which the seasons nourish.

Precise expression is given to this faith and hope through the imagery which centres on the cosmic alliance between nature and men. In the poem this imagery reaches its climax in *manly tempests* (line 10); but this is preceded by similar formations like *days and men* (line 3), *the rhythmic brotherhood of all peoples* (line 5), and recurs in *the seasons allied with men's bodies* (line 12). In these images the poet attempts to remind us of the elemental link between men and nature and to let us see in nature's activities indestructible hope for the oppressed.

Agostinho Neto

Agostinho Neto, the oldest and most eminent of the three Lusophone poets featured in this volume, was born near Luanda in the Icolo e Bengo region of Angola, in September 1922. His parents were both teachers. He received his secondary school education in Luanda and then worked for four years, between 1944 and 1947, in the Health Services of the colonial administration. Partly out of his own savings and partly with the support of the Angolan Working-men's Organisation, he proceeded to the University of Coimbra in Portugal to pursue his medical studies. Even before leaving Angola he had taken active interest in the emerging cultural nationalism which took the place of all political activity banned by the colonial administration. No wonder that in Portugal he soon joined the Portuguese opposition Movement for Democratic Youth Unity and was arrested and imprisoned briefly in 1951 and 1952 for circulating pamphlets critical of Portuguese colonialism. A third and longer spell of imprisonment kept him away from his studies between February 1955 and June 1957, and even then, he was only released when the Salazar government yielded to pressure from a number of international intellectuals and writers.

Neto finished his medical studies and returned to Luanda with his wife and first three children in December 1959. His medical practice went hand in hand with the resumption of his political activity as one of the leaders of the Popular Movement for the Liberation of Angola (MPLA). Consequently, he was arrested by the colonial authorities in June 1960, imprisoned in Lisbon and subsequently deported to Cape Verde Island where he was permitted to practise as a doctor but under constant police guard. But in February 1961, when the MPLA made its first military attack on the colonial administration in Luanda, Neto was returned to prison in Lisbon. Again mounting international pressure led to his release from prison in March 1962. Restricted to Lisbon, he finally escaped, making his way through North Africa to Congo Kinshasa (now Zaire) and joining the MPLA freedom fighters in north-eastern Angola.

When the armed struggle ended in 1975, Neto became the first President of independent Angola. Unfortunately, he became ill and died while receiving treatment in Moscow in November 1979.

Neto's poetry began to appear in various magazines as early as 1948. But it was not until 1961 that the poems written between 1948 and 1960 were brought together in a collection and published in Lisbon. A second collection called *Sacred Hope* (*Sagrada Esperanca*) came out in Dar-es-Salaam and Lisbon in 1974. Of the three poems anthologised here, the first two come from the 1961 collection and the third, "Hoisting the Flag" comes from *Sacred Hope*.

African poetry

Out on the horizon
there are fires
and the dark silhouettes of the beaters
with arms outstretched,
5 in the air, the green smell of burning palms.

African poetry

In the street
a line of Bailundu bearers
tremble under the weight of their load
10 in the room
a mulatto girl with meek eyes
colours her face with rice powder and rouge
a woman wriggles her hips under a garish cloth
on the bed
15 a man, sleepless, dreams
of buying knives and forks so he can eat at table
in the sky the glow
of fires
and the silhouette of black men dancing
20 with arms outstretched,
in the air, the hot music of marimbas

African poetry

and in the streets the bearers
in the room the mulatto girl
25 on the bed the man, sleepless

The burnings consume
consume
the hot earth with horizons afire.

Notes

line 1   *Out on the horizon*   The speaker seems to be watching, from a
distance, an outburst of fire which some people (*dark silhouettes* in line 3)
are attempting to put out. Against this distant background of rural fires
are set the succeeding images of smouldering desires in the city.

line 3   *beaters*   Those attempting to put out the fires with green palm
branches.

line 8   *Bailundu bearers*   A class of urban workers who hire out their casual
labour, by carrying loads on their heads often for long distance, for

which they are paid barely survival wages. In West Africa, they are
generally called Kayakaya.

lines 20–21 A deliberate recall of lines 3–4, since the dancing is another
form of 'putting out' the fires burning within.

line 26 the burnings Sum up the effect of the various fires, both real and
metaphorical with which the poem deals.

Questions

1 What do you think is the writer's attitude to the people he presents in the
poem?
2 Comment on the effectiveness of the repeated word *consume* in the last
section of the poem.
3 What do you think the writer is calling 'African poetry', and why?

Commentary

This is a very cryptic poem in which a series of images are presented, depicting
an aspect of African experience under colonial domination. The technique of
presentation resembles that of a quick motion camera which first focuses a scene
and ends up picking up details from the interior. The attempt is to distil the
common and binding element or essence of the scenes – that which the title of
the poem refers to.

Night

I live
in the dark quarters of the world
without light, without life.

They are slave quarters
5 worlds of misery. Dark quarters
where the will is watered down
and men have been confused
with things.

Anxious to live,
10 I walk in the streets
feeling my way
leaning into my shapeless dreams
stumbling into servitude.

I walk lurching
15 through the unlit
unknown streets crowded
with mystery and terror,

80

I, arm in arm with ghosts.
And the night too is dark.

Questions

1 Comment on the shifting meaning of the words *live, life* and *to live* as they occur in the poem.
2 What reasons does the poet provide for referring to his situation as *slave quarters?*
3 Pick out the various ways in which the speaker's walk is characterised, and describe the effect of this characterisation.
4 What do you think is the source of (a) the mystery and (b) the terror mentioned in line 17?
5 Compare this poem with Dennis Brutus's poem "Nightsong: City" on page 124.

Commentary

The most interesting thing about this short poem is the ambivalent target of its protest: both the oppressors and their victims. A similar ambivalence surrounds the use of the word *walk* to describe the only living activity of the speaker in the poem. Also, although the poem begins by referring vaguely to *the dark quarters of the world*, the rest of the poem gives a specific character to the speaker's situation. Yet the vague reference as well as the specific location are important for the total effect of the poem.

Compare the three Lusophone poets (Neto, Jacinto and de Sousa) represented in this anthology. They complement one another in a remarkable number of ways and together present us with an illuminating picture of the historic struggles of the peoples of Angola and Mozambique for liberation from Portuguese domination.

As poetry which developed among the intelligentsia during a period of growing national awareness, the poetry of these three writers is characterised by some unique qualities: first it is a poetry of acute observation of the social conditions of the masses of the people – the conditions of deprivation, of desperate waste and of self-hatred. Vivid and memorable pictures of the urban ghetto life which colonialism imposed on its victims are presented by these poets. Secondly, it is a passionate poetry, expressing the poets' love for their land and its people and, consequently, their denunciation of what colonial exploitation has made of both land and people. For that matter, it is a poetry of tremendous optimism, committed to inspiring a sense of worth in those demoralised by the conditions of the worst form of European colonialism. Finally, in keeping with the above commitments, it is a poetry popular and idealistic, rather than reticent, in its use of language, a poetry not afraid of emotion, because it seeks to move its mass audience by using the oral technique of repetition, parallelism and emphatic rhythms.

In Neto's "Night" and "African poetry", and in Jacinto's "Poem of alienation", vivid images of urban life under colonialism, which we hardly encounter in the poetry of African writers elsewhere on the continent, suddenly strike us. The poems are steeped in pity for the unfulfilled lives of the many who are compelled to sell both themselves and their labour for a pittance. Nevertheless, beyond the pity is the optimism which can affirm in the words of Jacinto:

my poem is not fatalist
my poem is a poem that already wants
and already knows.

A similar optimism links Neto's celebratory "Hoisting of the flag" with Jacinto's "Love poem" and de Sousa's "Poem of Joao".

Hoisting the flag

When I returned
the soldier ants had vanished from the town
And you too
My friend Liceu
5 voice gladdening with hot rhythms of the land
through nights of never-failing Saturdays
You too
sacred and ancestral music
resurgent in the sacred sway of the Ngola's rhythm
10 You too had vanished
and with you
the intellectuals
the Lingue
Farolim
15 the Ingombata meetings
the conscience of traitors betraying without love.

I came just at the moment of the dawning cataclysm
as the seedling bursts the rain damped ground
thrusting up resplendent in youth and colour,
20 I came to see the resurrection of the seed
the dynamic symphony of joy among men.
And the blood and the suffering
was a tempestuous flood which split the town.

When I came back
25 the day had been chosen
and the hour was at hand.
Even the children's laughter had gone
and you too
my good friends, my brothers,
30 Benge, Joaquim, Gaspar, Ilidio, Manuel
and who else?
hundreds, thousands of you, my friends,
some for ever vanished,
ever victorious in their death for life.

35 When I came back
some momentous thing was moving in the land
the granary guards kept closer watch,
the school children studied harder
the sun shone brighter,
40 there was a youthful calm among the old people,
more than hope – it was certainty
more than goodness – it was love.

Men's strength
soldiers' courage
45 poets' cries
were all trying to raise up
beyond the memory of heroes,
Ngola Kiluangi
Rainha Jinga
50 trying to raise up high
the flag of independence.

Notes

line 4   Liceu   The identity of this friend is not essential. He symbolises the
exuberant indigenous culture of music and dance which sustained the
resistance to colonial domination.

lines 13–15   the Lingue, Farolim, the Ingombata   Societies formed by the
educated Angolans which met for cultural activities like poetry reading,
under the guise of which political consciousness and resistance grew in
the nineteen-fifties. These societies were banned by the colonial
administration when the armed struggle began in 1961.

line 17   the dawning cataclysm   Perhaps a specific reference to the
4 February 1961 storming of the Luanda prison by the MPLA militants,
as a result of which the Portuguese unleashed tremendous violence
against the inhabitants of Luanda. It is reported that nearly 3 000 people
died on that day alone and the dead in the following few months of 1961
may have totalled 50 000. The names of some of those who lost their
lives in the early stages of the armed struggle against the Portuguese in
Angola are mentioned in line 30.

lines 48–49   Ngola Kiluangi   One of Angola's traditional rulers who fought
against the early Portuguese invaders of the territory; similarly *Raihna
Jinga* can be called the earliest queen who waged guerrilla warfare
against the Portuguese in the seventeenth century.

Questions

1 What does line 16 suggest as the cause of the changes that have overtaken
the cultural and intellectual life described in section 1 of the poem?
2 Section 2 of the poem contains a number of images drawn from nature.
Identify these images. What light do they throw on the poet's conception of
revolution?

3 *Beyond the memory of heroes*: how does the role of the speaker in this poem enhance the function of the poem?

Commentary

This is a poem that commemorates names and events connected with the struggle of the people of Angola for independence from Portuguese colonial rule. It is common to refer to this struggle as a revolution, but the word has been so frequently and loosely used that it has lost its precise meaning. This poem succeeds in restoring that meaning by presenting the dreams, actions, sacrifices and attitudes of the protagonists in a mass movement that deserves the name 'revolution'.

The poem is, of course, one individual participant's interpretation of the events, passions and changes that made up the revolution. For that reason, as we pay attention to the detailed structure of the poem, a pattern emerges. It begins with the ominous "vanishing of the soldier ants from the town" in section 1; unfolds in the violent uprising which is seen as the bursting of seeds in the rainy season in section 2; it blossoms in the sacrificial death of thousands in section 3; and bears fruits in the purposeful activity and optimism of section 4. Section 5 then sets this entire movement within a wider historical perspective, to which belong the fifteenth and seventeenth-century heroes of the resistance struggle. The poem is therefore more than a fitting memorial to the political struggle. It is also a celebration of the national culture that grew hand in hand with that struggle.

Antonio Jacinto

Antonio Jacinto, a white Angolan, was born in Luanda in 1924. He went to secondary school there and became an office worker. He identified himself with the movement of cultural nationalism in the fifties and his poems were subtle but powerful criticism of the Portuguese failure to educate and advance the social welfare of their colonial subjects. When the cultural movement entered its political phase, under the leadership of the MPLA, Jacinto was arrested with several others and sentenced to imprisonment in the Cape Verde Islands for fourteen years. He served his sentence from 1961 to 1972 in the infamous Tarrafal Concentration Camp, before being released and sent to Lisbon to work for the Portuguese government as an accountant. But he escaped from Lisbon and joined the MPLA forces in 1973. At independence in 1975 he became Minister for Education and Culture and later, Minister for Culture, a post he still holds. In 1986 his collection of poems, *Surviving Santiago's Tarrafal*, described as a "lyric testimony to the triumph of the human spirit over tyranny", won the coveted Norma Award.

Jacinto's poetry has a popular appeal not only because of its powerful lyricism and infectious optimism, but because he often uses the techniques of popular songs: emphatic rhythms, recurrent refrains and imagery drawn from nature and her regenerative processes. A good example of this type of poetry which became the MPLA marching song is "Love poem".

Poem of alienation

This is not yet my poem
the poem of my soul and of my blood
no
I still lack knowledge and power to write my poem
5 the great poem I feel turning in me

My poem wanders aimlessly
in the bush or in the city
in the voice of the wind
in the surge of the sea
10 in the Aspect and the Being

My poem steps outside
wrapped in the showy cloths
selling itself

selling
15 "lemons, buy my le-e-e-emons"

My poem runs through the streets
with a putrid cloth pad on its head
offering itself
offering
20 "mackerel, sardine, sprats
fine fish, fine fi-i-ish . . . !"

My poem trudges the streets
"here J'urnal" "Daily"
and no newspaper yet carries my poem

25 My poem goes to the cafes
"lott'ry draw-a tomorra lott'ry draw-a tomorra"
and the draw of my poem
wheels as it wheels
whirls as it whirls
30 never changes
        "lott'ry draw-a tomorra
        lott'ry draw-a tomorra"

My poem comes from the township
"On Saturdays bring the washing
35 on Mondays take the washing
on Saturdays surrender the washing and surrender self
on Mondays surrender self and take the washing"

My poem is the suffering
of the laundress's daughter
40 shyly
in the closed room
of a worthless boss idling
to build up an appetite for the violation

My poem is the prostitute
45 in the township at the broken door of her hut
"hurry hurry
pay your money
come and sleep with me."

My poem goes to market in the kitchen
50 goes to the workbench
fills the tavern and the gaol
is poor ragged and dirty
lives in benighted ignorance

my poem knows nothing of itself
55 nor how to plead

My poem was made to give itself
to surrender itself
without asking for anything

But my poem is not fatalist
60 my poem is a poem that already wants
and already knows
my poem is I-white
mounted on me-black
riding through life.

Notes

Title *alienation*   A term from Marxist thought and existentialist philosophy to
describe a social and psychological state in which men feel unfulfilled,
because their creative abilities are exploited by others and they are
compelled to lead basically unhappy lives and yet feel unable to change.
Thus they are made "other than" (alienated) they would wish to be.

lines 6–10 Describe a state of unrealised potentia. *Aspect* refers to the
individual's qualities, which are an expression of the life (Being) that
flows through or exists in him. In the first two stanzas therefore, "poem"
means the potentia or possibility of life that could be realised in the
speaker. But, instead of this potentia we have in stanzas 3–9 (lines
11–58) "alienated poems" which represent the various forms of
exploitation that the speaker's life is at present.

line 49–58 Summarise the state of exploitation and deprivation which the
preceding seven stanzas have presented.

Questions

1 In stanzas 3–7, *my poem* seems to refer to particular types of people. How
far do the activities attributed to these people help you to identify them?

2 What are the common features of the images presented in stanzas 3–7 and
how do they help to define the theme of the poem?

3 How does the poet convey his attitude to the theme of the poem?

Commentary

This is a philosophical poem which communicates its meaning through concrete
images of the colonial whites' exploitation of the colonised black. This exploi-
tation constitutes the "alienation" of both black and white from their true
humanity. The authentic "poem" (the "poem without alienation") would be a
just and equal partnership between black and white. But, since the speaker in
the poem knows this and also knows what is in his true interest he is not
"fatalist". He still hopes for a different future, when the great poem which
embodies his aspirations for true humanity will be written. Meanwhile, "the poem

of alienation" depicts and vehemently protests against colonial exploitation.

The poignancy of this poem is particularly striking when we remember that Antonio Jacinto is a white Angolan who completely identified himself with the black subjects of white Portuguese rule.

Letter from a contract worker

I wanted to write you a letter
my love
a letter to tell
of this longing
5 to see you
and this fear
of losing you
of this thing which deeper than I want, I feel
a nameless pain which pursues me
10 a sorrow wrapped about my life.

I wanted to write you a letter
my love
a letter of intimate secrets
a letter of memories of you
15 of you
your lips as red as the tacula fruit
your hair black as the dark diloa fish
your eyes gentle as the macongue
your breasts hard as young maboque fruit
20 your light walk
your caresses
better than any that I find here.

I wanted to write you a letter
my love
25 to bring back our days together in our secret haunts
nights lost in the long grass
to bring back the shadow of your legs
and the moonlight filtering through the endless palms,
to bring back the madness of our passion
30 and the bitterness of separation.

I wanted to write you a letter
my love
which you could not read without crying
which you would hide from papa Bombo
35 and conceal from mama Kieza

88

which you would reread without the coldness of forgetting
a letter which would make any other
in all Kilombo worthless.

I wanted to write you a letter
40 my love
a letter which the passing wind would take
a letter which the cashew and the coffee trees,
the hyenas and the buffalo
the alligators and the river fish
45 could hear
and if the wind should lose it on the way
the beasts and plants
pitying our sharp sorrow
from song to song
50 lament to lament
breath to caught breath
would leave you, pure and hot,
the burning
the sorrowful words of the letter
55 I wanted to write you.

I wanted to write you a letter
but, oh my love, I cannot understand
why it is, why, why, why it is my love
that you cannot read
60 and I – oh the hopelessness – cannot write.

Notes

Title   *contract worker*   Under Portuguese colonial rule, the contract worker
was often an uneducated adult, whose labour was "contracted" by the
colonial administration to the owners of South African mines. The South
Africans paid a lump sum to the Portuguese for each migrant worker.
Thus effectively enslaved, he was paid a small percentage of his wages
to live on in South Africa. The rest of his wages were supposed to be
saved for him. At the end of his contract, he was repatriated and his
"savings" were paid to him back home in Portuguese pesos after the
colonial administration had deducted what it regarded as tax. While
under contract, he could not return home voluntarily nor could his
family or relatives visit him in the exclusive male compound in which he
was housed.

line 16   *tacula fruit* (also translated 'henna')   The fruit of a tropical forest
plant which provides a red dye, used in cosmetics.

line 17   *diloa fish*   Mud fish.

line 18   *macongue*   Duiker, a variety of the antelope.

line 19   *maboque fruit*   A wild orange.

line 41   The passing wind is the beginning of an elaborate metaphor (often referred to as "pathetic fallacy") in which sympathetic nature becomes not merely the courier but the medium of the "unwritten" letter.

Questions

1 Describe, as exactly as you can, what constitutes the *nameless pain which pursues me a sorrow wrapped about my life* in the poem.
2 How does the ironical revelation in the last section of the poem affect the meaning of the poem?
3 How effective is the "conceit" in section 5 of the poem?
4 The poet speaks of *the sorrowful words of the letter*, but the effect of the poem is far from sorrowful. Do you agree? Why?
5 Do you think "Letter from a contract worker" and "Poem of alienation" have anything in common?

Commentary

The remarkable thing about this poem is that, although each section begins with the line *I wanted to write you a letter*, we never consider the meaning of the "wanting" until the end when we discover that the speaker cannot write and the addressee cannot read. But, by then, these limitations do not make the slightest difference to the love letter that has in fact been written and read. The feelings of romance, tenderness and admiration have been powerfully evoked, and the metaphor in section 5 demonstrates that these feelings do not require the written medium for their transmission: the world of nature more effectively carries the message of the heart.

Love poem

(*Like the earth, I belong to
everyone. There is not a single
drop of hatred in my breast.
Open wide, my hands scatter grapes
in the wind.*) Pablo Neruda

When I return to see the sun's light they deny me
my love
we shall go dressed in peace
and wearing a smile of flowers and fruit
5 entwined
along roads – twisting snakes
among the coffee groves
climbing from the mountain to the stars
and to our shining dreams
10 we shall go
singing the songs that we know and do not know

When I return to see the sun's light they deny me
my love
we shall go
15 then go briefly to weep
on the countless graves of countless men
who have gone
without funeral or wake
without hope for the sun's light they deny us

20 We shall go, my love
and tell them
I have returned, we are returning
because we love each other
and we love
25 those countless graves of countless men

When I return to see the sun's light they deny me
with standards raised
– freedom is a fruit of harvest –
we shall go
30 and gather corn cobs and colours
and offer flowers and resurrection to the dead
and to the living, the strength of our own lives
my love
we shall go
35 and draw a rainbow on the paper sky
for our son to play with:

        rain may come and rain may go
        if Our Lady wills it so
        rain for the father's farm will run
40   and never, never send for the sun

We shall go, my love, we shall go
when I return
– the bars undone –
and embraced together we'll make
45 life, undeniable, continue
in the gentle gifts of harvest
in the chirping of startled birds
in the march of men returning
in the rains' hosannas on the reborn earth
50 in the confident steps of a people resolved
my love
A fringe of new colour will dress the earth
we make kisses and smiles the tissue of life
and between the endless cotton fields

55 and the dance of a joyful feast

we shall go
my love.

Notes

The quotation from the Brazilian poet, Pablo Neruda, sets the tone of
sublime forgiveness and affirmation of life that runs through the poem.

line 1   the sun's light they deny me   The poem was apparently written while
    Jacinto was exiled and imprisoned in the Tarrafal Concentration Camp.
line 3   we shall go   Marks the beginning, in each stanza of a specific journey
    (recalling the historic march of the MPLA liberation forces) towards a
    goal presented in vivid images of triumph, celebration and renewal.
line 16   countless graves of countless men   An apparent reference to the
    thousands of Angolans killed during the liberation struggle. In the early
    months of 1961 alone, 50 000 people, including innocent civilians, were
    massacred in Luanda.
line 37   rain may come . . .   A nursery rhyme which fits snugly into the main
    poem, echoing its imagery.

Questions

1 Identify the images of forgiveness and triumph in the poem. Do they have
   anything in common?
2 One can hardly miss the love and tenderness towards the land and its
   people in Jacinto's poetry. Comment on this.
3 There are a number of phrases repeated and varied throughout the poem.
   Identify as many of them as possible and show what effect they have on the
   rhythm of the poem.

Commentary

Apparently written in prison and then smuggled to the MPLA militants, this
poem's popularity depends on a number of factors: its infectious confidence in
the success of the struggle against oppression, its emphatic and marching rythms
underlined by repeated phrases, its images of aspiration drawn from nature's
ability for renewal.

Noemia de Sousa

Noemia de Sousa, born in Mozambique in 1927, was in the vanguard of the movement for cultural nationalism which surged through Mozambique and Angola in the 1950s. She was in touch with the francophone writers in the 1950s and 1960s and elements of "poesia negra" (negritude poetry) are apparent in some of her poems. More than Neto and Jacinto, her poetry reflects some of the concerns of David Diop in denouncing all oppression, and in affirming the solidarity of the oppressed.

The poem of Joao

Joao was young like us
Joao had wide awake eyes
and alert ears
hands reaching forwards
5 a mind cast for tomorrow
a mouth to cry an eternal "no"
Joao was young like us

Joao was the father, the mother, the brother of multitudes
Joao was the blood and the sweat of multitudes
10 He smiled that same tired smile of shop girls leaving work
He suffered with the passivity of the peasant women
He felt the sun piercing like a thorn in the Arabs' midday
He bargained on bazaar benches with the Chinese
He sold tired green vegetables with the Asian traders
15 He howled spirituals from Harlem with Marion Anderson
He swayed to the Chope marimbas on a Sunday
He cried out with the rebels their cry of blood
He was happy in the caress of the manioc-white moon
He sang with the shilabos their songs of homesick longing
20 He hoped with the same intensity of all
For dazzling dawns with open mouths to sing
Joao was the blood and sweat of multitudes
Joao was young like us.

Joao and Mozambique were intermingled
25 Joao would not have been without Mozambique
Joao was like a palm tree, a coconut palm
a piece of rock, a Lake Niassa, a mountain,

an Incomati, a forest, a macala tree
a beach, a Maputo, an Indian Ocean
30 Joao was an integral and deep rooted part of Mozambique
Joao was young like us.

Joao longed to live and longed to conquer life
that is why he loathed prisons, cages, bars
and loathed the men who make them.
35 For Joao was free
Joao was an eagle born to fly
Joao loathed prisons and the men who make them
Joao was young like us.

And because Joao was young like us
40 and had wideawake eyes
and enjoyed art and poetry and Jorge Amado
and was the blood and sweat of multitudes
and was intermingled with Mozambique
and was an eagle born to fly
45 and hated prisons and the men who make them
Ah, because of all this we have lost Joao
We have lost Joao.

Ah, this is why we have lost Joao
why we weep night and day for Joao
50 for Joao whom they have stolen from us.

And we ask
But why have they taken Joao,
Joao who was young and ardent like us
Joao who thirsted for life
55 Joao who was brother to us all
why have they stolen from us Joao
who spoke of hope and dawning days
Joao whose glance was like a brother's hug
Joao who always had somewhere for one of us to stay
60 Joao who was our mother and our father
Joao who would have been our saviour
Joao whom we loved and love
Joao who belonged so surely to us
oh, why have they stolen Joao from us?
65 and no one answers
indifferent, no one answers.

But we know
why they took Joao from us
Joao, so truly our brother.

94

70 But what does it matter?
   They think they have stolen him but Joao is here with us
   is here in others who will come
   in others who have come.
   For Joao is not alone
75 Joao is a multitude
   Joao is the blood and sweat of multitudes
   and Joao, in being Joao, is also Joaquim, Jose
   Abdullah, Fang, Mussumbuluco, Mascarenhas
   Omar, Yutang, Fabiao
80 Joao is a multitude, the blood and sweat of multitudes

   And who will take Jose, Joaquim, Abdullah
   Fang, Mussumbuluco, Mascarenhas, Omar, Yutang Fabiao?
   Who?
   Who will take us all and lock us in a cage?

Notes

line 15   Marion Anderson   A famous Afro-American female singer/performer,
   especially, of the blues, the deep-felt lament of negro experience.
line 16   Chope marimbas   The infectious dance rhythms of a tribe from
   southern Mozambique.
line 19   shilabos   Contract workers recruited from their homes in
   Mozambique to work in the mines of South Africa.
lines 28–29   Incomati and *Maputo*   Names of rivers in southern Mozambique.
line 41   Jorge Amado   A Brazilian revolutionary poet.
lines 77–82   The names mentioned in these lines are drawn from various
   third world races, and the repetition underlines the solidarity the poet
   sees among the oppressed and exploited of the world.

Questions

1 What are the qualities of Joao, as an individual, presented in the poem?
2 Sections 2 and 3 of the poem present Joao in a contrasted way. Describe
   the contrast that emerges and show its effect.
3 *But we know why they took Joao from us.* From your reading of the poem,
   what do you know? ·
4 Does the poet succeed in reconciling the loss of Joao as an individual, with
   his survival as a symbol?
5 What does it mean to say that the poem is celebratory and its movement
   regal? Would you agree?

Commentary

On the surface, this is a poem in memory of a young man called Joao. But, on
closer reading, it becomes obvious that Joao is not only an individual, but also
an embodiment of the indomitable spirit of protest against oppression and exploi-
tation wherever these exist in the world.

As a celebration of a passionate faith and hope, therefore, the poem is based on a series of metaphorical statements, which are repeated through variation and summary. The poem's movement is regal and the constant reiteration of the name Joao has the effect of enacting the claim that he is the life-blood that pulsates through the multitudes of the oppressed and exploited throughout the world.

Abioseh Nicol

Abioseh Nicol was born in Freetown, Sierra Leone in 1924 as Davidson S. H. W. Nicol. Educated in Nigeria and Sierra Leone, he proceeded to Christ's College, Cambridge where he took a brilliant degree in Natural Sciences before embarking on the study of Medicine at London University. After obtaining his M.D. and Ph.D., he held a Fellowship in Christ's College for a while before returning home in the late 1950s first as Director of Medical Services and then as Principal of Fourah Bay College. From Fourah Bay he went to New York as a member of the Permanent Mission of Sierra Leone to the U.N. and subsequently served on many U.N. Commissions for Africa. Retired and now living in Cambridge, Nicol continues to teach and research at the University's Centre for International Studies.

Abioseh Nicol is rightly referred to as the doyen of African creative writing in English. He was one of the earliest recipients of the Margaret Wrong Prize and Medal for Literature in Africa. His stories and poetry have been widely anthologised. At the University of Ghana there is a prize for creative writing named after him.

His own poetry has the articulateness and poise characteristic of the older generation of African intellectuals and, although he may not dance to the tunes in fashion these days, his recent poems are still as keenly and sympathetically observant of the fortunes of Africa as his rightly celebrated poem "The Meaning of Africa".

The meaning of Africa

Africa, you were once just a name to me
But now you lie before me with sombre green challenge
To that loud faith for freedom (life more abundant)
Which we once professed shouting
5 Into the silent listening microphone
Or on an alien platform to a sea
Of white perplexed faces troubled
With secret Imperial guilt; shouting
Of you with a vision euphemistic
10 As you always appear
To your lonely sons on distant shores.

Then the cold sky and continent would disappear
In a grey mental mist.
And in its stead the hibiscus blooms in shameless scarlet

15 and the bougainvillea in mauve passion
entwines itself around strong branches
the palm trees stand like tall proud moral women
shaking their plaited locks against the
cool suggestive evening breeze;
20 the short twilight passes;
the white full moon turns its round gladness
towards the swept open space
between the trees; there will be
dancing tonight; and in my brimming heart
25 plenty of love and laughter.
Oh, I got tired of the cold northern sun,
Of white anxious ghost-like faces,
Of crouching over heatless fires
In my lonely bedroom.
30 The only thing I never tired of
was the persistent kindness
Of you too few unafraid
Of my grave dusky strangeness.

So I came back
35 Sailing down the Guinea Coast.
Loving the sophistication
Of your brave new cities:
Dakar, Accra, Cotonou,
Lagos, Bathurst and Bissau;
40 Liberia, Freetown, Libreville,
Freedom is really in the mind.

Go up-country, so they said,
To see the real Africa.
For whomsoever you may be,
45 That is where you come from.
Go for bush, inside the bush,
You will find your hidden heart,
Your mute ancestral spirit.
And so I went, dancing on my way

50 Now you lie before me passive
With your unanswering green challenge.
Is this all you are?
This long uneven red road, this occasional succession
Of huddled heaps of four mud walls
55 And thatched, falling grass roofs
Sometimes ennobled by a thin layer
Of white plaster, and covered with thin
Slanting corrugated zinc.

These patient faces on weather-beaten bodies
60 Bowing under heavy market loads.
The pedalling cyclist wavers by
On the wrong side of the road,
As if uncertain of his new emancipation.
The squawking chickens, the pregnant she-goats
65 Lumber awkwardly with fear across the road,
Across the windscreen view of my four-cylinder kit car
An overladen lorry speeds madly towards me
Full of produce, passengers, with driver leaning
Out into the swirling dust to pilot his
70 Swinging obsessed vehicle along.
Beside him on the raised seat his first-class
Passenger, clutching and timid; but he drives on
At so, so many miles per hour, peering out with
Bloodshot eyes, unshaved face and dedicated look;
75 His motto painted on each side: *Sunshine Transport,*
We get you there quick, quick. The Lord is my Shepherd.

The red dust settles down on the green leaves.

I know you will not make me want, Lord,
Though I have reddened your green pastures
80 It is only because I have wanted so much
That I have always been found wanting.
From South and East, and from my West
(The sandy desert holds the North)
We look across a vast continent
85 And blindly call it ours.
You are not a country, Africa,
You are a concept,
Fashioned in our minds, each to each,
To hide our separate dreams.
90 Only those within you who know
Their circumscribed plot,
And till it well with steady plough
Can from that harvest then look up
To the vast blue inside
95 Of the enamelled bowl of sky
Which covers you and say
"This is my Africa" meaning
"I am content and happy.
I am fulfilled, within,
100 Without and roundabout.
I have gained the little longings
Of my hands, my loins, my heart
And the soul that follows in my shadow."
I know now that is what you are, Africa:

105 Happiness, contentment, and fulfilment,
And a small bird singing on a mango tree.

Notes

line 1   once   Also repeated in line 4, refers to the period of the poet's stay
abroad, in the late 1940s and early 1950s, which saw the beginnings of
the agitation for self-government described in lines 5–11.

lines 7–8   Catch something of the initial reaction of sympathetic white
politicians to the demand for self-rule from the poineer African
nationalists.

line 9   vision euphemistic   A vision of Africa more pleasing than factual or
realistic.

lines 12–13   Signal the presentation of a picture of Africa which lays
emphasis on the pleasant and attractive.

lines 50–51   Pick up the contrast between once and now, first mentioned in
lines 1–2. The next section of the poem, consisting of lines 52–77,
presents a realistic picture of rural life in Africa.

line 78   Begins a section of reflections, prompted by the motto written on the
passenger lorry, but based on the contrast between the vision and the
reality of Africa presented so far. But, in view of Africa's experience
since the sixties, what is presented here as a sober reflection, now reads
like another dream. For who, on the continent of Africa, can claim:
"This is my Africa", meaning "I am content and happy . . ."?

Questions

1 Compare and contrast the sections of the poem that deal with the vision
and the reality of Africa, pointing to some of the elements that establish the
contrast.

2 The new cities mentioned in the section made of lines 34 to 41, do not
follow the actual geographical order. What is the effect achieved by the
arrangement the poet uses? Relate line 41 to this arrangement.

3 How do the speaker's reflections in the poem underscore the statement
"Africa you are a concept".

4 In the light of what Africa's experience has been in recent years what are
your reactions to the last portion of the poem beginning Only those within
you who know . . .?

5 "It is the genial attitude of the voice that we hear that constitutes the
poetry." Would you agree?

Commentary

This is a unique poem for several reasons. It chronicles and catches the flavour
of the aspirations and the genial spirit of the pioneering intellectuals who were
part of the movement towards African self-rule. In its combination of easy
narration, heightened description and sober reflection, it approximates to the
performance of the traditional griot. Its expansive mood remains infectious in
spite of the traumatic changes that Africa has experienced since the poem was
written in the early 1960s.

At the same time there are elements which date the poem. One can hardly speak of Africa as lying before one *with a sombre green challenge* after the recent experience of drought throughout the continent. Nor is the African in Europe ever likely to see the reaction of his hosts to him in terms of a fascination with his *grave dusky strangeness*. He is hardly welcome these days. Nevertheless, throughout the poem, it is the genial spirit of the observant mind, that goes *dancing on its way* (line 49) and that hears *a small bird singing on a mango tree* that creates the poetry we enjoy.

Words of wisdom and love

Words are like shells
Many see only their outer hardness
But the wise hold and open them
And sometimes find within them hidden pearls.

5 Words are like lightning strokes
Many see only frightening flashes
But the wise pause and wait
And hear the echo of their great thunder.

Words are like moonflowers by day
10 Many see only their bunched leafy fists
But the wise linger till after twilight
And watch them open spilling out their sweet fragrance.

Words are like high towering waves
Many see only the hurl of their long angry curl
15 But the wise stand waiting by the white sand
And feel the gentle soothing trickle of their spent force.

So, Africa, when you say to me
In quiet urgency you love me
(Oh you are a torn confused and ravaged land
20 Your strange uncertain love like shifting tides)
That I must stay and serve your needs
I pause and ponder
I stop and wonder.

Perhaps you hold within you
25 Some hidden gleaming pearl
Some future majesty
Some strange sweet fragrance of moonlit nights
I walk along your foam-flecked shores
Your words hold promise

30 And are not empty
   I have gained wisdom and shall wait.

Questions

1 Comment on the effectiveness of the poet's descriptions in stanzas 2 and 4 of the poem.
2 The similes used in these two stanzas seem to draw attention to one effect of the use of language. How would you characterise this effect?
3 What other word would substitute for *the wise* in this poem?
4 It is perhaps a mark of wisdom not to judge the shell by its outer hardness (stanza 1); but is it really a mark of wisdom to wait for the peal and echo of thunder that follow lightning flashes? (stanza 2)
5 Do you consider the response given in stanza 6 to the urgent appeal of stanza 5 adequate? Give reasons for your answer.

Commentary

This poem is remarkable for its clarity and beauty of phrasing, the aptness of its comparisons and its mature poise. Compare its hesitant tone with the commitment of Nicol's poem, "The Meaning of Africa".

Gabriel Imomotime Okara

Gabriel Okara was born in 1921 in Nembe in the Rivers State of Nigeria. After his secondary education at Government College, Umuahia, he became a book-binder. From then on he developed a remarkable personality through personal tuition, reflection and a deep interest in literature and in the language and culture of his people.

Okara is one of the most significant and serious early Nigerian poets. He started writing poetry in the early fifties and still writes. Some of his war poems are among the best of this class of Nigerian poetry. Okara is interested in music and this shows not only in the lyrical grace of his poetry, but also in some of his imagery. The motifs of childhood, innocence and nostalgia also run through many of his poems. He is often concerned about the identity of his people, and throughout his poetry there is evidence of the influence of their traditional folk literature. Indeed, some of his earliest writings were translations of this oral literature, and the subdued tone and rhythm of his poetry are as much a reflection of this inheritance as they are of the poet's withdrawn nature. His first published collection of poetry was *The Fisherman's Invocation*.

After the civil war, Okara served in several important capacities in the Rivers State of Nigeria. He was the first General Manager of the State Newspaper Corporation (publishers of the *Tide*) which he helped to establish, then Commissioner for Information, which provided him with more insight into human nature. These experiences form the material for his second series of poems *Fantasy*. He was particularly perturbed by his unjustified and ignominious removal as Commissioner. He later became the first writer-in-residence at the Rivers State Council for Arts and Culture. He has retired from the public service and now spends his time writing children's books for use in schools, and writing poetry.

The call of the River Nun

I hear your call!
I hear it far away;
I hear it break the circle
of these crouching hills.

5 I want to view your face
again and feel your cold
embrace; or at your brim
to set myself and
inhale your breath; or

10 Like the trees, to watch
my mirrored self unfold
and span my days with
song from the lips of dawn.

I hear your lapping call!
15 I hear it coming through;
invoking the ghost of a child
listening, where river birds hail
your silver-surfaced flow.

My river's calling too!
20 Its ceaseless flow impels
my found'ring canoe down
its inevitable course.
And each dying year
brings near the sea-bird call,
25 the final call that
stills the crested waves
and breaks in two the curtain
of silence of my upturned canoe.

O incomprehensible God!
30 Shall my pilot be
my inborn stars to that
final call to Thee
O my river's complex course?

Notes

line 4   crouching hills   This poem was written while the poet was working at
     Enugu. Enugu is hilly, much of it surrounded by parts of the range
     known as the Udi Hills.
line 5   Personification of the river.
line 12   span   Stretch from side to side, extend across; particularly in
     reference to rivers. Used figuratively here to mean the memory of early
     times. A man now, the poet remembers his youth. These two lines mean
     something like "Fill my life with childhood memories."
line 13   lips of dawn   Metaphor for songs sung by children, or childhood
     generally.
line 14   The gentle breaking of the surf on the river bank makes a *lapping*
     sound, which the poet refers to as the river's invitation to him.
line 18   silver-surfaced flow   The blinding whiteness of the river, caused by
     reflection.
line 19   Notice the change in tone and attitude. *River* here refers to "the
     river of life". The poem is reflective and the poet dwells on life and its
     inevitable end in death. The ceaseless flow of the river is compared to
     the continuous passage of time and life.

line 21 The poet is "declining into the vale of years" and death is near.
The image is that of a sinking canoe. The inevitability of death is shown
by the image of the canoe foundering though there is no turbulence.
The idea of death is clearly expressed in *each dying year* (line 23).
Passing through life is like sailing on a river.

line 25   the final call Death, which ends all, both the tribulations and
mysteries of life.

line 26   crested waves Ridge-like shape of the waves before they break.

line 33 There is a strong religious tone in this last meditative and climactic
stanza. This line refers to the *incomprehensible God* of line 29, and the
poet combines in it the inscrutability of God and life.

Questions

1 In what ways is the river in this poem symbolic?
2 This is an intensely personal poem and yet we react fully to it. We feel the
poet is expressing experiences that are important to us. How does the poet
succeed in involving us in his reflection?
3 Analyse the relationship between the call of the river and the sea-bird call.
Is it a physical call?
4 What change in structure and theme do you notice in the second part?
5 Discuss the use of repetition and alliteration in this poem.

Commentary

This poem starts off in a clear, dramatic, if subdued, tone but gradually becomes
complex. The repetitions in the first stanza achieve a kind of incantatory and
haunting quality. The use of apostrophe helps to heighten this mood which gives
the impression of some type of spiritual force compelling the attention of the
poet. This first stanza sets the scene.

In the second stanza the recalled river is presented as a concrete reality
through personification and other sensory images. There is unity of nature here,
and through the image of dawn the poet harks back to childhood innocence,
an experience realised in the third stanza where the tone becomes evocative
again.

In stanza four a symbolic dimension is introduced into the poem. The feeling
of longing changes to deep reflection as the poet now ponders the river of life
in which he sees mirrored his own inevitable end. The most significant quality
of this poem is not the romantic reference to the River Nun which has a great
fascination for the poet, but a subtle poetic exploitation of the idea of *call* which
is used euphemistically to refer to death. The poem then, is a serious meditation
on life and death and the poet uses a series of visual and concrete images and
metaphors associated with the river to explore this theme.

New Year's Eve midnight

Now the bells are tolling –
A year is dead.
And my heart is slowly beating

the Nunc Dimittis
5 to all my hopes and mute
yearnings of a year
and ghosts hover round
dream beyond dream

Dream beyond dream
10 mingling with the dying
bell-sounds fading
into memories
like rain drops
falling into a river.

15 And now the bells are chiming –
A year is born.
And my heart-bell is ringing
in a dawn.
But it's shrouded things I see
20 dimly stride
on heart-canopied paths
to a riverside.

Notes

line 1   The practice of ringing bells, shooting guns, beating drums, sounding
sirens or making some type of significant noise to announce the
departure of one year and the ushering in of another is common in
Nigeria and other parts of the world.

line 4   The reference here is to the prayer of Simeon as recorded in Luke
II, 29–32. Simeon was a devout old man who had been promised by the
Holy Spirit that he would not die until he had seen the infant Jesus
who was expected to redeem Israel. The *Nunc Dimittis* was Simeon's
song of gratitude and valediction.

line 17   The beating of the poet's expectant heart is metaphorically compared
to the ringing of a bell.

line 19   A *shroud* is a cloth used to cover a corpse. The idea in this line is
that ominous signs speak of another new year of failures, even before it
has begun. The use of *dimly* in the succeeding line is suggestive.

line 21   This line refers to those things which the poet would wish to
achieve in the new year.

Questions

1 Why does the poet use *tolling* and *chiming* in referring to the bells in lines
1 and 15 respectively?

2 In what ways does the poet suggest the idea of death in the first two
stanzas and how does he connect this with his unfulfilled hopes?

3 How does the poet express the idea that the new year offers no better
prospects than the old one?

Commentary

There are two essential facts about the origin of this poem. The first is that, like most of Okara's poems, it is occasional. Secondly, like most people, the poet seizes the opportunity provided by that critical moment of the celebration when one year is declared ended and a new one heralded to reflect upon his failures in the past year and express his anxious expectation of another year in which he hopes to make up for all the unaccomplished dreams of the previous year. But there are indications that this new year is not going to be as happy as the poet hopes, because *it's shrouded things I see*. The poet here then implicitly comments on the eternal cycle of hope and despair which make up the rhythm of life.

The snow flakes sail gently down

The snow flakes sail gently
down from the misty eye of the sky
and fall lightly lightly on the
winter-weary elms. And the branches,
5 winter-stripped and nude, slowly
with the weight of the weightless snow
bow like grief-stricken mourners
as white funeral cloth is slowly
unrolled over deathless earth.
10 And dead sleep stealthily from the
heater rose and closed my eyes with
the touch of silk cotton of water falling.

Then I dreamed a dream
in my dead sleep. But I dreamed
15 not of earth dying and elms a vigil
keeping. I dreamed of birds, black
birds flying in my inside, nesting
and hatching on oil palms bearing suns
for fruits and with roots denting the
20 uprooter's spades. And I dreamed the
uprooters tired and limp, leaning on my roots –
their abandoned roots –
and the oil palms gave them each a sun.
But on their palms
25 they balanced the blinding orbs
and frowned with schisms on their
brows – for the suns reached not
the brightness of gold!

Then I awoke. I awoke
30 to the silently falling snow

and bent-backed elms bowing and
swaying to the winter wind like
white-robed Moslems salaaming at evening
prayer, and the earth lying inscrutable
35 like the face of a god in a shrine.

Notes

line 4 *elms* Type of tree commonly found in temperate regions.

line 6 This is paradoxical. Snow flakes are weightless but as they accumulate, they become solid, hard and heavy:

line 8 Reference is to the white sheet of snow that covers (buries) everything in winter.

line 10 A poetic way of describing falling asleep.

line 11 In cold countries vessels known as *heaters* are used to keep rooms that do not have permanent fireplaces warm, especially in winter.

lines 15–16 *a vigil keeping* Staying awake at night especially for a particular purpose like watching over something or someone. The idea here is that the elms were awake and watching over the poet.

line 17 The term *inside* is Okara's peculiar rendering of an expression from his native Ijaw. It appears in many of his writings and for him it is a powerful code representing the sum total of the human being.

lines 19–20 The poet's own traditional roots are so strong and deeply entrenched that they resist the *uprooters' spades* (European culture).

line 25 An *orb* is a spherical object, often used to refer to heavenly bodies (poetic here for the sun), one carried by a monarch on special occasions.

line 26 Figurative way of describing the furrows that appear on the brow when one frowns. The reference is to the disagreements and divisions of opinions which the contemplation of the gift causes.

line 33 *salaaming* Bowing as usual among Moslems in prayer or greeting.

line 34 *inscrutable* Mysterious and impossible to understand. This refers to the expressionless face of a carved god in the priest's shrine. It is an excellent image of a monotonous winter landscape.

Questions

1 Winter is a bleak and dreary season in which all nature seems dead. How does the poet capture this atmosphere through rhythm and imagery in his description in the first stanza?

2 Attempt an explanation of the symbols used by the poet in stanza 2. Do you think they are effective in expressing the poet's meaning?

3 What gift do the oil palms give the uprooters and what is the latter's reaction to the gift? What do you think the poet means by this episode?

4 When the poet wakes up in the third stanza, the weather has changed. Describe what other change has taken place.

Commentary

This poem was written after the poet's first experience of snow during his visit to America. In this highly complex poem, the poet uses the technique of the dream in the second stanza to state a common theme for many African writers: the theme of the conflict of cultures, of the confrontation of Europe and Africa. In the second stanza, which contains the burden of meaning of the poem, the poet uses as symbols the images of the palm, sun, gold and roots. Through them the poet expresses preference for his African values to European values.

One interesting feature of the poem is its structure. The first stanza conjures up the atmosphere of winter in which the poet is lulled to sleep by the soothing warmth of the heater. The second stanza contains the dream which the poet had in his sleep, a dream which takes him back to his native home. In the third stanza the poet wakes; it is still winter, but a change has occurred in the weather.

Moon in the bucket

Look!
Look out there
in the bucket
the rusty bucket
5 with water unclean

Look!
A luminous plate is floating –
The moon, dancing to the gentle night wind
Look! all you who shout across the wall
10 with a million hates. Look at the dancing moon
It is peace unsoiled by the murk
and dirt of this bucket war.

Notes

line 7 luminous plate   A plate that emits bright light. A full moon looks like a flat, round plate, especially when it is reflected in water.
line 9   Not a physical wall, but a barrier of hatred and discord which people have erected and across which they cannot reach others.
lines 11–12   Although the water is dirty, it still reflects the moon and does not affect the image of the reflected moon.

Questions

1 The beginning of this poem is striking and arresting. What do you think it gains by such a dramatic opening? Is the repetition of *Look* monotonous?
2 One of the first things you notice about this poem is the difference in form between the first and the second verses. Comment on this difference and explain how each contributes to the effectiveness of the poem.
3 In what ways would you say this poem demonstrates the poet's keen sense of observation and descriptive ability? Why does he insist on minute details?
4 What does the poet mean by people shouting *with a million hates*? What type of figurative language is used here?

Commentary

Like the works of all true and great poets who are committed to their art and sensitive to human suffering, Okara's war poems show his deep concern for the violence and ravages of war and the destruction of human life. Ordinarily a quiet and peaceful man, the war sharpened his longing for harmony and his hatred for the divisions that plague human relationships. So, some of his war poems are pleas for sanity, truth and love, and this poem is a good example. One of its fascinations is its compact structure. Another is the use of the moon as a symbol of peace and concord.

Suddenly the air cracks

Suddenly the air cracks
with striking cracking rockets
guffaw of bofors stuttering LMGs
jets diving shooting glasses dropping
5 breaking from lips people diving
under beds nothing bullets flashing fire
striking writhing bodies and walls –

Suddenly there's silence –
and a thick black smoke
10 rises sadly into the sky as the jets
fly away in gruesome glee –

Then a babel of emotions, voices
mothers fathers calling children
and others joking shouting "where's your bunker?"
15 laughing teasing across streets
And then they gaze in groups without sadness
at the sad smoke curling skywards –

Again suddenly, the air cracks
above rooftops cracking striking
20 rockets guffawing bofors stuttering LMGs
ack-ack flacks diving jets
diving men women dragging children
seeking shelter not there breathless
hugging gutters walls houses
25 crumbling rumbling thunder
bombs hearts thumping heads low
under beds moving wordless lips –

Then suddenly there's silence
and the town heaves a deep sigh

30 as the jets again fly away and the guns
one by one fall silent and the gunners
dazed gaze at the empty sky, helpless –

And then voices shouting calling
voices, admiring jets' dive
35 pilot's bravery blaming gunners
praising gunners laughing people
wiping sweat and dust from hair
neck and shirt with trembling hands.

Things soon simmer to normal
40 hum and rhythm as danger passes
and the streets are peopled
with strolling men and women
boys and girls on various errands
walking talking laughing smiling –
45 and children running with arms
stretched out in front playing
at diving jets zoom past
unsmiling bombing rocketing shooting
with mouths between startled feet.
50 This also passes as dusk descends
and a friendly crescent moon
appears where the jets were.
Then simmering silence – the day passes –
And the curling black smoke,
55 the sadless hearts and the mangled
bodies stacked in the morgue
become memorials of this day.

Notes

line 3   bofors   This is a light anti-aircraft gun and *LMGs* means light
machine guns. *Guffaw*, which is a type of coarse laughter, modifies *bofors*,
while *stuttering* (a kind of repetition of initial sounds indicating some
difficulty in articulation) modifies *LMGs*. They imitate the sounds made
by these two weapons. Notice the use of alliteration.

line 7   To *writhe* means to roll, twist or contort the body in acute pain.

line 11   gruesome glee   The juxtaposition of two words which have opposite
meanings to heighten effect is a figurative use of language known as an
oxymoron. Gruesome refers to the jets that have caused so much terror
and destruction and *glee* to the unconcerned way in which they fly away
satisfied that they have carried out their mission. This emphasises the
ruthlessness of a mechanised air-attack.

line 12   babel of emotions   The reference is to Genesis Ch. XI and the
building of the city and tower of Babel. God introduced a confusion of
tongues during the project to frustrate the builders' vanity and to make

it impossible for them to achieve their plans. The implication here is a scene of confused emotions.

line 14 *bunker* Underground shelter commonly devised during wars to protect people from bullets, especially during air-raids.

line 21 *ack-ack* Colloquial term for light machine guns.

line 39 *Things simmer*, or "boil down" to normal, drawing attention to the state of suppressed agitation.

line 56 *morgue* A building where dead bodies are kept for identification.

line 57 *memorial* A significant object, landmark or event which commemorates particular historical incidents.

Questions

1 Describe the scene which the poet tries to depict.
2 Cite examples to show that the poet is able to see many sides of the experience.
3 What does the poet mean by the groups gazing *without sadness* and why is the smoke described as *sad* (stanza 3)?
4 Analyse the contrast which the poet draws between the moon and the jets.
5 Discuss the use of sound imagery, rhythm and punctuation.

Commentary

In all modern warfare, the agonies and destructions of war are increased a hundredfold by the role of war-planes. The ability to live with their harassments, having become used to their danger, and even to attempt to withstand their menace becomes a testimony to human courage and the inconquerable spirit of man. Air raids are frightening experiences and in this poem Okara captures vividly one such spell, observing the scene very closely and remembering to include the reactions of people, children not excepted, whose ability to make a joke of tragedy underlines the resilience of the human spirit.

In this poem, form, meaning and action are well integrated. The words used and their arrangements have an onomatopoeic quality (see for instance the first three lines which give the impression of hard rockets falling). And the "hanging" participial expressions give the feeling that the action is taking place (crumbling-rumbling, thumping). The punctuation is deliberately used to achieve a specific rhythm, which reflects the action of the aircraft and the confusion and destruction which they cause. Indeed the whole arrangement of the poem re-enacts the intermittent raids, the hurly-burly and the lulls that follow.

Piano and drums

When at break of day at a riverside
I hear jungle drums telegraphing
the mystic rhythm, urgent, raw
like bleeding flesh, speaking of
5 primal youth and the beginning,
I see the panther ready to pounce,

112

the leopard snarling about to leap
and the hunters crouch with spears poised;

And my blood ripples, turns torrent,
10 topples the years and at once I'm
in my mother's laps a suckling;
at once I'm walking simple
paths with no innovations,
rugged, fashioned with the naked
15 warmth of hurrying feet and groping hearts
in green leaves and wild flowers pulsing.

Then I hear a wailing piano
solo speaking of complex ways
in tear-furrowed concerto;
20 of far away lands
and new horizons with
coaxing diminuendo, counterpoint,
crescendo. But lost in the labyrinth
of its complexities, it ends in the middle
25 of a phrase at a daggerpoint.

And I lost in the morning mist
of an age at a riverside keep
wandering in the mystic rhythm
of jungle drums and the concerto.

Notes

Title Piano and drums are the two symbols around which this poem is
   organised. They are both musical instruments but whereas drums are
   important cultural and communication vehicles in traditional African
   society, the Piano is an important symbol of Western (European) culture.
   The drums symbolise simple, primitive ways while the piano symbolises
   complex modern and urban ways.
line 1 First line is significant in setting time and place – two factors that
   govern the working out of the theme of the poem. *Break of day* refers to
   morning, the early time of the day and by extension an innocent, pure,
   uncontaminated beginning. The poet is at a *riverside* and so is the "age"
   he is dealing with. Location at the riverside not only means the mist is
   heavier and his vision more blurred but, the river has not been crossed
   in pursuit of the invitation of the piano. It is this indeterminate poise
   that the poem explores.
line 3 mystic rhythm The drum not only expresses but also possesses some
   strong powers in African culture. Its rhythms do not only provide music
   for pleasurable dancing but can be a war cry or some occult
   accompaniment, expressing mysteries which only a few can understand.
   In this case the rhythms in particular ways carry a definite message,
   recreating the natural, untreated state of nature.

line 5   primal Belonging to the earliest time in the world.

line 11   suckling Young baby still taking milk from the mother. Image of
innocence, of the beginning.

line 17   wailing Long cry or sound that suggests grief or pain. There are
two possible meanings here. A piano note heard from a long distance
would give the impression of a wailing sound. Wailing here also gives
the impression of foreshadowing some problem to come or announcing it.

lines 19–23 Several terms associated with European music culture provide
the imagery of these lines.

concerto A piece of music composed for one, two or more solo instruments
and accompanied by an orchestra.

diminuendo Indicates a gradual diminishing in volume of sound.

counterpoint A musical arrangement in which a melody accompanies another
note for note or adding a related but independent melody or melodies to
a basic melody.

crescendo In music, gradually increasing loudness and fullness of tone.

labyrinth A network of narrow and twisting paths that criss-cross and form a
maze through which it is difficult to find one's way.

lines 24–25 A *daggerpoint* is a very sharp and fine point on which something
can only balance precariously. The poet is confused. He cannot cope
with the complex demands of the new ways which he understands only
dimly. He is caught in the middle (*of a phrase*) and cannot decide which
way to go.

phrase A short independent passage of music that is part of a longer piece.

line 26 He cannot see clearly through the mist.

lines 28–29 The conflict is not resolved.

Questions

1 Discuss the use of symbols and images in this poem.
2 How simple can we really say Okara's language is?
3 Discuss the structure of the poem and the way in which it reflects the
theme.
4 Discuss the theme of cultural conflict in two other poems in this
collection.

Commentary

In this poem, which treats the popular theme of conflict of cultures in Africa,
Okara uses the drums to symbolise simple primitive ways whose mysteries he
understands while the piano symbolises complex foreign ways which create
psychological problems for him. The first two stanzas present a primordial picture
of Africa in its natural state – related to childlike innocence – a time to which
the poet is transported on the wings of the music of the drum. Against this is
contrasted in the next stanza the new way represented by the piano. Its
complexity is reflected in the different musical directions, carefully spelt out, that
make up its rhythm while that of the drums is described with one word, *mystic*.
The last stanza brings the two ways together and with the image of *daggerpoint*
states the predicament in which the poet is. He is caught in a quandary.

In his attempt to make his contrast sharp, Okara goes to great pains to paint a picture of primitive Africa, employing words like *jungle, raw, bleeding flesh* and a forest full of wild animals. He may be cynical, but there is something conventional and stereotypical about this style which affects our final assessment of the poem.

Dennis Brutus

Dennis Brutus was born in Salisbury, Rhodesia, in 1924 of mixed parents, who, while Brutus was a child, migrated to South Africa and lived in Port Elizabeth. Brutus' early education was irregular but his mother introduced him to English poetry, reading to him from Tennyson and Wordsworth. He eventually entered Fort Hare University as an adult and graduated with a Bachelor of Arts degree. Subsequently he taught English and Afrikaans for fourteen years in South African high schools. But his active participation in protests against racism and the apartheid laws of South Africa led to his dismissal in 1962 and his arrest in 1963 in Johannesburg.

Released on bail he continued his agitation. His activities between 1963 and 1966, when he finally left South Africa for England, can only be described as that of an intrepid knight-errant, undeterred by all the formidable obstacles which beset his service to his cause – justice in South Africa. Banned by the South African Government from taking part in any social or political activities and under threat of being arrested and imprisoned without trial, he first moved to Swaziland where he tried in vain to obtain a residence permit. Then he tried to get to Germany through Mozambique, but was arrested and handed back to the South African police. He made a desperate attempt to escape, was shot in the back and sentenced to eighteen months imprisonment on the penal island of Robben. In 1965 he was freed from prison, but a total ban was imposed on his writing or publishing anything – a deprivation which finally led to his seeking exile in 1966. After a brief spell in England, he moved to the United States, where he now teaches and continues his campaign against racism and racial discrimination in South Africa.

Brutus writes simply and subtly. His style belongs to the main tradition of English poetry. His signal poem, as it were, "A troubadour, I traverse" is, for example, a sonnet. There are echoes of the Bible, of Tennyson, Wordsworth and Hopkins in his poetry. But he has his individual voice – resilient, sensitive, probing, controlled. Above all there is a persistent undercurrent of devotion to his home, South Africa, which enables a tenderness to come through even his most virulent denunciation and protest. This perhaps accounts for the unjustified criticism which some levelled against his work, that the brutalities of the South African experience are smoothed away by Brutus's subtle art and controlled passion. It is a criticism which misses the resonance of his voice.

A troubadour I traverse. . .

A troubadour, I traverse all my land
exploring all her wide-flung parts with zest
probing in motion sweeter far than rest
her secret thickets with an amorous hand:
5 and I have laughed, disdaining those who banned inquiry and
movement, delighting in the test
of will when doomed by Saracened arrest,
choosing, like unarmed thumb, simply to stand

Thus, quixoting till a cast-off of my land
10 I sing and fare, person to loved-one pressed
braced for this pressure and the captor's hand
that snaps off service like a weathered strand:
– no mistress-favour has adorned my breast
only the shadow of an arrow-brand.

Notes

line 1   *troubadour*   A medieval European knight who was also a poet and
who dedicated his life to the service of a lady (usually called a mistress)
and whose unattainable love he praised in his poetry. Often his service
entailed fighting in order to rescue the mistress from monsters and other
unfaithful knights. In this poem the land (South Africa) has become the
mistress and Dennis Brutus's restless fight for justice is behind the
poem.
   traverse
Travel across, but implying also the travail of the task.
lines 5–6   *banned inquiry and movement*   Imposed restriction on both the
freedom of speech and exchange of ideas and the freedom of movement
and association.
lines 6–7   *the test of will*   The ability to stand and suffer for one's
convictions.
line 7   The *Saracens* were Muslim Arabs, regarded as heretics and enemies of
the Christian faith, against whom medieval Christian knights fought the
Wars of the Crusades. Hence, since the speaker sees himself as such a
knight and a defender of justice, he describes his opponents as *Saracens*.
The armoured cars of the South African police are also called Saracens.
line 9   *quixoting*   From the name Don Quixote, the hero of the novel by the
16th century Spanish novelist, Cervantes. Don Quixote's pursuit of
imaginary monsters and enemies makes him a laughable figure. Hence a
quixotic act is a futile act as of a man fighting a losing battle.
line 11   *braced*   To be armed or dressed in readiness for action, to be alert.
line 13   *no mistress-favour has adorned my breast. . .*   Often the medieval
knight would bear embroidered on his breast an emblem of his mistress.
Here the speaker does not bear any such emblem except (line 14) the
scar of the wound he has received in the service of his mistress, South
Africa.

line 14   *arrow-brand*   In Britain the standard symbol of a convict, printed on his uniform, was the arrow.

Questions

1 How effective is the conceit of the knight-errant and his mistress in terms of the poet's relationship with his home country?
2 Comment on the comparison implicit in the line: *choosing, like unarmed thumb, simply to stand...*
3 Identify the instances of alliteration and assonance in the poem and describe how they contribute to the movement of the poem.

Commentary

Perhaps the best commentary on this poem is a passage from the poet's own *Childhood Reminiscences*: "there recur in my poetry certain images from the language of chivalry – the troubadour, in particular. The notion of a stubborn, even foolish knight-errantry on a quest, in the service of someone loved; this is an image I use in my work, because it seems to me a true kind of shorthand for something which is part of my life and my pursuit of justice in a menacing South Africa." (*The Modern Writer in Africa* ed. Per Wastberg, New York, 1969 p. 98.)

Using the complex and well-known form of the sonnet (fourteen mainly iambic pentameter lines with a regular rhyme scheme) the poet gives a deliberately measured expression to the defiant spirit behind his poetry. There is an effective use of alliteration and assonance to give the impression of a measured statement of the speaker's stand.

The sun on this rubble

The sun on this rubble after rain.

Bruised though we must be
some easement we require
unarguably, though we argue against desire.

5 Under jackboots our bones and spirits crunch
forced into sweat-tear-sodden slush
– now glow-lipped by this sudden touch:

– sun-stripped perhaps, our bones may later sing
or spell out some malignant nemesis
10 Sharpevilled to spearpoints for revenging

but now our pride-dumbed mouths are wide
in wordless supplication
– are grateful for the least relief from pain

– like this sun on this debris after rain.

Notes

line 4 Though our reason and will try to persuade us against the need of relief from continuous pain, our bodies and feelings acknowledge this need.

lines 5–6 The attempt is to present a concrete image of men broken by oppression and torture. *Slush* suggests a messy lump that the body and spirit has been reduced to.

line 7 *glow-lipped* A rather confused metaphor; the attempt is to convey an impression of the sun shining upon the partly muddy, partly watery surface of the rubble to which oppressed man has been reduced. But at the same time the revived body is imagined as regaining the power of speech.

line 8 *sun-stripped* Allowed to rot and be stripped bare of all flesh by the rays of the sun.

line 9 *some malignant nemesis* Some evil doom or catastrophe.

line 10 *Sharpevilled* Sharpened or stirred into an outburst of violence and bloodshed. The verb has been formed as a play on the name of the town Sharpeville, in South Africa, where on 21 March 1960, 67 black and coloured people, protesting against the pass laws, were shot dead by the South African police, and several others were wounded.

lines 11–12 Mouths made speechless by pride and unwillingness to beg for favours that are nevertheless welcome. The lines re-echo the earlier lines 3 and 4.

Questions

1 Why does the poet so clearly isolate the first and last lines of the poem?
2 What does the speaker mean by *our bones may later sing*?
3 Why are the mouths said to be *wide* in line 11?

Commentary

This poem is essentially a meditation upon the ways of nature and their possible implications for man. The starting point, to which the meditation finally returns, is the sun shining on a broken heap of earth after rain. The sun, symbolizing nature's periodic blessing, offers the hope of temporary respite to oppressed man.

Implied in this comparison of the ways of nature to the affairs of man is the welcome effect of any temporary relief in the pain suffered by men. Specifically there is an implied reference to the temporary relaxation of the oppressive pass laws of South Africa after the massacre at Sharpeville in March 1960. But the poem suggests that the ultimate outcome of the oppression remains unpredictable.

The structure of the poem is a variation on the fourteen-line sonnet which Brutus occasionally uses. There are echoes of the poetry of Gerald Manley Hopkins, in the formation of compound words and in the meditation on the marvellous and healing touch of nature (in Hopkins this is the work of God).

After exile (four selections)

1
I am the tree
creaking in the wind
outside in the night
twisted and stubborn:

5 I am the sheet
of the twisted tin shack
grating in the wind
in a shrill sad protest:

I am the voice
10 crying in the night
that cries endlessly
and will not be consoled.

2
I must conjure from my past
the dim and unavowed spectre of a slave,
of a bound woman, whose bound figure pleads
silently,
5 and whose blood I must acknowledge in my own:

fanciful wraith? imagining?
Yet how else can I reconcile
my rebel blood and protest
but by acknowledgement
10 of that spectre's mute rebellious blood.

3
"Bury the great duke,"
I piped from the floor
among my cotton reels:

"Yes?" he turned in surprise
5 and "Go on" he prompted gently
towelling the lather from a half-shaved cheek

"Bury the Great Duke
with a noise of lamentation."
But I faltered while he waited
10 and until he turned away.

And what other failures over ages
kept him turning half-away?

4
Today in prison
by tacit agreement
they will sing just one song:
Nkosi Sikekela;
5 slowly and solemnly
with suppressed passion
and pent up feeling:
the voices strong and steady
but with tears close and sharp
10 behind the eyes
and the mind ranging
wildly as a strayed bird
seeking some names to settle on
and deeds being done
15 and those who will do the much
that still needs to be done.

Notes on the first poem

lines 9–12 Compare with Matthew II, 18:

A voice was heard in Ramah
wailing and loud lamentation
Rachel weeping for her children
She refused to be consoled
because they were no more

Rachel's lamentation for the innocent children, massacred on
the orders of King Herod in his attempt to get rid of the baby
Jesus, has become representative of those who mourn
injustice and oppression.

line 6 Evokes a picture of the slum huts of the shanty-towns to which South
African blacks and coloureds are confined by the apartheid laws of the
country. The walls and roofs of these huts, made of rusted aluminium
and tin sheets and rattling in the wind, seem to cry in protest against
the inhuman laws they symbolise.

Questions

1 Comment on *creaking*, *grating* and *crying*, and show the various ways in which these verb forms are related.
2 What does the poet gain by comparing himself to three different things in the poem? Show how each of the three images contributes to the picture of oppression and suffering presented in the poem.

Notes on the second poem

line 1   *conjure*   Call forth from the past in order to account for a present fact.
line 2   *unavowed*   Unacknowledged; as yet not recognised to relate to oneself.
   spectre   Not necessarily a ghost; simply a remote figure from the past; here an ancestor.
line 6   *wraith*   A mere imaginary figure.

Questions

1 Comment on the phrase *mute rebellious blood* in line 10.
2 Discuss why the speaker feels compelled to acknowledge a slave maternal ancestor.
3 How does the poet create the impression that the speaker in this poem is communing with himself?

Notes on the third poem

line 1   First line of Lord Alfred Tennyson's ode on the death of the Duke of Wellington, the hero of Waterloo, in 1852.
   Tennyson's poem assumes a common grief for the imperial hero, shared by imperial rulers as well as colonial subjects. The opening lines of his ode are:

Bury the Great Duke
With an empire's lamentation
Let us bury the Great Duke
To the noise of the mourning of a mighty nation.

The imperial lord and the colonial slave are implicitly recalled in this poem of Dennis Brutus: the speaker on the floor (line 2) and his questioner towering above him with a half-shaved cheek (line 6). The poem can, of course, be imagined as set in a South African farm, so that it becomes a brief exchange between a white farmer and his black labourer.
line 3   *cotton reels*   Wheels for spinning cotton into yarn.

Questions

1 Why do you think the second speaker turned in *surprise* to the first in line 4?

2 What is the force of the word *gently* in line 5?
3 Does the faltering in line 9 mean anything more than an inability to recall the rest of the poem quoted in lines 7 and 8?
4 The speaker quotes the first line of Tennyson's poem twice (see note on line 1). Do you notice any difference in the quotations? What light does this throw on the speaker's attitude throughout the poem?

Notes on the fourth poem

line 4   A Zulu song usually regarded as a national anthem by Africans south of the Zambezi. Nkosi means the King or the Lord; and the phrase means "God guide the destiny of our land!"
line 2   tacit   Generally accepted without being spoken about.
line 7   pent up   Held in check and therefore more keenly felt.
lines 11–13   Convey both the anguish and near despair, as well as the fortitude, of the oppressed who, nevertheless, look to the future with hope. The search for the names of tribal heroes connects this poem with the previous one, where another "tribal hero", the Duke of Wellington, is recalled but rejected.

Questions

1 How far does the poet succeed in conveying the meaning of line 5 through the rhythm of the rest of the poem?
2 What is the meaning of line 14?
3 Comment on the syntax (the sense structure) of the last four lines of the poem.
4 Show how the poet's attitude to apartheid unfolds in the four poems.
5 Compare Dennis Brutus and Oswald Mtshali as commentators on the South African situation.

Commentary

These four poems written for South African Freedom Day, 27 June 1967, belong together and present a composite picture of life as an oppressed black or coloured person in South Africa.

The first poem presents three different images of oppression and protest. The second poem tries to see oppression and protest as an unavoidable heritage.

The third poem seeks a solution to oppression by the path of possible acculturation: if the oppressed adopted the same racial heroes as the oppressor perhaps a common bond of reconciliation could be forged. But this approach proves futile: "*I faltered . . . until he turned away; what other failures over the ages kept him turning half-away?*"

The final poem poignantly re-states the condition of the oppressed and the deprived, searching for their own tribal heritage of heroic deeds, through the simple ritual of a song which affirms hope deferred, but never destroyed: Nko-si Sikekela.

Nightsong: city

Sleep well, my love, sleep well:
the harbour lights glaze over restless docks,
police cars cockroach through the tunnel streets;

from the shanties creaking iron-sheets
5 violence like a bug-infested rag is tossed
and fear is imminent as sound in the wind-swung bell;

the long day's anger pants from sand and rocks;
but for this breathing night at least;
my land, my love, sleep well.

Notes

line 2 *glaze over* Give a common hue or shade to and, by so doing, hide
the details of normal daytime bustle.

line 3 *cockroach through* An apt description of the furtive movement of
police patrol cars (possibly VW beetle cars) in and out of the apparently
narrow streets which wind round the tall city buildings.
tunnel streets The impression of the streets seen below from the height
of the skyscrapers.

line 6 A very expressive simile. Just as the bell 'contains' sound all the time
which can be brought out even by its being merely swung by the wind,
so violence is endemic to the shanty-dwellings of the city.

line 7 The reference is to the heat, stored in the rocks during the day,
escaping at night; but this in itself becomes a symbol of the unwinding
of the tensions built up in human relationships during the city's working
day.

Questions

1 Describe in your own words the picture of the city and its surroundings
which the poem conveys.
2 What is the significance of the word *tossed* in line 5 of the poem?
3 Do you think the poet succeeds in resolving the tension between the desire
for peace and the fear of violence in the poem?

Commentary

This poem succeeds remarkably well in conveying an impression of night in the
urban centres of South Africa (possibly, Cape Town) with its harbour, skyscrap-
ers, surrounding slum dwellings and contained violence. An attempt is made
to catch the sound and sights of the city at night. This effect is created through
the impression of observing and listening from a distance, so that the stark lights
and startling sounds are blurred. Night is thus a period of lull in the normal
life of the city, as if a space has occurred for the city to pant and gather its breath

for the long day's anger ahead. There is also a deliberate attempt, through the tone of the speaker (as of a mother tenderly brooding over a loved child) to turn the blurred sights and sounds into a lullaby for the city.

A common hate enriched our love and us

A common hate enriched our love and us:

Escape to parasitic ease disgusts;
discreet expensive hushes stifled us
the plangent wines became acidulous

5 Rich foods knotted to revolting clots
of guilt and anger in our queasy guts
remembering the hungry comfortless.

In draughty angles of the concrete stairs
or seared by salt winds under brittle stars
10 we found a poignant edge to tenderness,

and, sharper than our strain, the passion
against our land's disfigurement and tension;
hate gouged out deeper levels for our passion –

a common hate enriched our love and us.

Notes

line 2   parasitic ease   Comfort for which one is dependent on others, for
   example, the comfortable life of a political refugee who relies on
   international charity.
line 3   expensive hushes   The silence exacted from an exile as the price for
   the offer of safety in a host country.
line 4   plangent   Intoxicating.
   acidulous   Having the effect of making one bad-tempered and sour.
line 5–6   clots of guilt   A powerful image of self-disgust, drawn from over-
   eating while one knows that others are starving.
   queasy   Fastidious; sensitive to guilt.
line 9   A vivid image of exposure.
line 10   a poignant edge   The harsh conditions of persecution had the effect
   of making the victims more affectionate to one another.

Questions

1 Against whom or what is the common hatred, mentioned in the first line of
   the poem, directed?

2 Compare and contrast the images and the experiences depicted in lines 2–7 and 8–13.
3 How does the poet convey his attitude to life in exile in the poem?
4 What light does the rest of the poem throw on the linking of love and hatred in the opening and closing lines of the poem?

Commentary

Through a series of powerful images, this poem presents the dilemma of the political refugee who seeks protection abroad, but feels guilty on account of the comfort of his new life in contrast to the harshness of his former life at home. The beauty of the poem lies in both the symmetry, the contrasts and the paradox it embodies.

The symmetry is seen in (i) the repetition of line 1 at the end of the poem, making it an outer framework of the entire poem; (ii) the four stanzas divided into two equal groups: lines 2–7 and lines 8–13. Lines 2–7 present the dissatisfaction with life in exile, and lines 8–13 recall with satisfaction the former life of persecution and exposure. Thus, while the structure of these two groups of lines is symmetrical, the experiences they present are contrasted. So are the images. The contrasts and the symmetry in the poem are brought together in the paradox of a love that is fed by the hatred of a common enemy: apartheid.

It is the constant image of your face

It is the constant image of your face
framed in my hands as you knelt before my chair
the grave attention of your eyes
surveying me amid my world of knives
5 that stays with me, perennially accuses
and convicts me of heart's–treachery;
and neither you nor I can plead excuses
for you, you know, can claim no loyalty –
my land takes precedence of all my loves.

10 Yet I beg mitigation, pleading guilty
for you, my dear, accomplice of my heart
made, without words, such blackmail with your beauty
and proferred me such dear protectiveness
that I confess without remorse or shame
15 my still-fresh treason to my country
and hope that she, my other, dearest love
will pardon freely, not attaching blame
being your mistress (or your match) in tenderness.

Notes

line 5   perennially   Constantly.
line 6   heart's-treachery   Refers to the betrayal of the public cause inherent in the speaker's yielding to the pleas of his loved one.
line 9   takes precedence   Deserves foremost attention.
line 10   beg mitigation   A legal phrase meaning someone admits his guilt but offers reasons for it.
line 11   accomplice of my heart   The one I cherish in my heart, hence one who is equally guilty of my heart's betrayal of the public cause.

Questions

1 What could *my world of knives* refer to?
2 Imagine that the speaker in this poem has been accused by his comrades of giving up the fight against apartheid. State in your own words the possible accusation and the arguments the speaker offers in defence.
3 Attempt an interpretation of the last line of the poem.
4 Comment on the conflict between the two loves presented in the poem.

Commentary

This is a characteristic Dennis Brutus poem both in theme and style. Two opposed impulses run through the poem: on the one hand, the commitment of a coloured South African fighting against the dehumanising conditions of apartheid and for whom everything else is secondary and, on the other hand, the temptation to relax, accept the ordinary blessings and the creature comforts of affection and tenderness. Thus there is a close link between this poem and "A common hate enriched our love". But whereas "A common hate . . ." concentrates on the public commitment which even personal feelings nourish, this poem admits the "guilt" of subordinating the public commitment to personal needs. This is a typical Dennis Brutus dialectic.

Of the two poems, this one places supreme value on beauty and love and tenderness and yet shows an awareness that an exclusive cherishing of these personal values may turn into a betrayal of responsibility to the wider world.

A striking feature of the poem is the careful and measured movement of its two stanzas. Each stanza is made of nine lines, and yet the lines in each case form an elaborate and complex sentence. The careful cadences of the phrases that make up the sentence convey the tender tone of the speaker.

Kwesi Brew

Kwesi Brew was born in Cape Coast, Ghana, in 1928. Educated in Ghana, he first entered the Civil Service before travelling widely as a diplomat for his country. The main qualities of his writing are studied simplicity, careful attention to detail and a highly controlled tone and rhythm. His poetry deals mainly with the recollection of moments of past experience which have really moved him.

He is represented in this anthology by poems which span the greater part of his writing career: from the early "Ancestral faces" to the recent occasional comment on the public scene in "A sandal on the head". His best poems such as "The dry season" or "The sea eats our lands" combine a bald description with implicit and often elegiac comment. His muted style stands in contrast to the two other major Ghanaian poets, Awoonor and Okai, also represented in this anthology.

The mesh

We have come to the cross-roads
And I must either leave or come with you.
I lingered over the choice
But in the darkness of my doubts
5 You lifted the lamp of love
And I saw in your face
The road that I should take.

Questions

1 Comment on the effectiveness of lines 4 and 5, paying attention to the function of devices like alliteration and assonance in them.
2 How is the title related to the rest of the poem?

Commentary

This brief but subtle poem is one of the frequently anthologised poems of Kwesi Brew. In his own collection *The Shadows of Laughter*, it occurs in the section subtitled "Today we look at each other" – a subtitle probably derived from John Donne's poem "The good morrow" in which Donne conveys the sense of wonder with which two people grasp the dawning of love between them. The poems in the subsection of Brew's collection deal mainly with love and "The mesh" particularly captures the moment of certainty and assurance when love is naturally given and accepted. Perhaps the most interesting thing about the poem is its title.

The dry season

The year is withering; the wind
Blows down the leaves;
Men stand under eaves
And overhear the secrets
5 Of the cold dry wind,
Of the half-bare trees.

The grasses are tall and tinted,
Straw-gold hues of dryness,
And the contradicting awryness,
10 Of the dusty roads a-scatter
With the pools of colourful leaves,
With ghosts of the dreaming year.

And soon, soon the fires,
The fires will begin to burn,
15 The hawk will flutter and turn
On its wings and swoop for the mouse,
The dogs will run for the hare,
The hare for its little life.

Notes

line 9 awryness Chaos, disorderliness, rich variety.
line 11 pools Thick layers.

Questions

1 A number of sounds are repeated at various stages in the poem. Identify
them and show how they contribute to the rhythm and meaning of the
poem.
2 What does the phrase *ghosts of the dreaming year* (line 12) mean?
3 Stanza 3 of the poem describes a number of energetic activities. How does
the description convey the poet's attitude to the "withering year"?

Commentary

This is a simple descriptive poem in which carefully observed details are brought
together to present a piece of landscape painting of a unified colour. Each stanza
of the poem provides a particular stroke of the brush different from the others
and yet related to them.

The first stanza, dominated by repeated and echoed sounds, concentrates on
the whispering wind. There is an emphasis on dryness, bareness and withering.
Simple direct statements lend the stanza a subdued tone.

The second stanza makes its appeal to our sense of sight and, by evoking a
rich and colourful scene, creates an impression of life amidst the dying year.

The third stanza begins on a note of excitement as the result of a few repeated or emphatic words. There is a lot of activity, in contrast to the end-of-life feeling of the previous two stanzas. Also, in contrast to the falling cadence on which the second stanza ends, the music of the third stanza soars: *the fires, the fires will begin to burn, The hawk will flutter and turn.* And that excitement is exquisitely summed up by the triple measure (dactylic foot) in *little life*, as it were, the little hop, upon which the poem ends.

The executioner's dream

I dreamt I saw an eye, a pretty eye,
In your hands,
Glittering, wet and sickening
Like a dull onyx set in a crown of thorns.
5 I did not know you were dead
When you dropped it in my lap.

What horrors of human sacrifice
Have you seen, executioner?
What agonies of tortured men
10 Who sat through nights and nights of pain
Tongue-tied by the wicked sappor,
Gazing at you with hot imploring eyes?

These white lilies tossed their little heads then
In the moon-steeped ponds;
15 There was bouncing gaiety in the crisp chirping
of the cricket in the undergrowth,
And as the surf-boats splintered the waves
I saw the rainbow in your eyes
And in the flash of your teeth.
20 As each crystal shone,
I saw sitting hand in hand with melancholy
A little sunny child
Playing at marbles with husks of fallen stars;
Horrors were your flowers then;
25 The blood-bright bougainvilleas,
They delighted you.

Why do you now weep
And offer me this little gift
Of a dull onyx set in a crown of thorns?

Notes

line 4   onyx   A quartz or cut stone of different colours used as ornament. The combination *dull onyx* ought to be compared with *glittering* and *sickening* in line 3.

line 11   sappor   Sharp sticks thrust through the under part of the jaw of the victim, pinning the tongue and making it immovable, so that the victim bleeds slowly to death.

line 18   the rainbow   A mark of triumph over his victims.

line 20   crystal   Possibly the glittering eye balls of previous victims.

lines 21–23   The little sunny child represents the executioner in his childish enjoyment of the sad lot of his victims.

line 24   your flowers   Your delight.

Questions

1 The poem embodies both the speaker's and the executioner's dream (see lines 24 and 27). Distinguish as clearly as you can the contents of the two dreams.
2 Identify some of the ways in which the poet creates the impression of a dream in the poem.
3 What is the executioner's dream? Give reasons for your answer.
4 Analyse the speaker's attitude to the executioner.

Commentary

This is one of the most popularly anthologised poems of Kwesi Brew. Its fascination lies in the haunting atmosphere which unifies the poem. Part of its appeal may also lie in the fact that it exemplifies the dark humour which is the obverse side of the otherwise bright realism of Brew. It also portrays something of the horror that traditional African life could have. For although the *sappor* (see notes) was reserved for criminals and the captives of war, the emphasis in this poem is on the innocent victims of ritual sacrifice. And our usual attitude of regarding such aspects of our life as nightmares is recreated in the fascination which the gift of a glittering eye holds for the speaker in the poem.

In the poem it is not only human beings, represented by the executioner, who exalt in power over others: even nature is seen as participating in the exaltation: the lilies toss their little heads, the crickets chirp and the surf-boats splinter the waves.

The sea eats our lands

Here stood our ancestral home:
The crumbling wall marks the spot.
Here a sheep was led to slaughter
To appease the gods and atone
5 For faults which our destiny
Has blossomed into crimes.

There my cursed father once stood
And shouted to us, his children,
To come back from our play
10 To our evening meal and sleep.
The clouds were thickening in the red sky
And night had charmed
A black power into the pounding waves.

Here once lay Keta.
15 Now her golden girls
Erode into the arms
Of strange towns.

Notes

line 1   ancestral home   Ancient family house, often in ruins, but normally the
   spot at which spirits are invoked and libation offered.
line 4   appease   Make peace with, pacify by means of a sacrificial offering.
line 5   destiny   That which has been ordained to happen.
line 6   blossomed   Ironical use, as if crimes were desirable fruits.
line 14   Keta   A town on the south coast of Ghana, built on a narrow strip
   of land between a lagoon and the sea and subject to constant sea
   erosion.

Questions

1 Describe the function and the effect of the words *Here* and *There*, in the
   poem.
2 Comment on the particular effectiveness of the word *Erode* in line 16.
3 "This is an elegiac poem". Show how the contrasting tone and movement
   of the last seven lines of the poem contribute to the elegiac effect.

Commentary

As is often the case with Brew, this poem is divided into sections, rather than
stanzas. The first section depicts the mind's random recall of the past frozen
around particular spots and incidents. But it is a past seen in the light of the
present: our destiny has blossomed former faults into present crimes. For even
as children we perversely regard our parents' natural concern for our well-being
as an intolerable interference. And it is this natural perversity which inevitably
turns initial faults into deliberate crimes.

The second section of the poem vividly evokes a particular moment of the past,
making an ordinary event suddenly symbolic of mysterious forces in nature and
the source of subsequent profound changes.

The third section quietly draws together the impersonal and the personal, the
natural and the human causes of disaster and change.

This is an elegiac poem lamenting the effects of a natural and perhaps
unavoidable disaster. At the same time it suggests a profound human implication
in and responsibility for changes which accompany or result from such disasters.
Natural disaster is matched by profound changes in the moral fibre of a people's

life. What starts as a lament for a particular place becomes a meditation on the passing away of a whole way of life and of an era. In a similar manner the sea as a natural part of the created universe becomes representative of an independent and hostile power up in arms against man. And the historical experience of a particular people and place takes on a universal meaning for all men.

A sandal on the head

The broken bones cannot be made whole!
The strong had sheltered in their strength
The swift had sought life in their speed,
The crippled and the tired heaped out of the way
5   Onto the ant hills
Had been bit by bit, half-eaten by termites.

The rough and ready were beginning
To tire of dancing to that one
Strange unfamiliar tune.

10 The Master of the House cracked his whip
In the realm of laughter and light,
And mopped his brow with a silken cloth

It is only the gods who know
Why the bones were broken;

15 It's only the old who know why
The goats skip homeward at evening
And the Master of the House
Now Master of Rags
Stays behind on the rocks
20 To rummage in the rubbish heap
For cast-away morsels of power!

Notes

Title   One of the rituals of enstooling a traditional ruler in Ghana is to put a
        pair of sandals on his feet. The reverse ceremony of dethronement is
        symbolised by touching the ruler's head with his sandals.

Questions

1 List and examine the distinctions which the poet makes between the
   supporters and the victims of the Master in the poem.
2 Comment on the distinction which the poet makes between what the gods
   know and what the old know.
3 Why would you call the poet's attitude in the poem complex?

This poem, written about the overthrow of President Kwame Nkrumah of Ghana in February 1966 and his subsequent exile in Guinea, conveys a powerful picture of the breakdown of civic responsibility among the supporters of the President before his fall. We also get an impression of how callous the President himself had become before his overthrow. But the poet's sense of humour keeps a tight rein on his outrage against the suffering imposed by the regime.

Ancestral faces

They sneaked into the limbo of time,
But could not muffle the gay jingling
Brass bells on the frothy necks
Of the sacrificial sheep that limped after them;
5 They could not hide the moss on the bald pate
Of their reverent heads;
And the gnarled barks of the wawa tree;
Nor the rust on the ancient state-swords;
Nor the skulls studded with grinning cowries;
10 They could not silence the drums,
The fibre of their souls and ours –
The drums that whisper to us behind the black sinewy hands.
They gazed
and sweeping like white locusts through the forests
15 Saw the same men, slightly wizened,
Shuffle their sandalled feet to the same rhythms,
They heard the same words of wisdom uttered
Between puffs of pale blue smoke:
They saw us,
20 And said: They have not changed!

Notes

line 1   *sneaked*   This suggests that the ancestors would rather escape
   notice, but they are only too well recalled to mind by the tradition of
   ceremonial obligations inherited by their descendants.
line 3   *frothy*   The thick white mane of the sacrificial sheep.
line 5   *the moss on the bald pate*   The reference is to the earthen images of
   the ancestors, on whose heads yearly sacrifices of food and oils are
   poured and which then decay and gather moss.
lines 5–10   A number of ritual objects are mentioned here, apart from the
   earthen images: state swords and skulls suggest that the ancestors were
   warrior-chiefs who brought home the skulls of war victims.
line 12   *black sinewy hands*   Of the skilful drummers who remember the
   ancient rhythms and the proverbial language of the talking-drums.
lines 17–18   *words of wisdom uttered Between puffs*   The utterances which

accompany the ceremony of libation to the ancestors are usually proverbs embodying the wisdom of the tribe.

Questions

1 Identify the various ways in which the poet suggests the ghostliness of the ancestors. What do these reveal about his attitude to them?
2 How does the poet's awareness of continuity *and* change show in the poem?
3 The poet's humour is registered through the precise descriptive details. Explain, with reference to descriptive verbs and adjectives.

Commentary

The background to this poem is the celebration of the funeral rites of the dead of an extended family or clan. During such celebrations the elders of the clan – the dead ancestors – are invoked through the offering of sacrificial animals, the pouring of libation, the firing of musketry, drumming and dancing. Since the funeral rites of each dead of the clan involve the repetition of this ceremony in the assumed presence of the ancestors, there is a suggestion of permanence and continuity, in the midst of the change and decay which death brings. It is the poet's keen awareness of this change that leads to his humourous mockery of both the living and the dead. The success of the poem lies in the distinction made between that which is really permanent and relevant and that which only pretends to be and therefore deserves to be mocked. The humour is registered by the precise descriptive details throughout the poem.

Joseph Kariuki

Joseph Elijah Kariuki was born in Banana Hill, Kenya in 1931 and educated at Makerere College, Uganda from 1950–54, and later at Cambridge University, England, from 1960–62. Between graduating from Makerere and going to Britain, he taught at various secondary schools in Kenya. On his return from Britain he went back to teaching, before he became the Principal of the Kenya Institute of Administration in 1966. In 1968 he joined the training section of the United Nations Economic Commission for Africa. And in the following year he became the Director of the Centre for Development Research and Information, Morocco.

Kariuki is an occasional writer whose poems have appeared in various anthologies. His most famous piece is the ode to President Kenyatta called "Ode to Mzee". He is represented here by the lyric poem "Come away, my love".

Come away, my love

Come away, my love, from streets
Where mankind eyes divide,
And show windows reflect our difference.
In the shelter of my faithful room rest.

5 There, safe from opinions, being behind
Myself, I can see only you;
And in my dark eyes your grey
Will dissolve

          The candlelight throws
10 Two dark shadows on the wall
Which merge into one as I close beside you.

When at last the lights are out,
And I feel your hand in mine,
Two human breaths join in one,
And the piano weaves
15 Its unchallenged harmony.

Questions

1 Comment on the meaning and the effectiveness of the following words and phrases: *mankind eyes, faithful room, opinions, being behind myself*.

2 There is a continuous reference, both direct and indirect, to light in this poem. Indicate the points in the poem where this occurs and show the effectiveness of the use of this device.

3 In what way do the last two lines of the poem sum up its theme and imagery?

4 Would you say that this poem is sentimental or escapist? Indicate some features of the poem to support your view.

Commentary

The background to this poem is the situation (now changing simply because of its familiarity) which faces the African student in a largely white community when he finds himself in love with a white girl. He walks the street with his girl friend and is aware that the wide glass windows of the shops reflect their colour difference. And compelled by the staring eyes of people who disapprove of such relationships, he seeks shelter and fulfilment in his room. Unable to face the light which is thrown on their relationship by outsiders, he prefers the candlelight; but this can only cast shadows of what the two are.

This is a simple poem embodying a wish-fulfilment and characterised by an understandable unwillingness to face realities. Its merit lies in the poet's attempt to find an imaginative solution for a genuine human problem. The problem is expressed through a series of contrasts, e.g. the outside world with the *faithful room*, the dark eyes with the grey. The imaginative solution comes out in phrases like *being behind myself* (formed on the model of "being beside oneself") or *the piano weaves its unchallenged harmony*.

David Rubadiri

Born in Malawi in 1930, David Rubadiri was educated at Makerere University and King's College, Cambridge where he took the English tripos. He returned home to deep involvement in the education and politics of his country; he was detained in 1959 during the state of emergency in Nyasaland. He was for some time ambassador to the United States of America but has since the mid-seventies lived in voluntary exile teaching at the universities of Makerere, Nairobi and now Botswana. He is keenly interested in the arts and the promotion of literature and is one of the early creators of modern African literature from East Africa. Apart from his poems, he has also written a novel, *No Bride Price*.

An African thunderstorm

From the west
Clouds come hurrying with the wind
Turning
Sharply
5 Here and there
Like a plague of locusts
Whirling
Tossing up things on its tail
Like a madman chasing nothing

10 Pregnant clouds
Ride stately on its back
Gathering to perch on hills
Like dark sinister wings;
The wind whistles by
15 And trees bend to let it pass.

In the village
Screams of delighted children
Toss and turn
In the din of whirling wind,
20 Women –
Babies clinging on their backs –
Dart about
In and out
Madly
25 The wind whistles by
Whilst trees bend to let us pass.

138

Clothes were like tattered flags
Flying off
To expose dangling breasts
30 As jagged blinding flashes
Rumble, tremble, and crack
Amidst the smell of fired smoke
And the pelting march of the storm.

Notes

line 6 A *plague* is a type of affliction or epidemic that causes a great deal of
discomfort. Locusts usually move in large numbers and they cause a lot
of destruction to vegetation.

line 7 *whirling* Spinning movement caused by strong wind.

line 13 *sinister* Evil. There is every suggestion from the association and
similes that the wind is a destructive one.

Questions

1 Examine the poet's use of similes, alliteration and onomatopeia. How do
  they contribute to the effectiveness of the poem?
2 Why are the clouds described as *pregnant* (line 10), and what picture is the
  poet drawing?
3 What differences do you notice between the forms of the first three stanzas
  on the one hand and the last stanza on the other hand? (Pay attention to
  the stress pattern in the last stanza.) How do these contribute to the
  progression of the poem?

Commentary

This poem is a vivid description of the disorder and havoc caused by an African
thunderstorm in which the poet through the use of suitable visual images, allit-
eration and onomatopoea successfully recreates the thunderstorm. The artistry
of the poem is skilful, because the form and rhythm of the stanzas represent the
progression of the thunderstorm from the moment it starts to gather with fury
from the west to the time it inevitably bursts, "pelting" rain drops. There is
strong local colour and flavour, and we feel the world of nature and man
tormented by this storm. Part of the strength of this poem lies in the manner in
which the poet uses varying line lengths to capture this physical incident. Notice
the weight and rhythmic force which short lines of a single word or two words
have in this poem.

Stanley meets Mutesa

Such a time of it they had;
The heat of the day,
The chill of the night

And the mosquitoes that followed.
5 Such was the time and
They bound for a kingdom.

The thin weary line of carriers
With tattered dirty rags to cover their backs;
The battered bulky chests
10 That kept on falling off their shaven heads.
Their tempers high and hot,
The sun fierce and scorching –
With it rose their spirits,
With its fall their hopes
15 As each day sweated their bodies dry and
Flies clung in clumps on their sweat-scented backs.
Such was the march.
And the hot season just breaking.

Each day a weary pony dropped,
20 Left for the vultures on the plains;
Each afternoon a human skeleton collapsed,
Left for the Masai on the plains;
But the march trudged on
Its khaki leader in front;
25 He the spirit that inspired.
He the light of hope.

Then came the afternoon of a hungry march,
A hot and hungry march it was;
The Nile and the Nyanza
30 Lay like twins
Azure across the green countryside.
The march leapt on chaunting
Like young gazelles to a water hole.
Hearts beat faster,
35 Loads felt lighter
As the cool water lapped their sore soft feet.
No more the dread of hungry hyenas
But only tales of valour when
At Mutesa's court fires are lit.

40 No more the burning heat of the day
But song, laughter and dance.

The village looks on behind banana groves,
Children peer behind reed fences.
Such was the welcome.
45 No singing women to chaunt a welcome

140

Or drums to greet the white ambassador;
Only a few silent nods from aged faces
And one rumbling drum roll
To summon Mutesa's court to parley
50 For the country was not sure.
The gate of reeds is flung open,
There is silence
But only a moment's silence
A silence of assessment.
55 The tall black king steps forward,
He towers over the thin bearded white man
Then grabbing his lean white hand
Manages to whisper
"Mtu Mweupe karibu"
60 White Man you are welcome.
The gate of polished reed closes behind them
And the west is let in.

Notes

line 6   There is a tinge of irony in this expression, and there are two
possible meanings implied. The party is bound for the Kingdom of
Mutesa; they are also on a quest to acquire more kingdoms for the
British government.

line 22   The *Masai* are a pastoral and warlike tribe in East Africa.

line 24   Refers to Stanley, dogged and determined. He was in khaki clothes.

line 31   *Azure*   Bright blue, often used to describe the colour of many rivers
and lakes.

line 32   *chaunting*   An old form of chanting. The party are now in high
spirits.

line 49   *parley*   To discuss terms with an enemy or foreign power.

Questions

1 The poet pays attention to details of the journey. What are these details
and how do they help you to realise the hardships the expedition
experienced? How do we know that, in spite of their hardships, the party is
hopeful?

2 Explain lines 32 and 33. What has happened, and why this sudden rise in
inspiration?

3 Lines 40 and 41 mark a bridge in this poem. Compare the scenes described
later with the earlier ones.

Commentary

This narrative poem, whose theme is usually regarded as the proto-type of the
conflict generated by the meeting of western ways and traditional African life,
is modelled on T. S. Eliot's *Journey of the Magi*. Basically, it describes the meeting
of Stanley, one of the great explorers of the interior of Africa in the nineteenth

century, with King Mutesa of Buganda. The contrast which the poet economically draws between the regal stature of the king and the puny build of Stanley is instructive. And the king's courteous reception of Stanley is ironically symbolic: for by this demonstration of nobility he let in the means of his own colonisation and dispossession. The first part of the poem describes the hardships and changing fortunes which Stanley's party experienced on their journey, while the second part describes the bewilderment and suspicion which the arrival of the party aroused in Mutesa's kingdom and their final, still unsure, welcome at the king's court.

Tchicaya U Tam'si

Gérald Félix Tchicaya U Tam'si was born in former Congo Brazzaville in 1931, but lived in voluntary exile in France from 1946 to April 1988 when he died. In spite of this long residence in France his work shows that he has not lost his roots in Africa. His imagination continually works upon and around both the physical and historical realities of Africa with profound intensity and tenderness. He is perhaps the most prolific and sophisticated African poet writing in French and, apart from his six books of verse, he has done a great deal of work as a freelance journalist and broadcaster while working fulltime for Unesco.

There are three aspects of his poetry to which he himself has drawn attention and which are useful guides to the reader. Firstly he has said that his poetry is spoken not written poetry. This is confirmed both by the dramatic and colloquial tone of voice continually behind his lines which, unlike the declamatory voice of David Diop's poetry, buttonholes as with an intimate and often self-mocking remark.

The second aspect of his poetry is what he calls his black humour. This is a self-mockery, which is nevertheless in keeping with the serious message of his poetry. For he is very much concerned with the appalling historical reality, down the ages, of being African and being black, and this has been intensified by reflection on the events in the Congo since the 1960s. Finally, and this constitutes the third aspect of his poetry, his keen awareness of what it is to be African and black is equally matched by his sense of the human condition as radically involved with suffering.

Thus U Tam'si's poetry is highly complex, blending humour with seriousness, accepting as well as mocking his Africanness, handling concrete images with symbolic repetition and re-echoing meaning, composing precise verse lines which nevertheless flow into elaborate sections. For example, *Viaticum*, from which two poems have been selected here, is divided into twelve sections altogether. It has the easy flow and carries as much of the human horror which the River Congo has borne to the sea down the ages. The river itself is in the background of the poem providing a concrete image of the turbulent history that the poem attempts to present.

Viaticum (1)

> They give you what they have eaten
> and what they have not known how to keep
> the shadow, like them, had a certain
> reticence
> I am full of spite with the sun.

You must be from my country
I see it by the tick
Of your soul around the eyelashes
and besides you dance when you are sad
5 you must be from my country

Keep moving time is waiting to seduce us
learn from this that the oil in your lamp
is really my blood brimming up
and that, if it overflows, you musn't light your lamp
10 We must have a dark corner somewhere
for our ancient orisons

All of us from the same umbilical cord
But who knows where we fetch
our awkward heads

15 Often the silences
reeking of iodine ravage us
with lecherous resolves
for my beardless conscience
ravage us alone

Notes

Heading
The heading, made up of five lines altogether, sets out the opposed values that are finally reconciled in the poem: what *they* (line 1), the colonialists, offer is a shadow, a leftover, which they have chewed up and found no more use for, i.e. Christian humility and forgiveness. In contrast, the speaker, like the sun (line 5), is full of bite and venom.

Main text
line 4 This is regarded in the poem as one of the unique qualities of being African.
lines 10–11 The lines express the need for the African to preserve something of his traditions, as he at the same time moves ahead with contemporary development (line 6). Here his colour and blood are accepted as defining

values opposed to the bright light of the lamp (line 7). Hence the need to preserve a dark corner for ancient rites and prayers.

line 12 umbilical cord The nerve which links a baby in the womb to the mother and through which the baby is directly fed; usually cut at birth. Hence the vital link to one's parents and ancestors.

lines 15–19 These are difficult lines. The flexibility of the arrangement of the lines in the French is difficult to retain in the English, if we want to arrive at the meaning of the lines.
Perhaps the following rendering might help:

> often the silences (echoes)
> of lecherous desires rightly suppressed
> for (from) my beardless conscience
> (rise) reeking of iodine (and) ravage us
> ravage us alone

The last line suggests that the revived memories and desires which are so overpowering (*reeking of iodine*) and tormenting belong to *us alone*: to us as a people distinct from other people. They are age-old crimes which the young and sensitive (the *beardless conscience*) would rather forget, but which we seem destined to repeat.

Questions

1 Is there anything striking about the marks of identity the speaker picks on in the first five lines of the poem? If you were identified by such marks, what would your reaction be?
2 What do you think is the meaning of the advice given by the speaker in lines 7 to 9?
3 Comment on the imagery of light and darkness in the poem.
4 Analyse the speaker's overall attitude to the common identity he claims with his audience.

Viaticum (2)

> The saltmaker, the well
> The soul of my desert – Anne!

To you your belly is a marvel
I am going to make there a slippery wound
so that you will never forget it:
the hydra in the pit of your belly secures
5 those she condemns to dismemberment.

As for you my shadow of flesh
take back my other cheek
mark it with your fingers
I laugh with sorrow
10 for once I will laugh at the sad gift of myself.

My cheeks were all my dignity
I offer one to your dingy cheek,
Woman,
dingy with the colour of three dinars
15 which have betrayed me
I give the other to your dirty hand,
Brother,
dirty with the colour of three histories
My cheeks like two hills
20 where the tree of my laughter had sprung.

The algae glide over my cheeks
a saltmaker there draws her ration of real salt

The saltmaker is she to whom I give
my other cheek
25 Anne has the foul cheek of a saltmaker!

Ah let them take my cheeks also
in exchange for a good easy sleep
so that I may yet keep
the night upon my soul!

Notes

Heading
line 1   *saltmaker*   From the salt tears of humility associated with orthodox
  Christianity.
line 2   *soul of my desert*   As the poem suggests, the Christian religion in
  demanding humility of its followers deprives them of all earthly pride
  and, within the colonial context, subjects them to a kind of sterility.
Anne   Most likely the Cathedral of St. Anne in Brazzaville, symbolizing the
  Catholic Church and the Christian religion.

Main text
line 1   *your belly*   The interior of the cathedral (by extension, the world of the
  Church); but possibly a reference to Jonah in the belly of the whale,
  where he learns obedience, marvellously, to the will of God (Jonah,
  Chapter I, 17).
line 5   The implication is that those who submit themselves to the Church are
  deprived of their physical attributes – such as the cheeks, which the
  speaker regards as his dignity in line 11.
line 6   *my shadow of flesh*   The shadow (the pale reflection) of the flesh; the
  soul; the personality under the control of the Christian religion.
line 7   Compare with Matthew V, 39 (Sermon on the Mount): "If any one
  strikes you on the right cheek, turn to him the other also."
line 13   *Woman*   St. Anne, the Church.
line 14   *Three dinars*   Ancient coins of the Mediterranean area. The numeral
  three is suggestive of the thirty pieces of silver for which Judas betrayed

146

Christ (Matthew XXVI, 15) and of the tricolour of the French national flag, the emblem of the colonial power to which the Church led, in betrayal, those who submitted to her teaching.

line 17   Brother   Congolese compatriots who have been responsible for so much of the Congo's troubles.

line 18   three histories   In the original French this rhymes with three dinars (trois deniers/trois derniers); the history of pre-colonial and post-colonial periods, equally marked by violence and bloodshed.

line 21   algae   Seaweed, therefore full of salt.

Questions

1 Comment on the difference implied by the offering of the cheek *to your dingy cheek* (line 12) and *to your dirty hand* (line 16).
2 What is the nature of the speaker's wish in lines 26–29?
3 Why does the speaker concentrate on the imagery of the body, although he is concerned with spiritual and religious issues in the poem?

Commentary

These two poems constitute *three* sections of the long poem *Viaticum*, which came out of the poet's experience of the Congo to where he had returned briefly between August and October 1960. Those were the first few months of independence for the former Belgium Congo, and the young state was torn by internal strife, violence and bloodshed. It was a time when Patrice Lumumba and Joseph Kassavubu were dismissing each other as Prime Minister and President respectively, leading to the house-arrest of the Prime Minister, his attempt to get away from the stalemate in Leopoldville, his capture and eventual murder.

U Tam'si, who had gone to Leopoldville to do his duty for the new nation, came away from this crucial period in the Congo's history, tormented and frustrated by his sensitive awareness of the causes of havoc for the new nation: the combination of international material interests with the volatile and violent passions of his fellow Congolese. *Viaticum* is therefore a poem of heart-searching, an attempt to come to terms with all these factors.

U Tam'si can only be truly appreciated when read in long stretches. For his images surge, recede, reappear and gather cumulative meaning. This is because there is a passion behind the lines which unite the various sections of his poems, and the sections are indeed headings which summarise the underlying passion.

First poem

Using the Christian ritual of the last sacrament (Viaticum), administered to the dying as a symbol of forgiveness and release from guilt, U Tam'si confronts the values and perils of being a Congolese. The Christian qualities of humility, forgiveness and mercy (expressed through offering the second cheek to be slapped) are first regarded as cringing and debasing values. But, as the poet considers the whole period of pre-colonial, colonial and post-independence experience in the Congo, he recognises the need for forgiveness and mercy.

This forgiveness is indeed a "night strange sacrament", because it can be mistaken for the weakness of an imbecile. The poet becomes reconciled to it only after a candid examination of his Congolese destiny and his colonial, Christian heritage.

147

Second poem
This second part of Viaticum is based on a contrast between an image of the
African full of the joy of life and laughter and an image of him after he had
become the victim of a double violation during the course of recent history. The
first violation came from the teaching of the Christian Church and its insistence
on humility and forgiveness – offering the second cheek to be slapped. The
second violation has been at the hands of the African's own compatriots – the
poet is thinking particularly of the mutually destructive tribal wars which have
plagued the Congo in pre-colonial, colonial and post-colonial times. So the
cheeks that had earlier expressed assurance and dignity in unrestrained laughter
become the symbol of humility. The tears of joy become tears of sorrow, and the
Cathedral of St. Anne in Brazzaville, symbolic of the Christian Church, makes
salt out of these tears of humility.

Forest

I
Barren head but heart
in the image of the multiplier
which by itself is a bushland
where roots at arm's length
5 go seeking rich earth
they turn into a tree
multiple of the one that burns.
Then comes the dark vaulting
that a bird of paradise fills with sun;
10 farther on there will be the hot-house
from where the flash of an orchid
catches me in distress.
These bindweeds will not make
that bloody fire more prosperous
15 in case the dance around it
should give withered arms
to the desire in search of earth
digestible after long mourning.

II
Life is for translating to the future
20 from that spring what is the good
of raising the weir of flesh and bone
before the soul grows lichened
and the heart as barren . . .
To love and multiply the daylight
25 by adding water and hormones
to romp through a farce at the top of one's voice.

Up above the most living flesh
the sun raises a striking objection
that sets the dawn achatter
30 and knots the hands under a skull
emptied by an orgasm of fierce love.

III
– Where are the flowers that smell
of the warm flesh under the armpits?
– In paradise on the victim's burial mound
35 Those that as a child I lapped
closed my burning eyes
the sun itself on my cropped head
though it was all red lead
ah! I still danced though I had no woman
40 hilarious toads and astounding pythons
as if my dead returned through them!

IV
Untranslatable into equation form
and yet that chemical formula
will dissolve me more violently than leprosy
45 I will be licked by the sun like you
blacks of Louisiana Jews of Dachau
but as soon translated into leaven.

Before that I will remember
my first still-born love
50 When I had from Sammy
her first lips I thought
her pearl dress was her only lie
Yet her body hid her heart . . .

Notes

line 1   Note the contrast between the barren head and the (fertile) heart
        with which the poem opens.
line 7   The tropical bushland is often subject to outbreaks of fire which
        destroy the vegetation.
line 8   *dark vaulting*   The deep shade formed by the canopy or arching
        branches of the trees.
line 9   *fills with sun*   Surrealist imagery in which the brilliant colours of the
        bird's feathers are equated with the rays of the sun.
lines 11–12   Compare with George Herbert's lines:
                Sweet rose, whose hue angrie and brave
                Bids the rash gazer wipe his eye.
line 13   *bindweeds*   (binding weeds) Creepers contrasted with the orchid.

line 14   that bloody fire   An extension of the imagery which begins with the flash of an orchid in line 11.

line 15   it   Refers to the orchid.

lines 13–18   The bindweeds restrain the excitement that the brilliant colour of the orchid generates, in case that excitement (*the dance*) exhausts (*give withered arms to*) the impulse of the vegetation in search of fertile (*digestible*) earth after a long period of drought (*mourning*). In short, to balance the beauty of the orchid there are the bindweeds, so that no single force or element might dominate life.

line 19   translating   Transforming and bequeathing to.

line 21   weir   Barrier.

line 22   lichened   Covered with moss, decayed, exhausted

line 28   objection   Antagonism.

lines 29–31   The sun starts off the dawn with all the signs of life, such as the birds chattering away. But it is also the sun that brings to an end a night of love-making. However, the resonance of the surrealist image in lines 30–31 lies in the suggestion that exhaustion and death lurk behind even the most enjoyable human activity. U Tam'si like John Webster, sees "the skull beneath the skin".

line 35   lapped   Adored (as a cat laps milk)

line 36   Closed their eyes to my burning desires.

line 40   These, presumably, are the child's fantasy of his jumping and playing around – what he 'danced'.

line 41   As if all losses were restored to the child through his excited play.

lines 43–44   The changes that affect life, under the sun, cannot be stated as a simple equation, yet they are real.

line 45   Compare with the description of the sun in line 28.

line 46   Louisiana stands for the lynching of blacks in the southern states of the USA, just as Dachau was the site of the concentration camp in which millions of Jews died during the Nazi regime in Germany.

Questions

1 The poem opens with a contrast between the head and the heart. Identify other contrasted ideas and images in the poem and show how the poet uses them to explore his theme.

2 There is something incongruous about the comparison of the fate of the speaker and that of the other victims mentioned in section IV of the poem. Would you agree?

3 What light does the title of the poem throw on its theme?

4 U Tam'si has been described as "a poet of lamentation without genuine sorrow". From your study of this poem would you say that this description is accurate?

Commentary

This is a poem from U Tam'si's sixth volume of poems titled *Arc Musical*, which Gerald Moore has translated Bow Harp but which can, with some justification, be rendered Musical Rainbow. This particular poem from the sixth volume embodies a balancing and harmonising of themes and images as happens in both music and the rainbow.

It is, also a poem which is full of some of the disturbing elements of U Tam'si's vision of life and his art. There are two basic ideas expressed in the poem: (i) that all life, vegetable as well as human, is a cycle of procreation which is laughable (lines 24–26); and (ii) that life is subject to change and suffering, but this *may* lead to a new beginning (lines 45–47). These two ideas are balanced but not reconciled in the poem, as U Tam'si himself seems to be aware of (lines 43–45).

But the poem also illustrates U Tham'si's surrealist art: his use of imagery which at first strikes us as very odd but, nevertheless, reveals a fascinating insight. Examples are found in lines 11–12, lines 29–31, lines 32–33 and in that most striking description of the child's fantasy of jumping and playing around as *hilarious toads and astounding pythons* in line 40.

The basic metaphor (conceit) of the poem is the swarming luxuriant life of a tropical forest, full of tall trees which provide deep shade suddenly illuminated by the brilliant colours of exotic birds and flowers. The vegetable imagery, however, does not quite exhaust life as U Tam'si sees it – it only conveys an impression of the fertile heart. The barren head observes the striking antagonism of the sun overhead and Section III of the poem begins:

> Where are the flowers that smell
> of the warm flesh under the armpits?

Here the vegetable and the human imagery are fused together, but not for long. For U Tam'si is not content with observing change, suffering, and decay as the human condition under the sun. He *believes* there is a transmuting of life into leaven for the future. However the evidence for this belief is not provided by the poem. Instead the poem ends with a poignant series of contradictory images: the still-born love, the kiss that is betrayed by the pearl dress, the body that hides the heart.

Okot p'Bitek

Okot p'Bitek is probably the most outstanding poet from East Africa and certainly one of Africa's greatest poets. Born in Uganda in 1931, he was educated in his native country and later in England, where he graduated in Education, Law and Social Anthropology. The latter became an abiding passion and in some senses enabled him to study in great depth the oral literature, culture and traditions of his people. His poetry is not only an outcome of his findings, but is also fortified by a rich blend of native traditional literary forms and acquired European forms. p'Bitek's poetry represents one of the best examples of African poetry to successfully express African ideas in European forms, retaining the lyric freshness and simplicity of the songs of his own tribe, the Acholi, and using personal imagery. The distinctive result has no comparison in the whole range of African poetry.

Okot p'Bitek wrote his poetry first in his indigenous Acholi language and then translated it himself into English – a distinctive practice which he shared with Mazisi Kunene. His publications include *Song of Lawino* and *Song of Ocol, Two Songs*, a collection of folk tales, *Hare and Hornbill* and Acholi oral poetry in *Horn of my love*. He was active in the educational, cultural and political life of his country. He was at one time the Director of the National Theatre in Kampala and taught in the universities of Makerere, Nairobi and Ife in Nigeria. For many years he lived in exile but returned to his home country shortly before he died in 1982.

Cattle egret

My children gather stars
Into their soft songs
And woo the young moon
With their white teeth.

5 The moon kisses
My daughter's emerging breasts
And my son's dimples dimples.

I plead guilty
To pride,
10 I was not born to this,
I am a great soul

My mother knows this
My uncle told me so
And my father was proud
15 Of me ...

My children call me
Papa!
They run to me
And fall into my arms,
20 They sing and dance for me
And play games with me.

The testicle of the bell
Knocks hard against
His round thighs
25 And he screams in sharp pain.

Tired teachers wipe
The chalk dust
Off their faces,
The school dam bursts
30 And floods of hungry children
Melt into their mothers' bosoms.

My children are
Not among them,
My children do
35 Not go to school
My children will
Never go to school.

The teacher's cane
Will never touch
40 Their buttocks,
They will grow up
With the wild trees
Of the bush
And will be burnt down
45 By the wild fire
Of the droughts!

The proud cattle egret
Flourishes his long
And colourful tail
50 And dances between his
Wives and chicks ...

Look at my athletic thighs,
My chest was broad
And without a scar,
55 My teeth were the
White okok birds
Standing on the back
Of a buffalo bull . . .

Have you heard me
60 Playing the mother drum?
Have you seen me
In the dancing arena?
Cut off this rope,

Free my hands and feet,
65 I want to clap my hands
And sing for my children
So that they may dance,
I want to drum the wall
With my hands,
70 I want to jump up
And dance . . .

Let me beat the rhythm
Of the orak dance,
Let my wife shake
75 Her soft waist before me
And remind me of our first meeting
At the dancing arena . . .
I want to join the youths
At the "get-stuck dance"
80 I want to suck the stiff breasts
Of my wife's younger sister,
I want to wrestle
With my wife-in-law
And crush the young grass
85 Beyond the arena . . .
Is today not my father's
Funeral anniversary?

My clansmen and clanswomen
Are gathering in our village,
90 They sit in circles
In the shades of granaries,
But who will make
The welcome speech?

Men drink kwete beer,
95 Women cook goat meat
And make millet bread,
But I am not there
To distribute the dishes
Among the elders!
100 The priests throw morsels
Of chicken meat,
They squirt goat blood
And pour libations
To the assembled ghosts
105 Of the dead,
But how can I address
The ghosts of my fathers
From here?

How can they put chymes
110 On my chest and back?
How can my grandmother
Spit blessing on me?

My age-mates have donned
White ostrich feathers,
115 They are singing a war song,
I want to join them
In the wilderness
And chase Death away
From our village,
120 Drive him a thousand miles
Beyond the mountains
In the west,
Let him sink down
With the setting sun
125 And never rise again.

I want to join
The funeral dancers,
I want to tread the earth
With a vengence
130 And shake the bones
Of my father in his grave!

Notes

line 56   *white okok birds*   Like egrets: they also visit cattle grazing and can
   be seen standing on the backs of cattle at times.
line 73   *orak dance*   Native traditional dance.

line 79 *"get-stuck dance"* A popular dance among the youths of Northern
    Uganda. Sexy and entertaining.
line 94 *kwete beer* A local brew, usually strong and meant for men.
line 109 *chymes* Hurtful and dangerous fluid.

Questions

1 Explain the imagery in lines 1–6 and 22–31. What do they contribute to
  the poem?
2 What is the cattle egret symbolic of in this segment, and how is it reflected
  in the concern of this section?
3 What picture of the fate of his children does the poet paint and how?
4 What is the relevance of the poet's preoccupation with his father's death?

Commentary

"Cattle egret" is the thirteenth segment of a long poem, "Song of prisoner",
regarded by many critics as p'Bitek's finest poem. It is a poem in which the poet
imagines himself in jail, a deprivation which he sees as a sign of gross injustice
and against which he cries out. The poem then is a complaint, a political poem
in which the poet castigates the ills of a newly independent African nation with
all the pious talk of freedom by her leaders: oppression of the poor, assassin-
ations, corruption, falsehood, ostentatious living, etc.

   The measure of p'Bitek's success is the way in which he artistically transforms
what would have been a mere catalogue of political ills into good and serious
poetry by means of his cynical humour, wit and arresting imagery. Of particular
interest is his varied use of nature imagery. Sometimes the peace and quiet of
nature – and there is a constant reminder that this recalls the village life –
contrast with the crimes of the new order. At other times the brutalisation of
nature reflects the indignities which the common people suffer. And sometimes
elements of nature play symbolic roles, particularly in the titles of the different
sections. Throughout the poem local scenes and local flavour and the rhythm
of the poem, which recalls traditional lyrics, help to ensure the authenticity of
the piece.

Song of Malaya

Sister Prostitutes
Wherever you are

I salute you

Wealth and Health
5 To us all

I Karibu

156

Welcome ashore
You vigorous young sailor,
I see you scanning the horizon
In search of dry land

I hear your heart drumming
tum-tum-tu-tu-tum . . .

That time bomb
Pulsating in your loin
Surely weighs you down!
Oh . . . oh!

* * *

You soldier
Home bound,
I hear your song . . .
I see the girls
On the platform
Waving a farewell . . .

You reprieved murderer
You prisoner and detainee
About to be released,
Your granaries full
To overflow . . .

Welcome home!

* * *

You drunken Sikhs
The night club
Your battle ground,
Turbans, broken heads
And broken glass
Strewn on the floor . . .

Are your wives here?

* * *

And you skinny
Indian vegetarian
Your wife breeding
Like a rat,
40 Welcome to my table too,
I have cooked red meat
With spices . . .
You hairy
Thick-skinned white miner
45 At Kilembe, at Kitwe . . .

You sweating engineer
Building roads and bridges,
I see the cloud of dust
Raised by your bumping Land Rover
50 Heading for the City.

Karibu, Come in,
Enter . . .

* * *

All my thanks
To you
55 Schoolboy lover,
I charge you
No fee . . .

That shy smile
On your face,
60 And . . .

Oh!
I feel ten years
Younger . . .

Hey! Listen . . .
65 Do not let the
Teacher know . . .
Mm . . . mmm?
He was there
Last night . . .!

* * *

Welcome you teachers
Teaching in bush schools,
I see you in buses
And on bicycles
Coming into the City
Your trouser pockets
Bulging with wallets . . .

Chieftain,
I see your gold watch
Glittering on your wrist,
You are holding
Your wife's waist
And kissing her
Goodbye.

Your shimmering briefcase
Is pregnant . . .

How long
Will your Conference last?
You bus drivers
And you taxi men
Driving away from your home towns,
Will you be back
Tonight?

* * *

You factory workers
Do you not hear
The bells?
Is that not the end
Of your shift?

You shop assistants
Standing there all day
Displaying your wares
And persuading the customers
With false smiles

When do you close?

* * *

Brother,
105 You leader of the People,
How is our Party doing?
How many rallies
Have you addressed today?
How many hands
110 Have you shaken?

Oh – oh . . .
Your blue shirt
Is dripping wet with sweat,
Your voice is hoarse,
115 You look a bit tired
Friend . . .

I have cold beer
In the house,
I have hot water
120 And cold water,
You must rest
A little,
Drink and eat
Something . . .

125 Brother,
Come!

* * *

Sister Harlots
Wherever you are,
Wake up
130 Brighten up
Go gay and clean,
Lay
Your tables
Bring in fresh flowers . . .

135 Load your trays
With fresh fruits
Fresh vegetables
And plenty of fresh meat . . .
The hungry lions
140 Of the World
Are prowling around . . .
Hunting!

Notes

line 9   scan(ning)   To examine closely or look searchingly at something.
line 23   reprieved   Suspension or delay of capital punishment.
line 26   granaries   A granary is a store house for grains. It is used metaphorically here to refer to the testes which hold the male sperm which are released during intercourse. It is as if the receptacles are too full and have become uncomfortable because they have not been emptied. It is possible to see a play on *release* in line 25.
line 29   Sikhs   Members of a Hindu religious sect in India. The turban they wear is one of their distinctive marks. Can be fanatical.
line 77   Chieftain   Big and important public officer or business man.
line 85   Full of documents but especially money that needs to be delivered on to the laps of the prostitute.
line 104   There is an implied and serious criticism here. The prostitute addresses the politician with words of endearment – *brother, friend* – and this would seem to indicate that they have some close relationship. Both groups are hecklers who try by stealth and guile to attract and devour men. But more significant, politicians are likened to prostitutes because it is thought these two classes of people have no moral qualms, are unreliable and exploit their victims.
line 140   This refers to all the classes of men who run to prostitutes to satisfy their sexual needs.
lines 129–142   Prostitutes are said to know how to look after their men and this is one reason men feel attracted to them.

Questions

1 Discuss the tone of this poem. What does it contribute to the total impact and meaning of the poem?
2 Explain lines 13–16.
3 Discuss this poem as a piece of social criticism.

Commentary

Prostitution is one of the by-products of urban life and development, whatever else may be said about its antiquity. It is often used by moralists and social critics as one of the indices for measuring the moral health of a society. The tendency almost always is for most people to condemn the practice.

It is clear that reprehensible as prostitution may be, society's attitude to it is hypocritical. Far too many people than can be easily imagined are engaged in it especially as clients. This satirical poem aims to expose the popularity of the trade, as if to insist that the derided trade persists because there is no end to the customers who patronise it. These customers cut across all sections of the society: from sex-starved sailors, soldiers, reprieved murderers and prisoners, to Sikhs and Indians noted for their fanatical religious observances and active sexual lives in their homes. They also include schoolboys, teachers, public servants and tycoons, drivers, factory workers, shop assistants and politicians who find the prostitute an attractive means of releasing pent-up passion.

The poem is couched in the form of an address by the leader of the prostitutes welcoming their various customers and advising the prostitutes to be ready for

161

their part. Karibu, the leader, does a run-down of their different patrons, taking swipes at individual groups as she goes down the register. The tone is mocking and ironical and the humour dark. There is something particularly cutting in the close relationship between the prostitutes and the politicians. The poem ends on a defiant and exhilarating note. Rather than urge her fellow prostitutes to hide their heads in shame, Karibu calls on them to prepare themselves lushly to receive *the hungry lions of the World* who *are prowling around*. This is a bold poem with prostitutes as theme. The table is turned on society because the prostitutes are not at the receiving end as is usually the case. Society is and the prostitutes are offering the criticism.

Lenrie Peters

Lenrie Peters was born in Bathurst, Gambia in 1932. He was educated in the Gambia, Sierra Leone and England, where he eventually qualified as a surgeon. A talented man, he has always been interested in literature and has written plays, poems, short stories and a novel, *The Second Round*. Many of Lenrie Peters' poems bear the mark of his profession in the use of anatomical and physiological imagery. Even the contexts within which he explores specific ideas relate to his training. Apart from writing, which has become for him a passionate pastime, he also sings and broadcasts. He is the first Gambian chairman of WAEC.

His early poetry is very much concerned with Africa, its destiny and especially its political, moral and cultural health. He is also concerned about the image of Africa in the eyes of the world. His poetry is sophisticated, even when his diction is simple, and this sometimes requires quite some intellectual effort to appreciate. He has published three volumes of poetry: *Satellites, Katchikali* and *Collected poems*.

We have come home

We have come home
From the bloodless wars
With sunken hearts
Our boots full of pride –
5 From the true massacre of the soul
When we have asked
"What does it cost
To be loved and left alone"

We have come home
10 Bringing the pledge
Which is written in rainbow colours
Across the sky – for burial
But it is not the time
To lay wreaths
15 For yesterday's crimes
Night threatens
Time dissolves
And there is no acquaintance
With tomorrow

20 The gurgling drums
   Echo the stars
   The forest bowls
   And between the trees
   The dark sun appears

25 We have come home
   When the dawn falters
   Singing songs of other lands
   The death march
   Violating our ears
30 Knowing all our loves and tears
   Determined by the spinning coin

   We have come home
   To the green foothills
   To drink from the cup
35 Of warm and mellow birdsong
   To the hot beaches
   Where the boats go out to sea
   Threshing the ocean's harvest
   And the hovering plunging
40 Gliding gulls shower kisses on the waves

   We have come home
   Where through the lightning flash
   And thundering rain
   The famine the drought,
45 The sudden spirit
   Lingers on the road
   Supporting the tortured remnants
   Of the flesh
   That spirit which asks no favour
50 Of the world
   But to have dignity.

Notes

lines 1–2 This poem commemorates African students who have returned to
    their country after a period of study in overseas European countries. To
    overcome all manner of prejudice and hardship in a hostile environment
    to get an education and return alive, was like surviving a war.
line 3 Dejected, sad, humiliated, yet they were proud they were victorious
    and survived.
line 5 Their souls have been destroyed through indoctrination; they have
    been educated out of their culture and almost brought up to look down
    on themselves.

lines 7–8 Colonial powers claimed that they came out of love to enlighten and save the colonised. But in view of the adverse effects of the experience of colonialism the poet would wish Africans had been left alone to make their own choices and mistakes and be the architects of their own fortunes. They should not have been indoctrinated and brutalised in such a way as to make them lose their dignity.

line 10 The diploma and all it symbolised about European civilisation (cf. the proverbial Golden Fleece). Returning students will need to give up much of what they learned to be themselves again.

line 15 Colonialism and its many destructive effects on the mind.

lines 18–19 The future is uncertain.

line 26 To falter is to walk or move unsteadily as through weakness or fear.

line 29 Disturbing, grating on the ear. The sound is unpleasant.

lines 30–31 To spin a coin is to determine something by chance. They have no control over their fortunes which are determined by the fancies of others – the colonial powers.

lines 39–40 The repetition of the *-ing* forms in *hovering, plunging* and *gliding* gives the effect of the actual motion of the birds.

line 45 The sudden spirit His spirit is shocked into a realisation of the new situation. In spite of the harsh circumstances the brave spirit and the beaten body are sustained by determination, refusing to die or surrender and pleading for or insisting on his humanity being recognised. Protest in this poem is muffled; it is a complaint against the indignities to which Africans are subjected.

Questions

1 Give a detailed explanation of the structure of this poem.
2 Identify the elements of tone, mood and imagery that go to make up the meaning of this poem.

Commentary

One of the concerns of Peters in his early poetry is the destructive effect of colonialism on the Africans. For the African, subjugation by colonial powers and the numerous changes this has brought into his life has left him in a state of war with himself, of spiritual and psychological conflict. Colonialism bruised the African spiritually, destroyed his self-pride and dignity and instilled in him a sense of insecurity. He has had to fight to ensure that his humanity is recognised in the modern world.

This is an early poem by Peters written soon after he returned home from his studies in Britain. Although the students are proud that they successfully completed their courses, they return with trepidation in their hearts because of their earlier experiences overseas and the uncertainties that await them at home. They are painfully aware of the fight they need to put up in view of their immediate past and present situations. This brooding atmosphere is established in the first few lines which also hint clearly at the sad and deeply reflective tone of the poem. The sense of foreboding in the poem is heightened by the symbolic use of time (evening and night). For it is night now and it is not the beautiful moon that shines but the *dark sun*.

The fence

There where the dim past and future mingle
their nebulous hopes and aspirations
there I lie.

There where truth and untruth struggle
in endless and bloody combat,
there I lie.

There where time moves forwards and backwards
with not one moment's pause for sighing,
there I lie.

There where the body ages relentlessly
and only the feeble mind can wander back

there I lie in open-souled amazement

There where all the opposites arrive
to plague the inner senses, but do not fuse,
I hold my head; and then contrive
to stop the constant motion.
my head goes round and round,
but I have not been drinking;
I feel the buoyant waves; I stagger

It seems the world has changed her garment.
but it is I who have not crossed the fence,
So there I lie.

There where the need for good
and "the doing good" conflict,
there I lie.

Notes

line 2   nebulous Blurred and indistinct. Hopes can hardly be certain.
line 15 The poet manages or tries to stop the unheaval in him through
different devices.
line 19 There is some irony here. *Buoyant* does not imply gaiety and
gladness, but rather the type of light-headed dizziness that comes from
worries.

Questions

1 Discuss the structure of this poem and comment on its effectiveness in contributing to the feeling of a dilemma.
2 Discuss the images which the poet uses and examine how he manages to create this poem from ordinary and commonplace statements.

Commentary

This is a reflective poem based on the proverbial "fence-sitting". It is a moral poem which deals with the dilemma which the poet faces, the spiritual battles and agonies which the poet suffers because he cannot cross the fence. The poem is built on a structure of opposites, and the poet's irresolution is shown by his inability to move from the centre and to take the decisive step on the side of the good and morally right.

This is a picture of man's state; far too many people are plagued by a moral weakness which incapacitates them. The first four stanzas present statements and moral questions, each ending on the short refrain *there I lie*. The fifth stanza through a series of images, provides a picture of the poet's struggles with the forces of evil and good and gives the impression that he has not mastered them. So in the last stanza, neater and more stinging than the first four, we return to the state of moral indecision and the sitting on the fence.

Lost friends

They are imprisoned
In dark suits and air-conditioned offices
Alsatians ready at the door
On the saliva carpeted floor

5 They spend their nights
In jet airlines –
Would change them in mid-air
To show how much they dare

Drunk from the vertigo
10 Of never catching their tails
They never seem to know
When not to bite their nails

Their new addiction
Fortifies their livers
15 They are getting there
While the going's good
They have no time for dreamers.

Notes

line 1   *Imprisoned*   The use here is metaphorical. To imprison is to confine in prison or any place where one is deprived of one's freedom and contact with the rest of society. The word is used here in two senses: the formality of suits which do not give the wearer the freedom of casual clothes. He is also imprisoned in the sense that all the windows and doors of his air-conditioned office are shut and his guard dog shields him from intruders. It is as if he were in a fortress. This is the typical outfit of modern–day fast businessmen. The poet considers them with sympathy and contempt.

line 3   *alsatian*   A large dog also known as a German Shepherd. Commonly used as a guard dog, especially by the police and other security agents.

line 4   Dogs drop *saliva* as they pant and guard dogs do this a great deal. The area around them is usually soaked with saliva.

lines 9–12   *Vertigo* is a feeling of unsteadiness and dizziness as if one's head were spinning round. The image here is that of a dog trying to scratch or catch its tail. It often turns around in a circle several times to do so. "Biting their nails" shows they are nervous or childish. These are not the decorous type, anyway. Notice the rhyming of the words *tails* and *nails* to emphasise their lack of class and the poet's contempt.

line 13   *addiction*   A harmful habit from which one is unable to free oneself. In this case it is the quest for wealth.

line 14   The *liver* is the seat of courage.

Questions

1 Discuss this poem and any other two poems by other poets in this volume, that criticise African society.

2 Carefully examine the contribution of each stanza to the picture of reckless quest after wealth.

3 The language and the attitude of the poet contribute to the effect of the poem. Discuss any three points that strike you about these qualities of the poem.

Commentary

Post-colonial Africa seems marked by one main unfortunate disease: the destruction of the sound moral ethics of traditional society and the elevation of materialism to an unhealthy and unprecedented height. The result of this situation has been the phenomenal increase in the number of people who run after money recklessly, determined to acquire wealth, to "make it", to "get there" in the shortest possible time. In the process they display no scruples of conscience and respect no moral codes. The poet expresses his disgust at and contempt for this breed of people, former friends with whom he shared some ideas or ideals about society and humanity at some stage. Now he has lost them to greed and mammon. They behave like maniacs, people possessed, opportunists who are preoccupied with exploiting every circumstance to make fast money.

In a compact and pungent poem in which every stanza contributes a particular negative picture, the poet builds his comment to a climax in the last stanza in which the daredevilry of these fortune seekers is expressed in a telling sarcastic undertone. The last line sums up the bitterness of the poet's satiric criticism.

These men are so lost to the world of money that they despise all who talk of ideals and the need for moral standards that will sustain society, revealing the depth of their own degeneration. The bland language and tone of the piece gives added weight to the poet's lamentation.

It is time for reckoning Africa

It is time for reckoning Africa
time for taking stock
never mind New York, America –
it's ours; is here, and running short

5 too long we have dragged
our slippered feet
through rank disorder
incompetence, self defeat

in the high capitals
10 the angry men; angry
with dust in their heads
a dagger at each other's throats.

"Maudors" sit on wicker thrones
ghosted by White ants
15 a hundred Marabus at hand
living on the fat of the land

all threatening coups
and claiming vast receipts
like winsome children
20 feeding on mother's milk.

The seats of Government
levelled at the dice
they get the most
who tell the biggest lies

25 while honest men stand
waiting at the door
or rot in prison cells,
the vultures feed on sturgeon's eggs.

The riot squads
30 parade the avenues
like lion prides
testing their sinews

and every trembling heart
retires as evening falls
35 crushed by the weight of hours
till daylight comes

oh country of great hopes
and boundless possibilities
will the seed grain
40 perish for ever

will rivers run
endlessly with blood,
saints resort to massacre
and all your harvests burn?

45 will no one see
no sign instruct
till Noah's ark
comes sailing on in flood?

between Alpha and Omega
50 is now; Africa
this is the lost time
and future time; Africa.

In this all revolutions end
and the straight path
55 from world to better world
branded across the sky.

Notes

line 2 taking stock Means to consider the situation of things to be able to
take a decision.

line 6 slippered feet To denote easy going, unserious, uncaring and
indifferent attitude.

line 10 The *angry men* are empty-headed and unintelligent. Reference is to
soldiers who overthrow governments and seize power.

lines 13–14 Maudors are puppets, weak and unimaginative rulers hence they
sit on *wicker thrones* – thrones made by weaving twigs and reeds. The
fragility of the throne is a reflection of the intrinsic ineffectiveness of
the rulers. Maudors are similar to Maurides who are pupils or followers
of the leader of a Muslim order. Power lies elsewhere – with the *White
ants*, that is the Europeans who are still manipulating and controlling
African governments. There is an interesting play on *White ants* here
because it can also be referring to the insects. They eat up wicker
works that are not properly treated. So the white ants can and do
undermine the throne.

line 15 Marabus Itinerant Muslim leaders in the Senegambia area who play many roles: teachers, diviners, medicine-men, traders, politicians. Some become wealthy and acquire much political power.

line 16 Living comfortably, even luxuriously, with plenty to eat.

lines 19–20 winsome Attractive, well-fed. This is a biting remark which refers to the immaturity of the soldiers who take over power (seen as children) and also to their exploitative tendency.

lines 21–22 Governments are changed easily and frequently at the whims and caprices of some adventurers. The reference here is to frequent *coups d'état* and the consequent changes of governments.

line 28 a sturgeon A kind of large fish. Its eggs (caviar) make a very expensive dish. It is considered a delicacy and mark of class. *Vultures* here refer to all who pretend to serve their countries in positions of power but are, in fact, predators, selfish and only interested in exploiting the country for their own wealth.

line 35 Curfews, which are common features of military governments in Africa, compel people to stay indoors for unnecessarily long hours.

lines 39–40 The poet wonders whether it would be impossible to nurse the germs of nationhood to maturity or whether African countries will drift perpetually.

line 43 saints This is a sarcastic reference to those, especially soldiers, who seize power and invariably start off by claiming Messianic roles, condemning those before them and calling themselves saviours. But they soon settle down to a reign of terror in which they kill, maim and abuse the country more than those before them.

line 47 The story of Noah's ark in the Book of Genesis. Noah was ordered by God to build an ark and stow away in it a pair of each species of all created living things to save them from destruction by the flood which was punishment for the sins of man.

line 49 Alpha and Omega The beginning and the end. The tone of the poem becomes urgent. Africa must not delude itself, thinking that there is time to waste. Much time has already been lost because of the blunders that have disturbed its progress.

lines 53–56 Because of the urgent need for Africa to organise itself to achieve an assured greatness it must resolve to stop all the pretensions about revolutions. The prospects for Africa are great, what is lacking and must be cultivated, is the determination and honesty to exploit the glorious possibilities by taking the obviously correct actions. It is only by governments walking the straight paths of dedicated and genuine leadership that Africa can achieve the growth which all its potential points to.

Questions

1 What picture of Africa does the poet present? What images does he use in various parts of the poem to convey his ideas?

2 Comment on the development of the ideas in the poem, particularly the change in tone in stanza 10.

3 Is the poet opposed to change? Discuss his attitude to change.

4 Compare and contrast the emotions and ideas expressed in this poem with those expressed in "We have come home".

Commentary

In the eyes of the world, Africa is probably the least developed of all the continents. Black Africa has also suffered more colonial pillage and oppression than any other place. But what is worse, its political development has been problematic because many African governments have shown greed, incompetence and rabid adventuresomeness symbolised in frequent *coups d'état* and in many cases oppression by whites has been exchanged for oppression by Africans. This pattern started in the 1960s and is continuing. Africa as a continent of new nations has remained for a long time a study in political incompetence and economic mismanagement. The poem is a plea for good government.

This poem is different from many other poems written on the fate of Africa (cf. Diop's "Africa" for instance) because it does not seek to put the blame for Africa's current travails outside Africa. He draws attention to the lapses that have destroyed African nations and urges them to take stock and mend their ways, so that the latest hopes will be realised. Africa's problem is that of bad government by Africans themselves.

This poem is a forthright expression of discontent and impatience. It is in two parts. After a general statement about the disorder and incompetence that characterise African countries and governments, the poet focuses on the soldiers whose rule typifies this situation. Working through appetitive images and others that reflect the combative attitude of the military to show the immaturity of the soldiers and his abhorence of their pretensions, he depicts the topsy-turvy environment which they perpetuate, the enthronement of liars and sycophants in positions of power and the relegation of honest men, ending in their needless intimidation of the people through acts of murder and high-handedness and the general terror and fear that rule the land.

But the poet does not only express disgust at the situation, and see Africa as being incapable of any good. Rather, he thinks there are vast possibilities and a glorious future ahead for the continent. So in the second part, in the tenth stanza, there is a change of tone, attitude and imagery. The poet becomes reflective and this is seen in the rhetorical questions that dominate. The controlling image in the twelfth stanza refers to the warning signs in the Bible. God sent the flood to purge the earth of impurities caused by man. There is hope; what is necessary is to take urgent and right actions to achieve the great good ahead. There is a new tone of urgency as seen in the repetition of *now* and *time*. Time is telescoped so that the future is seen in the present. Africa has floundered for a long time. It is now time to get on the right and straight road – through good government – which is clearly emblazoned for all to see, so that Africa can realise itself fully. There has been enough of the military and political revolutions that have always pretended to improve conditions but ended up creating more chaos, oppression and corruption. This is a poem that speaks to our times.

Christopher Okigbo

Christopher Okigbo is one of the most enigmatic and yet fascinating modern African poets. Born in 1932 at Ojoto in the Eastern part of Nigeria, he attended Government College, Umuahia and University College, Ibadan where he read Classics. After leaving university he worked for short spells as a secondary school teacher, civil servant, librarian at the University of Nigeria, Nsukka and as the West African Representative of Cambridge University Press. When the Nigerian Civil War broke out, he threw his lot on the side of seccessionist Biafra and was one of the early casualties of the war in 1967. His death was a great loss to the cause of literature in Nigeria; the poems that were written in his memory by admirers and fellow poets all over the world represent a significant portion of the literature of war in Nigeria.

Okigbo was greatly involved in the development of literary culture in Nigeria. He was in the centre of the literary ferment that characterised the Ibadan of his time and gave rise to such contemporaries as Clark, Soyinka and Imokhuede. He was one of the pioneers of the Mbari Club and contributed to *Black Orpheus* which was then the organ of Mbari. He was also involved in the founding and editing of *Transition* which was later christened *Chin'daba*. But, perhaps Okigbo's most enduring impact was exerted at Nsukka where he influenced many of the younger poets who were coming up at the time. His influence is the most pervasive on the younger generation of Nigerian poets. Apart from some early pieces, Okigbo's poetry is made up of long sequences intricately and subtly connected, published as *Labyrinths*. *Labyrinths* contains the posthumous sequence "Path of Thunder" which gives a clear indication of the line along which his poetry was to move. A great lover of music and a composer himself, music is one of the enchanting qualities of his poetry. It was an ingredient of the craft which he saw as an inalienable part of art.

The passage

BEFORE YOU, mother Idoto,
    naked I stand;
before your watery presence,
    a prodigal

5 leaning on an oilbean,
    lost in your legend.

Under your power wait I
  on barefoot,
watchman for the watchword
10   at *Heavensgate*;

out of the depths my cry:
give ear and hearken . . .

DARK WATERS of the beginning.

Rays, violet and short, piercing the gloom,
15 foreshadow the fire that is dreamed of.

Rainbow on far side, arched like boa bent to kill,
foreshadows the rain that is dreamed of.

Me to the orangery
solitude invites,
20 a wagtail, to tell
the tangled-wood-tale;
a sunbird, to mourn
a mother on a spray.

Rain and sun in single combat;
25 on one leg standing,
in silence at the passage,
the young bird at the passage.

SILENT FACES at crossroads:
  festivity in black . . .

30 Faces of black like long black
  column of ants,

behind the bell tower,
into the hot garden
where all roads meet:
35 festivity in black . . .

O Anna at the knobs of the panel oblong,
hear us at crossroads at the great hinges

where the players of loft pipe organs
rehearse old lovely fragments, alone –

40 strains of pressed orange leaves on pages,
bleach of the light of years held in leather:
174

For we are listening in cornfields
　among the windplayers,
　listening to the wind leaning over
45　　its loveliest fragment . . .

Notes

line 1　Mother Idoto　A river goddess of a village stream in Ojoto, Okigbo's
　　birth place. Okigbo claimed that his maternal grandfather was the chief
　　priest of his village and he (Okigbo) assumed this responsibility since he
　　was a reincarnation of his maternal grandfather. Okigbo, then, saw
　　himself as the priest of Idoto.

line 3　watery presence　Describes the essence and environment of Idoto as a
　　water goddess.

line 4　prodigal　The reference here is to the story of the prodigal son in the
　　Bible, St. Luke 15, 11–32. In returning to his cultural roots after many
　　years of alienation in the form of study and immersion in foreign
　　cultures, Okigbo likens himself to the prodigal son who in his extremity
　　remembered the steadfastness, comfort and love of his father's house and
　　returned to beg forgiveness for his misdemeanour, confident that he
　　would be forgiven. He had realised his folly.

line 5　Oilbean　A large tropical tree whose fruits (cooked, sliced and
　　dressed) are edible and considered a delicacy in some African
　　communities. Here it is an emblem and representation of the goddess.

line 6　The poet persona is either completely absorbed in his contemplation
　　of the goddess or is confused either because he is overwhelmed or does
　　not know. He is seeking clarification.

lines 7–8　Sign of absolute humility.

line 10　Heavensgate　The reference here is to Shakespeare's Sonnet 29
　　wherein the thought of the poet's love for his friend enlivens him and
　　lifts his spirits from his dejected, forlorn and hopeless state so that he
　　"sings hymns at Heaven's gate". The implication here is the confidence
　　and expectation of good which the poet is certain will accompany the
　　goddess's utterance to him.

line 12　Biblical ring. This diction agrees well with the biblical image we
　　have seen so far.

lines 13–15　So far, the earlier part of this poem has been some kind of
　　invocation, a homage and dedication to the goddess Idoto before the
　　poet persona sets out on his quest. His quest is multi-pronged, all
　　aspects of which are intertwined and conducted almost simultaneously.
　　This is what partly accounts for the complexity of the poem. His quest is
　　a spiritual journey of personal self-discovery which he attempts to do
　　through a reconciliation or resolution of the traditional and foreign
　　cultural forces on him; he must forge a personal path through these
　　claimant forces. His is also a quest for growth as a poet, with his own
　　style and strong voice, becoming his own myth-maker, through which he
　　can comment on his society and speak to society and his people in the
　　clear voice of vision and prophecy.

　　The poetry here is considered a ritual and the incantatory litany of the
　　lines helps to project the poem to the level of the visionary. The romantic
　　transluscence which the generous imagery and symbolism of nature

provide help to transport the poet and the experience to the level of the transcendental. Yet throughout, there is a very strong and pervasive use of traditional folklore and mythology, underscoring the fact that Okigbo was, indeed, one of the most African of our modern African poets.

DARK WATERS *of the beginning*, in mythic quest can refer to the darkness and chaos that existed at the very beginning of creation, of the Book of Genesis and Milton's account in *Paradise Lost*. This spiritual journey is then supposed to start at this time. But it can also refer to the fact that nothing is clear at the beginning and that the poet is still groping his way through. His vision is not clear and he can only see partially. It is going to be a struggle but there are signs that enlightenment and purification (fire) will come.

lines 16–17 One significant feature of Okigbo's procedure in this poem is the juxtaposition of two opposing forces or ideas as a way of showing the conflict which he is striving to resolve in himself. In traditional Igbo mythology the rainbow which is always likened to the boa is a premonition of some great or mysterious event, especially connected with death, and in Yoruba mythology the rainbow is the sign that the boa has excreted and whoever got hold of a piece of the excrement was sure to be in wealth. In Ghanaian mythology, the rainbow is the result of the communion between the sun and moon. There is some duality involved here: death/life, beauty/death, hope/mystery since, in spite of everything else the boa constrictor's deadliness is ever present. In Christian mythology on the other hand, the rainbow was the sign given by God to Noah promising him that the world would not be destroyed by flood.

lines 18–23 The scene shifts to an orange grove or an orchard where the poet now pictures himself as a solitary bird (a *wagtail*) who has a difficult story to tell (*tangled-wood-tale*) and has to lament his abandonment of his tradition (*mother*). The bird is perched on a spray which is a slender branch such as most orange tree branches are. The image or symbol of the bird as the young poet who is struggling to acquire his own style and achieve his own distinctive voice is one of the most significant in this sequence of poems.

line 24 This suggests the conflict between traditional and foreign cultures. But the idea of the combat is taken from an Igbo folktale about the formation of the rainbow and contrasts with the scientific explanation of the rainbow as a series of refractions and reflections of the sun through the prism of rain drops.

line 25 This is also taken from an Igbo folktale and expresses a situation of doubt and uncertainty. A young fowl got to a strange land and because it did not know the custom of the place or how the inhabitants walked or stood, it decided to stand on one leg. It was upbraided and was, in fact, to be killed for offending the custom of the land. But it pleaded ignorance and argued that it had to take that caution because it wanted to be sure of what to do. It was spared. At the initial stage of the poet's progress, he was still afflicted by dilemmas and uncertainties.

lines 28–35 crossroads Are important and symbolic in traditional ritual practice. Because it is a point at which several roads intersect, it is significant in traditional lore or religion for sacrifice and as the meeting place of the spirits. This then is a scene of sacrifice. But note that this is also juxtaposed with the Christian Church (behind the bell tower).

lines 36–39 Okigbo's parents were devout Roman Catholics. Here, Okigbo appeals to his mother (Anna), pictured here holding the knobs of the Church door, to listen to him from the crossroads, aptly represented by the hinges of the door. The door shuts out and also shuts in two contiguous landscapes: the traditional rural landscape (cornfields, wind) and the Christian Church represented by pipe organs and leather-bound hymn books. The natural music of the cornfields is compared to the music produced by the pipe organs in the church. The poet is moving towards the fusion of these two worlds.

lines 40–41 The pages of the leather-bound hymn book used by the organist have been bleached by the stains of orange leaves over a long period of time. Here the two worlds are imaginatively brought together and Okigbo seems to be saying that tradition and Christianity are not exclusive. They have been in contact for a long time.

Questions

1 Discuss the verse form of this poem paying particular attention to those features that strike you. Give reasons why you think the form is either suitable or unsuitable for the poet's theme.
2 Identify the images and symbols used here and discuss how the poet uses them to work out his theme.
3 We have observed that Okigbo drew a great deal from the folklore of his people. Do you have similar tales as those he has employed in this poem?

Commentary

This is the first movement of the first part ("Heavensgate") of Okigbo's sequence of poems known as *Labyrinths*. These poems celebrate Okigbo's attempts to resolve the antagonistic foreign and traditional cultures which he had acquired and through this effort achieve personal understanding and self-discovery. He is also anxious to grow and mature as a poet with a strong voice and distinctive art through which he can speak to his people in the voice of prophecy. As in the cases of serious poets who set out on some important enterprise by dedicating themselves and their endeavour to the muse, this portion is Okigbo's ritual invocation and supplication to the goddess Idoto whose presence and approval are crucial in his spiritual journey. The context of the quest is religion and this quest is conducted through the exploration and juxtaposition of the Christian religion (representing foreign culture) and traditional images bathed in all-suffusing and powerful nature (which provides both solace and continuity).

Okigbo was noted for his concern with the craft of his poetry. He paid particular attention to the form of his art so that the totality of the form of the poem was an integral part of the meaning. This early poem shows Okigbo still experimenting, still fusing elements from foreign poets. The poem is incantatory and throughout this piece there is strong evidence of the influence of modern European poets, especially T.S. Eliot and Pound. In these poems, Okigbo ransacks European, Sumarian, Classical and African heritages for myths and symbols to convey his anguish and quest. But some of the more obviously modernist qualities of his poetry derive from T.S. Eliot and are traceable in the musical quality of his poetry, use of repetitions, the visionary nature of his poem and especially the fact that his poetry seems to achieve its meaning and impact by the association of images and symbols and not by rational argumentation borne out by the syntax of the poem. The impression is that the mind is at a high imaginative point where gulfs can be traversed easily.

His poetry remains one of the stoutest defenders of African culture. He is also one of the most creative African poets as he gradually sheds his borrowed early style and fashions out an art form uniquely his.

Come thunder (1967)

Come Thunder
Now that the triumphant march has entered the last street corners,
Remember, O dancers, the thunder among the clouds . . .

Now that the laughter, broken in two, hangs tremulous between the
 teeth,
5 Remember, O dancers, the lightning beyond the earth . . .

The smell of blood already floats in the lavender-mist of the
 afternoon.
The death sentence lies in ambush along the corridors of power;
And a great fearful thing already tugs at the cables of the open air,
A nebula immense and immeasurable, a night of deep waters —
10 An iron dream unnamed and unprintable, a path of stone.

The drowsy heads of the pods in barren farmlands witness it,
The homesteads abandoned in this century's brush fire witness it:
The myriad eyes of deserted corn cobs in burning barns witness it:
Magic birds with the miracle of lightning flash on their feathers . . .

15 The arrows of God tremble at the gates of light,
The drums of curfew pander to a dance of death;

And the secret thing in its heaving
Threatens with iron mask
The last lighted torch of the century . . .

Notes

The date of composition of this poem is significant. The Nigerian Civil War broke out in July 1967 and this poem was composed before the actual outbreak of war. It prophetically warns of the death and destruction which the charged political situation will inevitably lead to.

line 2 *thunder* The god of thunder and lightning among the Igbos of
  Nigeria is a destructive and implacable god of vengeance.
line 6 *lavender* Plant with purple, pleasant and strong smelling flowers.
line 8 The atmosphere was pregnant with rumours of terrible incidents.

line 9   *nebula*   A mass of gas and dust in space among the stars.

lines 11–14   Present a vivid picture of desolation and abandonment. There were many acts of arson that forced people to run away from their homes; farms were neglected because people were afraid to go out. The affliction in the human society is reflected in forlorn nature. It is as if nature mourns man's state, a degree of pathetic fallacy.

line 15   Reference to the title of Achebe's third novel, *Arrow of God*.

line 16   In the uncertain and dangerous period preceding and during the civil war, curfews were common features of governments.

line 19   Before the upheaval that overtook Nigeria, the tendency was to see the country as the show-piece of the success of British colonial administration and the glory of the British parliamentary system transplanted on to a new soil in Africa.

Questions

1 What do you think is the significance of the long lines of the first four stanzas and the concluding shorter lines?

2 Select any four images in the poem and comment on how they contribute to the general atmosphere described here.

3 Attempt a comparison of the form and imagery of this poem with those of "The passage" by the same author.

Commentary

This poem is the third in the sequence of Okigbo's poetry entitled "Path of Thunder". It was published posthumously and represents Okigbo's reaction to a very difficult and unpleasant period in Nigeria's history: the political and social upheavals that gathered force in 1965 and culminated in the civil war that started in July 1967. This was a period of reckless and fierce political rivalry and victimisation in which many horrendous acts were committed either as proof of political ascendancy or in revenge. It was the period of the first military *coup d'état* and its terrible aftermath.

The poem is a prophetic warning to factions, who drunk on their successful ravages were celebrating in mirth and dance, to be aware of the terrible destructions that will inevitably result because all the signs were evident. What they were glorying in was, after all, a lurking sinister force that threatened to destroy the country and bury it totally. Starting with this warning then, the poet follows in the next three stanzas with a string of images and metaphors that show that all the heralds of destruction were present and that the situation was highly inflamable. Of special note are the images of thunder and lightning, blood and death, night and deep waters, iron and stone. The structure of the poem is determined by the tone, rhythm and imagery of the piece. From the long lines of the earlier part of the poem giving details of the warning and describing the situation, the poem ends with short crisp lines that express the near certainty of the destruction to come.

One other remarkable and fascinating point about this poem is that it represents a new Okigbo. He has matured from the derivative poetry of his earlier period, such as we see in "The Passage" and achieved his own voice. The form of his poetry, the images he coins and the rhythm of the poem are original and fresh.

179

Wole Soyinka

Wole Soyinka is black Africa's foremost dramatist and one of the most controversial and distinguished writers of this generation. As playwright, actor, producer, poet, film maker, musician, essayist, author of scathing satirical revues (*Before the Blackout*) and editor, Soyinka has been a champion of the responsibility of art and the artist to society. This has made him a bitter critic of society and the establishment and has involved him in some activist episodes which cost him his freedom on two occasions.

Born in 1934 in Ake in Abeokuta, Ogun State of Nigeria, Soyinka was educated at the University College, Ibadan and Leeds University, England where he took a degree in English. He showed interest and ability in poetry and drama while in the university. He was part of the literary harvest in Ibadan of the 1950s and early 1960s and his considerable literary and dramatic potential was remarked upon while he was in Leeds. His involvement with the Royal Court Theatre at a time when it was the focus of revolution in English drama and later work on Nigerian culture and literature through a Ford Foundation grant greatly influenced the course of his own development. He founded his own theatre company known as "1960 Masks" – producing and acting in his own plays and others. In later years at Ife he started the guerilla theatre which was taken to the market place for popular consumption.

He was a Fellow at Churchill College, University of Cambridge, at various times Head of the English Department, University of Lagos, Head of Theatre Arts, University of Ibadan and Professor of Comparative Literature, University of Ife. He has retired from his University chair and is now devoting his time to the pursuit of the arts, especially film making. A prolific writer, Soyinka has so far published fifteen full-length plays and numerous sketches spanning the various forms of drama including *A Dance of the Forests, The Lion and the Jewel, Brother Jero, The Road, Death and the King's Horseman, Opera Woyonsi* and *A Play of Giants*. He has also published two novels, *The Interpreters* and *Season of Anomy*, a celebrated memoir *Ake*, a book on his prison experience, *The Man Died*, and three volumes of poetry: *Idanre, A shuttle in the Crypt* and *Ogun Abibima*. Other publications are: an anthology, *Poems of Black Africa* and a book of critical essays, *Myth, Literature and the African World*.

Soyinka's writings are sophisticated and show a profound exploration of human themes and concerns through a unique exploitation of his cultural milieu. He has won many international prizes for his contribution to literature. The crowning point was the coveted Nobel Prize for Literature (1986). He is the first African to be so honoured.

Telephone conversation

The price seemed reasonable, location
Indifferent. The landlady swore she lived
Off premises. Nothing remained
But self-confession. "Madam", I warned,
5 "I hate a wasted journey – I am African."
Silence. Silenced transmission of
Pressurized good-breeding. Voice, when it came,
Lipstick coated, long gold-rolled
Cigarette-holder pipped. Caught I was, foully.
10 "HOW DARK?" . . . I had not misheard. . . . "ARE YOU LIGHT
OR VERY DARK?" Button B. Button A. Stench
Of rancid breath of public hide-and-speak.
Red booth. Red pillar-box. Red double-tiered
Omnibus squelching tar. It was real! Shamed
15 By ill-mannered silence, surrender
Pushed dumbfoundment to beg simplification.
Considerate she was, varying the emphasis –
"ARE YOU DARK? OR VERY LIGHT?" Revelation came.
"You mean – like plain or milk chocolate?"
20 Her accent was clinical, crushing in its light
Impersonality. Rapidly, wave-length adjusted,
I chose. "West African sepia" – and as afterthought,
"Down in my passport." Silence for spectroscopic
Flight of fancy, till truthfulness changed her accent
25 Hard on the mouthpiece. "WHAT'S THAT?" conceding
"DON'T KNOW WHAT THAT IS." "Like brunette."
"THAT'S DARK, ISN'T IT?" "Not altogether.
Facially, I am brunette, but madam, you should see
The rest of me. Palm of my hand, soles of my feet
30 Are a peroxide blonde. Friction, caused –
Foolishly madam – by sitting down, has turned
My bottom raven black – One moment madam! – sensing
Her receiver rearing on the thunderclap
About my ears – "Madam," I pleaded, "wouldn't you rather
35 See for yourself?"

Notes

line 2 Indifferent The location of the apartment was not of great
   importance.
lines 6–10 The landlady is shocked at the prospect of having an African
   tenant, but she tries to control herself and reply. The poet can feel this
   tension coming through over the telephone.
line 12 Describes the odour in the public telephone booth from where he is
   speaking.

line 14 Describes the crushing sound of the tyres of the buses on the tarred street. It is onomatopoeic. The poet could not believe that he heard the lady correctly; but the physical realities around him convinced him that it was all true.

line 16 To be *dumbfounded* is to be made speechless by an experience. The poet asked for further explanation.

line 20 The image here is taken from medicine. The point is the detailed enquiries of the landlady.

line 21 To be *impersonal* is to be distant, cold and calculating. Following from *clinical* in the previous line the word is apt because the physician has to avoid becoming involved with his patient. Moreover, the word is correctly used because the poet cannot see the lady at the other end of the telephone.

line 22 *sepia* Describes a shade of brown.

line 23 a *spectroscope* Instrument, like a small telescope, for forming and analysing the spectrum of rays. The analysis would show the distinctive colours that combine to make up the rays. This reference continues the image of investigation twice referred to before. The colour which *sepia* describes does not register on the landlady's memory.

line 26 *brunette* A term used among Europeans to describe brown-haired women.

line 30 *blonde* Term used by Europeans to describe fair-haired women. Here the fair colour according to the poet, is like that caused by bleaching with a peroxide compound. Notice the poet's cynicism here and the way in which he confuses the lady by drawing attention to those parts of the typical African's skin colour which do not conform to the general notion of black and which at the same time do not quite approximate to the colour distinctions Europeans are familiar with. The poet aims to expose the stupidity of the concept of racial colour. Notice also that although Africans tend to refer to all peoples of the caucasian race as "white", they themselves make distinctions among the varying shades of their own colour.

line 32 a *raven* A big black bird. It is supposed to be something of an evil omen. Does the poet go beyond the physical reference to the bird? One of the reasons the African is despised is that his colour is dark, which connotes evil. The devil is always represented as black!

line 33 She bangs her telephone receiver in despair. Notice the way the alliteration in this line reinforces the action.

Questions

1 Do you think this poem represents a real conversation between two people? Give reasons for your answer.

2 Comment on lines 1–4 and describe how they contribute to the form of the poem.

3 Discuss the techniques the poet uses to achieve dramatic effect in this poem.

4 How is the mutual suspicion that exists between the speakers in this poem conveyed? What is the development from this feeling in the last eight lines of the poem?

Commentary

This poem is a dramatic monologue probably born out of actual experience. It dramatises the dilemma and frustration which the African faces when seeking accommodation in England. Such an occasion usually betrays the bottled up colour prejudice of many white landladies or landlords who are generally reluctant to rent out their apartments to Africans. Often, distinctions are made between shades of black, and the nearer an African's complexion is to white the more acceptable he is. In this poem, cast in the form of an imaginary conversation between a "well-bred" landlady and the poet looking for accommodation, Soyinka captures admirably the tension which accompanies this type of negotiation between two mutually suspicious parties. Through a carefully graded argument and play on colours, he exposes the absurdity of the insistence on skin colour. There is a good dose of satirical humour, cynicism and even open mockery in this poem. The landlady's confused ideas about colour differentiation go to the heart of the poem. By adroitly varying the tone of this poem, commenting in places, using apt punctuation, paying attention to details around him, the poet successfully recreates the situation.

Night

Your hand is heavy, Night, upon my brow,
I bear no heart mercuric like the clouds, to dare
Exacerbation from your subtle plough.

Woman as a clam, on the sea's crescent
5 I saw your jealous eye quench the sea's
Fluorescence, dance on the pulse incessant

Of the waves. And I stood, drained
Submitting like the sands, blood and brine
Coursing to the roots. Night, you rained

10 Serrated shadows through dank leaves
Till, bathed in warm suffusion of your dappled cells
Sensations pained me, faceless, silent as night thieves.

Hide me now, when night children haunt the earth
I must hear none! These misted calls will yet
15 Undo me; naked, unbidden, at Night's muted birth.

Notes

line 2 mercuric Here means lively, active, quick. The clouds are constantly
      changing. The poet sees this phenomenon as evidence of the clouds having
      some power to do as they please. He cannot toy with night (notice the use

of the word *dare*) because its almighty power is irresistible; night steals in and overwhelms the earth.

line 3 exacerbation Used in the sense of irritation or annoyance. The poet cannot afford to confront night. It is a way of admitting his powerlessness at the approach of night. The rest of the line fortifies this point through the image of sowing.

lines 4–6 A *clam* is a species of bivalve mollusc or shellfish (i.e. having two separate pieces hinged at a point and which can close and open automatically). The image here is very subtle, approaching the type used by the English Metaphysical poets. The reference is to the fact that women are jealous and the action of the clam closing its two halves (shutting itself up in its own world of darkness) is seen as night snuffing out the lingering brightness of the sea surface to bring in complete darkness, as if it (night) were jealous of light, its antithesis.

line 6 fluorescence refers to the shining surface of the sea. *Dance* gives the image of the movement caused by the waves. Notice the use of *pulse* to describe this movement and the way in which it agrees with the human element introduced in the use of *woman*.

line 8 brine Salt water; the sea. Also possibly sweat from exertion or heat or fear.

line 10 Picturesque way of describing the shadows that are cast. They have jagged edges like a saw. Shadows cast by leaves usually appear in this way.

line 11 dappled Made up of patches of colour or shade. It follows here from the *shadows* of the former line.

lines 13–14 Calls that come through the mist. They are eerie and unsettling cries. There is a sense of mystery and disaster implied in this last stanza. *Night children* suggests several possibilities: the insects and animals whose cries make the night terrifying, night marauders who work under the cover of night, the "abiku" or other evil forces which are believed to operate at night.

line 15 naked Defenceless, unprotected and undisguised.
   unbidden Not invited.
   muted birth Silent approach.

Questions

1 What do you think is the setting of the poem?
2 What do you notice about the way the stanzas are related to one another? Comment on the significance of this relationship as far as the structure of the poem is concerned.
3 What do you think the last stanza means?
4 Discuss Soyinka's descriptive ability as shown in this poem.

Commentary

In this subtle and exquisite poem, the poet describes nightfall and its effect on him. Through a series of images he conjures up a picture of the insidious yet overwhelming approach of night to which he must submit, the silhouettes that are characteristic of night due to the play of light, the mist that announces evening and the warmth that is generally felt in the early part of night in the tropics. There is an impression of self-identification, of the poet being merged in the landscape he is describing. But paradoxically there is a hint of terror, because night is also the time when evil people operate. And the poet asks to be hidden and protected from all evil forces. There is here a suggestion of the complexity of night – it provides rest, it terrifies, it provides cover.

The structure of the poem is noteworthy. It is written in triplets, the first and third lines of each stanza rhyming. The first stanza represents a complete statement of the overpowering effect of night. The next three stanzas, which constitute the descriptive part of the poem, are cleverly linked and enact the idea of the stealthy and relentless progress of night. The final stanza is a plea. The dangers that come with night are indicated in the last line of the fourth stanza and the poet wants to be protected from them. The manner in which stanzas two, three and four are syntactically linked together suggests and enacts the imperceptible and indeterminate progress of night.

I think it rains

I think it rains
That tongues may loosen from the parch
Uncleave roof-tops of the mouth, hang
Heavy with knowledge.

5 I saw it raise
The sudden cloud, from ashes. Settling
They joined in a ring of grey; within,
The circling spirit

O it must rain
10 These closures on the mind, binding us
In strange despairs, teaching
Purity of sadness.

And how it beats
Skeined transparencies on wings
15 Of our desires, searing dark longings
In cruel baptisms.

Rain-reeds, practised in
The grace of yielding, yet unbending
From afar, this, your conjugation with my earth
20 Bares crouching rocks.

Notes

lines 2–3 This is condensed metaphorical writing involving a number of
ideas. First the use of *parch* (dry) means that the rain will bring relief
and will invigorate nature, just as saliva in the mouth helps us. *Uncleave*

185

means to unfasten. What the poet is saying here is that the rain releases the tongue which indeed has a great deal to divulge.

lines 6–7 The stirring of ashes caused by the rain is likened to the thoughts that trouble the mind of the poet. Note the use of *grey*, a colour which conventionally denotes cheerlessness. The poet must remain bottled up.

line 10 Refers to the restrictions which make it difficult for him to speak out and therefore cause him sadness and despair.

line 12 The very essence of sadness.

lines 14–15 The fourth stanza of this poem is the most difficult because of the use which the poet makes of ambiguity and paradox. *Skeined* means tangled and confused and *transparencies* are things that can be seen through clearly. A drop of rain is transparent and the drops reach the earth in a disorderly manner. *Skeined transparencies* then refers to the rain falling. *On wings of our desires* is a poetic way of imagining the effect of the rain on people generally, their thoughts and desires. It underlines the flightiness of wishes, hence the use of *wings*. It is as if the rain had analytic power.

lines 15–16 *searing dark longings* This is a paradoxical expression, as the rain would be expected to cool and not *sear* (wither or scorch) anything. But it is *dark longings* that are disposed of, and this effect of the rain in expelling evil thoughts is seen as *cruel baptisms*. The baptismal image agrees with the *purity of sadness* of the previous stanza. It is that pure state that is achieved by the *searing* away of *dark longings*.

lines 17–18 When the atmosphere is saturated and pressure is low, rain inevitably falls. The rain *yields*. There is a sexual image here with the rain standing for the male principle (the phallus) and the earth the female principle. It is unbending because it falls in straight shafts. There is some implied relationship between the rain and the poet here. The sexual act itself releases tension.

lines 19–20 The sexual image is clearly hinted, and *my earth* refers to both the physical earth and the poet. The washing of the rocks symbolises the exposure of the poet's thoughts under the influence of the rain.

Questions

1 One interesting quality of this poem is the delicate style through which the ideas of the poem are developed. Comment on this, paying particular attention to the way in which each stanza begins.

2 Can you see any relationship between the rain and the poet? Describe that relationship.

Commentary

What makes this poem difficult is that the poet explores a state of mind by using rain as a symbolic image. We must be able to see the quick parallels and associations which the poet draws. Rain is used in this poem as a bringer of relief and as an agent of good. Through the symbolic image of the rain the poet narrates the burdensome thoughts that are stifling him and causing him so much despair and sadness. But circumstances dictate that he must keep his peace.

Procession I – hanging day

Hanging day. A hollow earth
Echoes footsteps of the grave procession
Walls in sunspots
Lean to shadows of the shortening morn

5 Behind, an eyepatch lushly blue.
The wall of prayer has taken refuge
In a peace of blindness, closed
Its grey recessive deeps. Fretful limbs

And glances that would sometimes
10 Conjure up a drawbridge
Raised but never lowered between
Their gathering and my sway

Withdraw, as all the living world
Belie their absence in a feel of eyes

15 Barred and secret in the empty home
Of shuttered windows. I know the heart
Has journeyed far from present

Tread. Drop. Dread Drop. Dead.

What may I tell you? What reveal?
20 I who before them peered unseen
Who stood one-legged on the untrodden
Verge – lest I should not return.

That I received them? That I
Wheeled above and flew beneath them
25 And brought them on their way
And came to mine, even to the edge
Of the unspeakable encirclement?
What may I tell you of the five
Bell-ringers on the ropes to chimes
30 Of silence?
What tell you of rigours of the law?
From watchtowers on stunted walls,
Raised to stay a siege of darkness
What whisper to their football thunders
35 Vanishing to shrouds of sunlight?

Let no man speak of justice, guilt.
Far away, blood-stained in their
Tens of thousands, hands that damned
These wretches to the pit triumph
40   But here, alone the solitary deed.

Notes

line 1   *Hanging day*   This is, in fact, the title of this poem. It gives the
impression of an endless day that will last longer than the length of a
normal day. The title also refers to the main topic of the poem; the day
on which those five hopeless prisoners were hanged.

line 6   *The wall of prayer*   Wall which separated one of the yards in the
prison. In this yard the inmates said prayers and sang hymns every night.
This wall is in the shadow cast by other walls in the morning sun.

line 10   *drawbridge*   Bridge hinged at one end for drawing up to prevent
passage. The image here describes the frightened look of the detainees
who tended to stare vacantly.

line 14   This means "tell lies about the disappearance of these detainees". *In
a feel of eyes* expresses the fact that people are afraid to speak out their
feelings; their reactions are expressed with their eyes.

line 20   He was peeping at this procession through a small opening in his
own cell.

line 22   He was on the brink of death and had to be careful lest any excuse
be found to kill him.

line 29   A gruesome image of the five men who were hanged that day.

line 33   The walls seem deliberately erected to shut out light so that the
prisoners remain in perpetual darkness.

lines 34–35   *football thunders*   Refers to the heavy sounds of the boots worn
by the police and warders. He cannot appeal to them. A *shroud* is a
cloth used in covering the dead, and its use here is strongly suggestive
of death. Sunlight does not bring cheer and warmth; rather it brings
death. The execution took place in daylight.

Questions

1   Line 18 is outstanding in a number of ways and is probably the most
powerful line in the poem. In what ways does it strike you as being special?
2   In what ways does the poet convey the horror of the detainees?
3   Attempt an analysis of lines 23–35. Who does *them* refer to?
4   How does the poet condemn injustice in the last stanza? Why does he refer
to *tens of thousands*?

Commentary

This is the first part of a two-part poem which appears as a sub-section of
Chimes of Silence which is one of the major divisions of Soyinka's collection of
poetry: *A Shuttle in the Crypt*. But for two or three poems, the poems that make
up this volume were written while the poet was in prison detention for almost
two years during the Nigerian civil war. It is a collection of poems which through

the image of the "shuttle" (weaving implement with two pointed ends which shoots the weft-thread across between threads of warp) records the restlessness and torment of an extremely sensitive mind in a solitary confinement that could have harmed his sanity permanently.

This particular poem concerns the fate of a group of eleven fellow inmates, who the poet listened to tramping up and down the prison corridor for three days, as they were being led out and in under heavy guard by warders. On the morning of the third day after he had started counting from the thud of heavy feet how many people were in this procession, five of the men were hanged at the gallows, an event which he describes as the "greatest travesty of the loom" (in which the shuttle works).

There are clearly three sections to this poem. The first section is descriptive and ends on the evocative and harrowing line *Tread. Drop. Dread Drop. Dead.* The second section, through a series of rhetorical questions, analyses his precarious fate and their fates, ending with a wholesale castigation of the machinery of justice.

Abiku

In vain your bangles cast
Charmed circles at my feet;
I am Abiku, calling for the first
And the repeated time.

5 Must I weep for goats and cowries
For palm oil and the sprinkled ash?
Yams do not sprout in amulets
To earth Abiku's limbs.

So when the snail is burnt in his shell
10 Whet the heated fragment, brand me
Deeply on the breast. You must know him
When Abiku calls again.

I am the squirrel teeth, cracked
The riddle of the palm. Remember
15 This, and dig me deeper still into
The god's swollen foot.

Once and the repeated time ageless
Though I puke. And when you pour
Libations, each finger points me near
20 The way I came, where

The ground is wet with mourning
White dew suckles flesh-birds
Evening befriends the spider, trapping
Flies in wind-froth;

25 Night, and Abiku sucks the oil
From lamps. Mothers! I'll be the
Suppliant snake coiled on the doorstep
Yours the killing cry.

The ripest fruit was saddest;
30 Where I crept, the warmth was cloying.
In the silence of webs, Abiku moans, shaping
Mounds from the yolk.

Notes

line 1 *Abiku* Is a Yoruba word for a child born to die young and to be
reborn by the same woman over and over again. There is something
other worldly in the *abiku*. Magic and ritual are used in the struggle to
keep him on earth to live like a normal child. One strategy is to shield
the child from fellow *abiku* spirits that will tend to invite him back to the
spirit world. Because the clanging sound made by bangles is supposed to
repel these spirits, an *abiku* wears bangles on his ankles. This opening
line strikes the note of mockery and indifference which runs throughout
his poem. Indeed, *abiku* is mischievous and taunting, stating clearly that
no art can bind him to man's desire.

lines 5–6 Futile ritual sacrifices are performed (with goats, cowries, palm
oil and sprinkled ash) to placate the spirits and persuade *abiku* to stay
on earth.

lines 7–8 As is common in many parts of this poem, a lot of meaning is
condensed here by the poetry of the piece. First, there is reference to
the practice of hanging amulets on the neck of an *abiku* to charm him to
stay. As usual *abiku* dismisses this action as useless. Secondly, in Yoruba
system of thought, the *abiku* is likened to yam. To propagate yam, a
tuber is cut and the pieces buried. These later germinate. Similarly,
abiku is marked, "cut" in several places when he "dies" and buried. But
he is born again with those marks. No amulets can stop this process. Just
as you cannot plant yams in amulets, so you cannot bury *abiku* in them.
Abiku's limbs should be buried in mother earth – where it will be sure to
wake in the other world and be born again. This is an important
statement of the theme of death and renewal, and of continuity, central
to Soyinka's poetry.

lines 9–12 Reference to the crude implement used in making the marks on
an *abiku*. See note on Clark's "Abiku" for reason for this action.

lines 13–14 A defiant note on the efforts of diviners who claim to have
found the answer or remedy for *abiku*. The metaphor of *the squirrel teeth*
is instructive. The squirrel teeth are small but they are able to crack
hard palm nut shells which human beings are unable to do with their
teeth. The medicine man thinks he has solved the problem with his

190

divination but *abiku* makes nonsense of his knowledge. Abiku continues his sarcastic attitude in the succeeding lines, warning or reminding them precisely of some of the unnecessary steps they take.

line 16   The earth is said to be the footstool of God. The earth, the mound of earth which forms on graves. An *abiku* is buried in either an extraordinarily deep grave – as if this will prevent its coming back – or thrown away in an evil forest.

line 18   To *puke* is to vomit like a small child, but the *abiku* is indeed very old (ageless) because it has been on this journey of coming and going for a long time – has been there from the beginning, but apart.

line 19   Even the pouring of *libations* only point the child to the underworld from where it came. Nothing can contain *abiku*, every palliative action taken by man only furthers his own irrevocable designs.

lines 21–24   This stanza thickens the tragic environment in which *abiku* likes to operate and through the images associates him with death, especially that caused by dark chances.

The ground is made wet by the tears from the mourners (line 21); *Flesh-birds* refer to witches which are agents of darkness and death. Witches are said to feed on human flesh and especially blood (line 22), *the spider* figures here (line 23) as a predatory evil creature that snares and kills with its frothy webs. cf. Soyinka's use of the spider and its web in *The Road*.

lines 26–28   In the Yoruba tradition, some *abiku* are thought to work through snakes. Here the snake coiled at the doorstep is the *abiku*. The mother seeing a snake on her doorstep at night would instinctively utter a shrill cry accompanied by an attempt to kill the snake. *Killing cry* then refers to the cry by the mother either before or as the snake is killed. Killing the snake is ironically returning *abiku* to the spirit world; it is aiding him to continue in his antics.

lines 29–32   *The ripest fruit was saddest* is a paradox that summarises all the anxieties and heartaches *abiku* causes. Using the metaphor of a fruit, a ripe fruit is mature but it is also strangely ready to be plucked. Many *abiku* children die at the most promising stages of their lives for example on their birth days or wedding days and this is added reason why their death causes so much sorrow. As if to clinch this image of death in life the *abiku* finds the *warmth* of the womb *cloying*, that is unpleasant because it is having too much of it. Finally, the egg *yolk* is a symbol of life and generation but *abiku* only finds it good for shaping burial mounds. *Abiku* is preoccupied with death (line 31) and like the spider's web (whose main duty is to trap flies to be killed), *abiku* is busy forging death (*mounds*) out of the substance of life (*yolk*).

Questions

1 Discuss any four images or symbols that associate *abiku* with death.
2 Describe the structure of the poem.

Commentary

This is a very different poem from Clark's "Abiku". In Clark's poem, a very human attitude is adopted, the *abiku* is recognised for what he is among the people and is begged to stay to end the agony of the mother. Soyinka's attitude is completely different. His poem explores the myth and essence of the *abiku* and highlights the capricious and elusive, clairvoyant, tyrannical and uncontrollable qualities of *abiku* whose spirit-side and close association with death are emphasized all the time. It is the *abiku* that speaks as the persona in this poem and his whole demeanour and tone are chilling and demoralising, almost satiric.

Soyinka focuses on the inexplicable and unalterable cycle of birth and early death which is the hallmark of *abiku*, in poetry that is dense with images drawn from beliefs and practices about *abiku*. The cycle of *abiku's* birth and death determines the structure of the poem, life and death providing poles between which the actions and thoughts of the poem oscillate until the last stanza where these two ideas unite in the paradox of destruction in life. Notice that although the individual lexical items are not difficult, the ways in which they are used and the syntax of the poem (in places) make the poem appear difficult to understand or unravel.

To my first white hairs

Hirsute hell chimney-spouts, black thunderthroes
confluence of coarse cloudfleeces – my head sir! – scourbrush
in bitumen, past fossil beyond fingers of light – until . . .!

Sudden sprung as corn stalk after rain, watered milk weak;
5   as lightning shrunk to ant's antenna, shrivelled
off the febrile sight of crickets in the sun –

THREE WHITE HAIRS! frail invaders of the undergrowth
interpret time. I view them, wired wisps, vibrant coiled
beneath a magnifying glass, milk-thread presages

10   Of the hoary phase. Weave then, weave o quickly weave
your sham veneration. Knit me webs of winter sagehood,
nightcap, and the fungoid sequins of a crown.

Notes

line 1   *hirsute*   Shaggy, coarse. The tumble of words in this first stanza
constitutes a proud description of the volume and colour of the hair that
crowns the head. In contrast, Stanza 2 contains a series of images
suggesting the feebleness of the emerging grey hairs.

line 8   *interpret time*   Signify the passage and effect of time.

lines 9–10   *presages of the hoary phase*   Signs of the on-coming period of grey
hairs.

line 11   *sagehood*   Wisdom.

line 12   *sequins*   Small spangles used to ornament a crown. The combination
fungoid sequins, suggests the speaker's ambivalent attitude to the grey
hairs as both signals of decay and wisdom.

Questions

1 The poem is made up of four main utterances, the first two of which can
be recast as follows:

> My head, sir, was like (a) hirsute chimney-spouts, (b) black
> thunderthroes, (c) confluence of coarse cloudfleeces, (d) scourbrush in
> bitumen, (e) past fossil, beyond fingers of light

> (until) THREE WHITE HAIRS sudden(ly) sprung as (a) corn stalk
> after rain, (b) weak, watered milk, (c) lightning shrunk to ant's antenna,
> shrivelled off the febrile sights of crickets in the sun, (d) frail invaders of
> the undergrowth (which) interpret time.

Identify the two remaining utterances, along the pattern set above and give
reasons for the poet's choice of the complex structure.
2 What effect does the poet achieve by the repeated use of exclamations in
the poem?
3 Do you consider the dense, difficult language used by the poet justified by
the theme that he is handling?

Commentary

This poem works through a torrent of words, to convey the speaker's dramatic
shock at discovering his first crop of grey hairs and his gradual reconciliation
with the coming of old age that this event implies. The poet's final attitude is,
however, not a simple one: it consists of self-mockery and a sardonic trusting
to the conventional belief that old age brings with it wisdom and respectability.

The speaker goes through three contrasted moods in the course of the poem:
first there is the exaggerated admiration for the pile of thick, black hair, seem-
ingly impregnable to the invasion of any grey; then there is the near-panic
reaction to the appearance of the milk-weak shrivelled wisps of three grey hairs
and, finally, there is the sober assessment of the self in venerable decay.

Post mortem

there are more functions to a freezing plant
than stocking beer; cold biers of mortuaries
submit their dues, harnessed – glory be! –

in the cold hand of death . . .
5 his mouth was cotton filled, his man-pike
shrunk to a subsoil grub

his head was hollowed and his brain
on scales – was this a trick to prove
fore-knowledge after death?

10 his flesh confesses what has stilled
his tongue; masked fingers think from him
to learn, how not to die.

let us love all things of grey; grey slabs
grey scalpel, one grey sleep and form,
15 grey images.

Notes

line 1 *freezing plant*   A refrigerating machine.
line 2 *biers*   Cases or stretchers for carrying and storing corpses.
line 3 *harnessed* (ironical use)   Dressed up, as it were, in armour.
line 5 *man-pike*   Penis.
line 6 *subsoil grub*   A worm.
line 8 *a trick*   A devise, an attempt.
line 11 *masked fingers*   The gloved hands of the doctors, performing the
    post-mortem operation.
line 14 *scalpel*   A small light knife used in surgical operations.

Questions

1 In what ways does the humour of the poet show in this poem?
2 What is the poet's attitude to the knowledge gathered through post-mortem
examinations? What do you think of his attitude?
3 What is meant by describing the last verse of the poem as "a litany of
acceptance"? Do you agree with this description?

Commentary

This is a poem in which the humorous attitude of the poet to death, and the
usual human attempts to circumvent it, leads him to a mature acceptance of its
inescapable reality. Note particularly the matter-of-fact opening statement, the
play on the words, beer and bier, (which hides a profound irony) and the
absence of any capital letters at the beginning of each line. A similar humorous
detachment characterises the itemising of the results of the post mortem. This
is crowned by the scepticism with which the so-called scientific knowledge,
yielded by the examination, is regarded.

The unity of the tone in the poem is indicated by the fact that in verse 1 the
sight of the corpse, *harnessed in the cold hand of death*, evokes the exclamation
glory be!, and anticipates the litany of acceptance which begins in the last verse
with *let us love all things of grey* . . .

John Pepper Clark

John Pepper Clark was born at Kiagbodo in the Ijaw country in 1935. He was educated at Government College, Ughelli and has an English degree from University College, Ibadan. He was the founding editor of *The Horn*, a student poetry magazine which played a crucial role in the history of literary development in Nigeria. He worked for a while as a newspaper editor, was a Parvin Fellow at Princeton University in the United States and a Research Fellow at the University of Ibadan. He taught at the University of Lagos where he became Professor and Head of Department. He retired voluntarily in 1980 and set up the first Repertory theatre in the country, PEC Repertory Theatre. He was for ten years editor of *Black Orpheus*.

Poet, playwright and essayist, Clark has published an impressive range of books. His plays include *Song of a Goat, Masquerade, The Raft, The Wives Revolt* and a triology called *The Bikora Plays* comprising "The Boat", "The Return Home" and "Full Circle"; *Ozidi*, a journalistic piece, *America their America*, a collection of critical studies, *The Example of Shakespeare* and a highly commended translation of the Ozidi Saga. His published volumes of poetry include *A Reed in the Tide, Casualties, A Decade of Tongues, State of the Union*, and a sixth book of poems, *Mandella and other poems*.

Streamside exchange

CHILD
River bird, river bird,
Sitting all day long
On hook over grass,
River bird, river bird,
5 Sing to me a song
Of all that pass
And say,
Will mother come back today?

BIRD
You cannot know
10 And should not bother;
Tide and market come and go
And so shall your mother.

Notes

line 3 This expression aptly describes the loop that is formed by the river
bird that is perched on a long stalk which bends under the bird's
weight.

line 11 *Tide and market* Here are measures for time. The poet is expressing
    the transcience of things. There is even a deeper implication in the line
    because *tide* (in the sense of the ebb-tide and full-tide of the river) and
    market (a place where people go to buy and sell, a necessary social
    institution) are features that mark the unending rhythm of life, over
    which man has little control.

Questions

1 What does the poem gain by being put in the form of a conversation?
2 The poem is supposed to be an "exchange" between a child and a bird;
  but we know that birds do not talk the way human beings do. What type of
  conversation is actually meant here?
3 Discuss the structure of the first stanza and the significance of line 7.
4 Compare the forms of the question and the answer. Discuss whether you
  think that the bird answers the child's questions.

Commentary

One of the fascinating features of Clark's short poems is the manner in which
he manages to say a great deal in a short space by using symbolic image. In this
poem Clark sets a scene as well as reflects on it. In this way he fulfils one of
the best distinctions of a lyric: that of presenting an intense moment and emotion
as an experience and at the same time as an imaginative comment on human
nature in general. In this simple but deeply disturbing poem, cast in the form
of a conversation between an anxious child and a bird, Clark touches on the
perennial problems of loneliness, anxiety, uncertainty about the future and the
humbling knowledge of the transcience of life. The finality of the bird's reply
puts a seal on the child's enquiries and underlines the child's helplessness.
There is a strong plaintive and fatalistic note about this poem, clearly emphasised
by the reply. The lyrical and elegiac tone of the first stanza contrasts with the
epigrammatic terseness of the second stanza, which clinches the exchange and
makes it impossible for any more to be said.

Fulani cattle

Contrition twines me like a snake
Each time I come upon the wake
Of your clan,
Undulating along in agony,
5 Your face a stool for mystery:
What secret hope or knowledge,
Locked in your hump away from man,
Imbues you with courage
So mute and fierce and wan
10 That, not demurring nor kicking,
You go to the house of slaughter?

Can it be in the forging
Of your gnarled and crooked horn
You'd experienced passions far stronger
15 Than storms which brim up the Niger?
Perhaps, the drover's whip no more
On your balding hind and crest
Arouses shocks of ecstasy:
Or likely the drunken journey
20 From desert, through grass and forest,
To the hungry towns by the sea
Does call at least for rest –
But will you not first reveal to me,
As true the long knife must prevail,
25 The patience of even your tail?

Notes

line 1 Contrition twines me like a snake Picturesque way of expressing his
sympathy and therefore sense of guilt at the pain caused to the cattle by
their drovers. *Contrition* (meaning penitence) is personified and the simile
that follows conjures up the picture of a snake that coils itself either in
agony or as a sign of withdrawal. The deep feeling of contriteness is
clearly indicated. Notice the way in which the alliteration and the rhythm
of the line suggest the action.

lines 2–3 upon the wake of your clan This refers to a large herd of moving
cattle and the characteristic path they leave behind.
Clan is used in the sense of species.

line 4 Undulating A geographical term used to describe an uneven, gently
rolling landscape. This is a graphic description of a herd of cattle
moving sombrely, the rhythm of their different movements and the
contours of their backs giving the impression of an undulating landscape.
It seems as if a part of the landscape is moving.

line 8 Imbues Saturates or fills completely.

line 9 wan Looking tired and exhausted.

line 10 not demurring Not raising any objection or protest.

lines 12–13 The image is from the blacksmith's profession. The poet
imagines that the horns of the cattle have been hammered and beaten
into their curious shapes by a skilful smith. *Gnarled* means twisted and
knotted.

line 14 passions Means strong feeling either of anger or love. It is also
used to describe Christ's painful experience in the moments leading to
his death.

line 17 balding hind This refers to the backs of the cattle that are losing
their hair under the insistent lashing of the drover's whip.

line 18 shocks of ecstasy There would seem to be some ambiguity in this
elegant expression. The poet is making a very fine point relating to the
fleeting excitement which shocks provide. The pain comes later. The
cattle have become used to the thrashing and so no longer feel any pain;
they no longer react, having become benumbed.

line 19 *drunken journey* This is a metaphorical expression referring to the appearance of the cattle that have walked several hundred miles. The wobbling and unsteady steps of the tired cattle call up the image of a drunk. This expression could also mean that the cattle are drunk with pain and tiredness so that they no longer feel. The expression is a good example of the figure of speech known as a *transferred epithet*.

line 24 *must prevail* Must win; the butcher's knife will surely end the life of the cattle.

Questions

1 This poem progresses by a series of images. Identify them and comment on their functions in the poem.
2 Does the poet achieve any particular result by the use of rhetorical questions?
3 What does the fact that the cattle are uncommunicative, have no choice in, and are unaware of what is to become of them add to your appreciation of this poem?
4 Notice that the first two lines and the last two lines of the poem are in couplets. What do they contribute to the poem?

Commentary

In this poem the poet expresses the sympathy and anger he feels at seeing cattle driven all the way from northern Nigeria to the south to be slaughtered. There is something mysterious about these cattle that trudge along to their death, their faces expressionless and uncomplaining. The poet is struck by the cattle's patience and in his admiration of their capacity for endurance hints at such themes as pain, suffering, fate and death.

The patterning in the poem is exquisite and can be divided into three types of movements. There is the progressive description of the cattle, the sense of geographical movement from north to south and finally the sense of an inevitable movement from life to death. This last suggestion is fortified by a subtle image in the first four and the last five lines of the poem: the crashing of the spent waves on the shore is compared to the slaughtering of the cattle in the south. Is Clark hinting at man's journey to death?

The problem in judging this poem is that, although the rhetorical probing of the mystery of the cattle's patience is artistically done, Clark does not seem to be able to communicate this experience to the reader. The poem appears not to go beyond the occasion for his own meditation and, as if to confirm our questioning of the true quality of the poem, ends on what sounds a bathetic note.

Song

I can look the sun in the face
But the friends that I have lost
I dare not look at any. Yet I have held
Them all in my arms, shared with them

5 The same bath and bed, often
Devouring the same dish, drunk as soon
On tea as on wine, at that time
When but to think of an ill, made
By God or man, was to find
10 The cure prophet and physician
Did not have. Yet to look
At them now I dare not,
Though I can look the sun in the face.

Notes

line 1 "To look the sun in the face" is a saying which implies a courageous and impudent, but risky act. We usually avoid the sun because it dazzles our eyes. It is therefore bold to dare to look at it directly. On the other hand when we have either offended someone or our own feelings have been hurt, we are unable to look the person squarely in the face. To be able to look the sun and not his former friends in the face implies the degree of unfriendliness that now separates them because of their different views and positions in the civil war. But there can be no self-justification here, because either party could have caused the loss of love.

lines 6–7 Notice the almost hyperbolic way in which the poet states the affectionate relationship that tied him to his friends. *Devouring* conjures a picture of conviviality, of careless abandon. It is literally unthinkable for people to be *drunk* on tea, but again this is a way of putting across the merriment and deep experiences he shared with his friends. The poet's technique is to intensify these former intimacies in order to contrast them with the present strife.

line 10 There is interesting "logic" in the occurrence of the word *cure* in this line, because it maintains the image of disease in the use of *ill* in line 8. The point being made is that the present estrangement could not have been predicted by anybody. *Prophet* is also used in the biblical sense of one endowed with some healing power.

Questions

1 The poet calls this poem a song. What do you think are the relationships between a *poem* and a *song*? What type of *song* is this poem and can you point to the qualities that make it a song? (Consider the sound pattern of the poem.)
2 Who has been wronged in this poem? Do you think the poet overstates his points?
3 What strikes you about the way in which the poet organises his ideas in this poem? (Look at the first three and the last three lines and compare them with the lines in between.)

Commentary

This is the first poem in J. P. Clark's volume of poems entitled *Casualties*. The poems that make up *Casualties* were inspired by the social strife that led up to, and the actual civil war that rocked Nigeria for thirty odd months. "Song" is a good introduction to these poems because it captures adequately the deep feelings of grief, loss and estrangement which went with the war. Even in form this poem heralds a new note in Clark's art. It is a deeply moving poem in which the poet mourns the loss of former bosom friends. The two extreme states of formerly intimate friendship and present hostility are conveyed through this image. The poem is tightly structured and the contrary states are forcefully indicated.

The casualties

The casualties are not only those who are dead;
They are well out of it.
The casualties are not only those who are wounded,
Though they await burial by instalment.
5 The casualties are not only those who have lost
Persons or property, hard as it is
To grope for a touch that some
May not know is not there.
The casualties are not only those led away by night;
10 The cell is a cruel place, sometimes a haven,
No where as absolute as the grave.
The casualties are not only those who started
A fire and now cannot put it out. Thousands
Are burning that had no say in the matter.
15 The casualties are not only those who escaping
The shattered shell become prisoners in
A fortress of falling walls.

The casualties are many, and a good number well
Outside the scenes of ravage and wreck;
20 They are the emissaries of rift,
So smug in smoke-rooms they haunt abroad,
They do not see the funeral piles
At home eating up the forests.
They are wandering minstrels who, beating on
25 The drums of the human heart, draw the world
Into a dance with rites it does not know

The drums overwhelm the guns. . .
Caught in the clash of counter claims and charges
When not in the niche others have left,
30 We fall.
All casualties of the war,
Because we cannot hear each other speak,

Because eyes have ceased to see the face from the crowd,
Because whether we know or
35 Do not know the extent of wrong on all sides,
We are characters now other than before
The war began, the stay-at-home unsettled

By taxes and rumours, the looters for office
And wares, fearful everyday the owners may return,
40 We are all casualties,
All sagging as are
The cases celebrated for kwashiorkor,
The unforeseen camp-follower of not just our war.

Notes

line 1   casualties A number of people killed or wounded in an accident or a
war. Here it is used in the overall sense of "victims".

line 4 This refers to people fatally wounded in battle who are given
treatment in a determined attempt to save their lives. Since they are sure
to die, the meaning is that they die gradually, by degrees, compared to
the sudden death of being killed outright.

line 7   to grope To search blindly for something without certainty, to feel for
something in the dark with no definite knowledge of its whereabouts.
The tragedies of war carry with them a great sense of loss.

line 10   a haven A refuge, a place where one finds rest, comfort and
security. Ironic here, yet somehow true; certainly better than death.

line 14   burning Used both literally in the sense that people were actually
burnt to death by various means and metaphorically in the sense of
severe suffering.

line 17   fortress A place strongly protected by fortifications. Poetically any
place that provides or seems to ensure safety is referred to as a fortress.
Here it refers to houses or other buildings where people used to run for
safety from lethal shells. But invariably such buildings were also targets
and were destroyed. It could also refer to any rickety building on the
point of collapse in which people in panic sought refuge.

line 20   emissaries of rift Messengers of dissension and division. One of the
public relations acts of the two sides engaged in the civil war was to
send delegations overseas and to other African countries to canvass for
military and diplomatic support.

line 21   smug Self-satisfied, narrow-minded. Describes the behaviour of
these *messengers* who were well provided for and who thoroughly enjoyed
themselves in the circumstances of physical comfort provided for them in
their luxury hotels. Notice the alliteration.

line 24   wandering minstrels Singers who perform from place to place.
The poet is here referring to the writers who were sent out by both
sides to plead the causes of their various governments. There is a strong
satirical note in this statement.

line 27   drums overwhelm To surpass a thing in number or volume. This is a
continuation of the image of the drum. What the poet means is that the

emotional appeals made by both sides trying to win support abroad have become so clamorous that the physical war going on at home seems less important. The clamour and insistence drown all sense and reason.

line 28 Claims, counter claims and charges by either side to the dispute were the stock-in-trade of these emissaries. They endeavoured to sway their potential supporters with these, each side getting the ear of the eager audience with its stories. But sometimes the delegations *clashed* and sounded quite contradictory. At such times it was clear falsehood had a hand in the wicked game; the masks fell off and the lies were exploded, making the tellers also casualties of the war! These ideas are expressed in an exquisite alliterative and onomatopoeic line.

line 33 This refers to the mass hysteria which operated during the war. Anger made people blind and unable to differentiate sensible and well-meaning individuals and friends from the unthinking crowd.

line 38 Various types of levies, some compulsory, others voluntary, were instituted to provide money for the war.

line 42 *kwashiorkor* Deadly disease caused by protein deficiency. Very common during the war.

Questions

1 You will notice that there is a great deal of variation in the length of the lines. What do you think is the effect of this device?
2 Discuss the imagery of this poem, paying particular attention to the guns and drums.
3 Why does the poet consider that *we are all casualties*?
4 This piece reads like a prose passage. How would you set about justifying it as a poem?

Commentary

In this poem Clark expresses in an objective way the tragedy of the Nigerian war. The subject is that *we* are *all* casualties of the war and not only those who died while fighting the war. In the poet's view, all classes of Nigerians (both the Federalists and the Secessionists) were authors, aggravators and victims in various ways of the catastrophe. Clark conducts his castigation in a subdued, controlled and modulated tone. This feature adds greatly to the poetic quality of a piece, which may strike some as prosaic. He proceeds by first seemingly eliminating the obvious cases from the list of casualties, then goes on to state positively those he considers the casualties, taking time to satirise and digress on the propagandist roles played by agents of both sides, using the telling image of people beating on "the drums of the human heart". He finally gives reasons why the casualty rate was so all-inclusive. The last line of the poem seems to expand the bounds of the poem and make accomplices of even non-Nigerians. This is an obvious reference to the international implications of the war.

Night rain

What time of night it is
I do not know
Except that like some fish
Doped out of the deep
5 I have bobbed up bellywise
From stream of sleep
And no cocks crow.
It is drumming hard here
And I suppose everywhere
10 Droning with insistent ardour upon
Our roof thatch and shed
And thro' sheaves slit open
To lightning and rafters
I cannot quite make out over head
15 Great water drops are dribbling
Falling like orange or mango
Fruits showered forth in the wind
Or perhaps I should say so
Much like beads I could in prayer tell
20 Them on string as they break
In wooden bowls and earthenware
Mother is busy now deploying
About our roomlet and floor.
Although it is so dark
25 I know her practised step as
She moves her bins, bags and vats
Out of the run of water
That like ants filing out of the wood
Will scatter and gain possession
30 Of the floor. Do not tremble then
But turn, brothers, turn upon your side
Of the loosening mats
To where the others lie.
We have drunk tonight of a spell
35 Deeper than the owl's or bat's
That wet of wings may not fly
Bedraggled up on the iroko, they stand
Emptied of hearts, and
Therefore will not stir, no, not
40 Even at dawn for then
They must scurry in to hide.
So let us roll over on our back
And again roll to the beat
Of drumming all over the land

45 And under its ample soothing hand
    Joined to that of the sea
    We will settle to sleep of the innocent and free.

Notes

line 4 Dope is a narcotic or stimulant. But here it refers to a fish-poison
used for fishing in the riverine areas. Spread on the river at appropriate
places, it kills any fish that comes into contact with it instantly, making
them float on the river. *Doped* here is an apt image to depict the fact
that the poet was awakened suddenly from his deep slumber by the rain
which has entered their poor house through the leaking roof.

line 5 *bob up* To move up and down, as if with a jerk; it indicates sudden
consciousness. It continues the image introduced in *Doped*.

line 6 *stream of sleep* Sleep, like consciousness or time, has no physical
reality and is best referred to as a continuum or a stream.

line 10 To *drone* is to make a continuous deep humming sound like the
buzzing of bees. *Droning* is one of the many apt words which the poet
uses to create the right atmosphere.

line 22 *Deploy* is a military term which means to spread out to take charge of
strategic positions. The picture here is that of the poet's mother fighting
off the invasion of the rain by moving things out of the way of the
rivulets that have formed on their floor.

line 35 These are nocturnal birds of ill-omen. They are usually perched on
high trees such as the iroko. The poet, using the poetic technique of
exaggeration, or hyperbole as a way of drawing attention to their misery,
implies that his household has been soaked by the rain more than the
bats or the owls that have been out in the trees all night. The condition
of these creatures is an indication of how heavy the rain has been.

line 41 To *scurry* is to run hurriedly. The bats and owls "run" fast to
escape light at dawn if they have "over-slept".

Questions

1 Discuss the poet's use of imagery, alliteration and onomatopeia. In what
sense do they succeed in conveying meaning?

2 With what success does the poet use repetition in this poem? Support your
answer with specific references from the poem.

3 What pictures of rural life does Clark present in this poem and "Abiku"?
How does he present these pictures?

Commentary

This is one of Clark's best poems, because of the way in which he successfully
fuses sound, meaning and atmosphere in the form and imagery of the poem. Its
impact also rests on the way in which the poet is able to realise tender feelings
and to hint at broader implications in the poem. For the poem is not a mere
description of a rainstorm in a village, but rather a subtle depiction of the living
conditions of a people and of a broader identification of man and nature. Of
particular interest, as far as the technical competence of this poem is concerned,

is the torrential rhythm achieved through the run-on lines and the generous use of the -*ing* forms of the verb. The overall effect of these techniques is to give the poem an almost prosaic rhythm, which paradoxically emphasises its poetic quality. Also of interest is the use of alliterative and onomatopoeic words, which help to build the mood and to fill in details of the scene.

Abiku

Coming and going these several seasons,
Do stay out on the baobab tree,
Follow where you please your kindred spirits
If indoors is not enough for you.
5 True, it leaks through the thatch
When floods brim the banks,
And the bats and the owls
Often tear in at night through the eaves,
And at harmattan, the bamboo walls
10 Are ready tinder for the fire
That dries the fresh fish up on the rack.
Still, it's been the healthy stock
To several fingers, to many more will be
Who reach to the sun.
15 No longer then bestride the threshold
But step in and stay
For good. We know the knife scars
Serrating down your back and front
Like beak of the sword-fish,
20 And both your ears, notched
As a bondsman to this house,
Are all relics of your first comings.
Then step in, step in and stay
For her body is tired,
25 Tired, her milk going sour
Where many more mouths gladden the heart.

Notes

Title   Abiku   Yoruba word for a child born to die young and to be reborn
by the same woman over and over and again. Among the Igbo such a
child is known as *Ogbanje* and among the Akan (Ghana) as *Kosama*. A
child suspected of being an *abiku* is given several marks when it dies.
line 1   Coming and going   Gives the impression of a continuous process. The
same child comes several times. *Seasons* means years.
line 2   baobab   A large African tree reputed to be the abode or meeting
place of witches, wizards and *abiku*.

line 3   *your kindred spirits*   Fellow *abiku.*

line 6   *brim*   Fill to overflowing. The poet comes from the riverine area of the country where many rivers easily overflow their banks during the heavy rains of the rainy season. This setting accounts for some of the other details and images in the poem.

lines 12–14   It is a poor and humble family but it has produced generations of healthy people who have grown up and become successful. Many more will grow out of this lineage. *Several fingers* here is a synecdoche, the use of part for whole, since fingers represent the children born into the family who have grown up.

line 15   *bestride the threshold*   To stand or sit on or over something with legs apart, one leg on either side. In this case one leg is in the house and the other is out. .

line 17   An *abiku* is identified by the marks made on him in one of his earlier comings. These marks are supposed to disfigure the child; some traditions maim the child, to make him unattractive in the spirit world. He will then be rejected and the only option left him will be for him to remain on earth when he comes again. (In the Igbo tradition an *abiku* is usually very handsome.) An *abiku* is given funny and unusual names also to make him unattractive to his kindred who will tend to lure him away.

line 18   To *serrate* means to cut in such a way that a surface has a row of connected teeth-like shapes as in a saw.

line 20   *notched*   A notch is a V-shaped cut.

line 21   *bondsman*   A slave. Slaves were usually branded in some parts of the body to show ownership. The ear lobes were popular parts.

line 22   *relics*   Something old that reminds of the past.

line 26   This is a very striking ending, characteristic of Clark. Nigerians or Africans like large families. Notice the use of alliteration here; also the length of this line compared to the three short ones before it. The effect is to reflect through its relaxed form, the joy and happiness in the home to which the *abiku* is being invited.

Questions

1 Comment on the poet's tone and attitude in this poem.
2 Discuss the poet's style and technique in this poem.
3 How does the poet present a vivid picture of the household?

Commentary

The *abiku* syndrome is one of the cultural beliefs common to peoples of southern Nigeria. Clark accepts the reality of the *abiku* and so addresses it directly. Usually, an *abiku* is considered wicked and the source of much sorrow, a perverse child (part-spirit, part-human) whose mother is to be pitied. Clark's simplicity and tenderness in this poem gives the difficult experience a humane treatment that makes this poem one of his most successful and memorable, in which language, imagery and structure bear out the theme ever so engagingly.

The poem is a moving plea to the *abiku* (the child is confirmed an *abiku* because it has been born with tell-tale scars) to be considerate and decide whether to live like a normal child and bring comfort to the mother or *stay out* permanently (die and be buried and not return again) instead of tormenting the woman who has the misfortune of being the vehicle of its entrances. Employing a good rhetorical technique which ensures the tight structure of the poem, the poet starts by ironically asking the *abiku* to *stay out* if it will not come in. Then follows a vivid portrayal of the home in which it is being invited to stay. The poet then asks it to stay among the warmth, love and friendship of the family where it is welcome instead of tormenting with its antics, a mother who is physically tired from many frustrating births. The masterly use of repetitions in this part of the poem, especially in the last quatrain contribute greatly to the tender tone of the poem and its total effectiveness.

This is one of Clark's best poems. The simplicity and clarity of language, the deft use of caesuras and enjambments, the use of repetitions, alliteration, assonance and the modulated tone which all contribute to the rhetorical structure of the piece, make this a satisfying poem.

Olokun

I love to pass my fingers
As tide thro' weeds of the sea
And wind the tall fern-fronds
Thro' the strands of your hair
5 Dark as night that screens the naked moon:

I am jealous and passionate
Like Jehovah, God of the Jews,
And I would that you realize
No greater love had woman
10 From man than the one I have for you!

But what wakeful eyes of man,
Made of the mud of this earth,
Can stare at the touch of sleep
The sable vehicle of dream
15 Which indeed is the look of your eyes?

So drunken, like ancient walls
We crumble in heaps at your feet;
And as the good maid of the sea,
Full of rich bounties for men,
20 You lift us all beggars to your breast.

Notes

Title Olokun (literally "Owner or queen of the sea") is a river goddess, worshipped in Bendel State and among the Yorubas of Nigeria. She is a very kind and bounteous goddess. She gives fertility to the barren, health, wealth and bountiful harvest; cures the sick and gives long life.

She is extremely beautiful, with dark long hair and gives her worshippers beautiful children. Everything connected with her is white – symbol of purity. She is worshipped by both male and female devotees.

lines 1–5   Nature images create a romantic and dissolving atmosphere, which accords well with the fanciful environment of the goddess's habitat.

lines 6–10   Biblical: Jehovah, God in the Old Testament, is depicted as a strict, fierce and jealous God who exacted penalty and punished misdemeanour. Lines 9–10 are a reference to the New Testament declaration "Greater love hath no man than this that a man lay down his life for his sheep" – to show degree of devotion.

The language of this stanza raises some critical issues. We must ask ourselves whether it adds to the seriousness of the poem or detracts from it. Is it an attempt at elevated language or is it melodramatic and incongruous?

line 11   *wakeful*   Sleepless, not able to sleep.

line 12   *mud*   Not only refers to popular belief about the creation of man "earth thou are and to earth must return", but also to the weakness of the flesh.

line 13   *stare*   Remain open.

line 14   *sable*   Black.

lines 11–15   The presence of the goddess is over-powering and her beauty is hypnotic, it dims all sleepless eyes. Also refers to the dreamy eyes of the goddess.

line 16   *So drunken. . .*   Intoxicated by her beauty they totter and fall just like old walls (made of either mud or stones) that have been long exposed to rain and sun and other agents of the weather.

line 20   *breast*   Symbol of comfort and life. Used here both in sense of bosom and in the sense of granting them their request from her bounty which flows with milk.

Questions

1 Discuss the poet's use of simile in this poem.
2 What kind of relationship exists between the poet and the goddess?

Commentary

This poem is a celebration of Olokun in the form of a daring, almost sacrilegious profession of love to the goddess. The poet worships her romantically. Who would not fall for a creature who combines beauty with kindness?

The human level at which the poet expresses his love and the mythic level which presents the popular image of the goddess represent the two levels of the poem that are sustained throughout. The language of the poem confirms this because the profane and erotic mingle with the religious (Christian) to emphasise the duality and reality of Olokun – a kind-hearted goddess who listens to the needs of man. For the poet persona like other devotees, needs bounties, not just emotional love from "the good maid of the sea". Whereas the first two stanzas express the poet's deep affection for the goddess, the last two express her nature and the fascination which she exerts on her worshippers. She does not attract in order to destroy like a *femme fatale*, she attracts in order to bless and feed. The ordered structuring of the poem (each stanza contains five lines) is one of the good qualities of Clark's poetry.

Kofi Awoonor

Kofi Awoonor (also known as George Awoonor Williams) was born in 1935 in the Volta Region of Ghana and educated in Ghana, the United Kingdom and the United States. He has taught literature at the State University of New York and at the University of Cape Coast, Ghana. He is now Ghana's ambassador to Brazil.

His earliest collection of poems, *Rediscovery and other poems*, was published in 1964, and since then his poems have appeared in various anthologies of African poetry. He is a prolific writer, very conscious of his roots in traditional Ewe poetry and folk songs and, among Ghanaians writing poetry, he is perhaps the most successful in attempting to recover the rhetorical vehemence and the metaphorical intensity of vernacular poetry. His poems, often difficult, but powerful and mysteriously moving, are predominantly rituals of lament over the "senseless cathedral of doom" which educated Africans have allowed to usurp the shrines of their ancestral gods.

The cathedral

On this dirty patch
a tree once stood
shedding incense on the infant corn:
its boughs stretched across a heaven
5 brightened by the last fires of a tribe.
They sent surveyors and builders
who cut that tree
planting in its place
A huge senseless cathedral of doom.

Notes

line 1   *dirty patch*   A piece of earth, a plot of land which could be used for building.

line 3   *shedding incense*   Blessing and, as it were, providing the power for growth.

lines 4–5   The impression created is of a giant family tree underneath which flourished the life of the tribe. *The last fires of a tribe*, however, suggests that life was somehow doomed. The *fires* could be the last lit for cooking by the tribal owners of the land before they were evicted for the construction of the cathedral; or they could be the fires of the last burnt offering to the gods. The main point is that the religious and the ordinary life existed side by side.

line 8   *planting*   An ambiguous and possibly ironical use of the word. The
point of the whole poem is that the earlier religious life of the tribe
grew naturally out of its ordinary existence; whereas the foreign religion
which the cathedral symbolises, was imposed. *Planting*, however, suggests
natural growth or, at least, the ability to grow – something emphatically
denied by the last line of the poem.

Questions

1 The poem consists of two sentences. Analyse the co-ordination of the
various portions of these two sentences, and show how this helps the poet
to obtain maximum emphasis.
2 Comment on the position, the effect and the meaning of the last line.

Commentary

This poem expresses in a compact and persuasive way disapproval of the change
from the complex life of Africa's past to her more modern environment and prac-
tices. The cathedral is taken to symbolise not only foreign (and therefore empty
and meaningless) religious practices, but other changes that accompany the inter-
ruption of the spiritual and commonly shared experiences of a people.

Rediscovery

When our tears are dry on the shore
and the fishermen carry their nets home
and the seagulls return to bird island
and the laughter of the children recedes at night,
5 there shall still linger here the communion we forged,
the feast of oneness which we partook of.

There shall still be the eternal gateman
who will close the cemetery doors
and send the late mourners away.
10 It cannot be the music we heard that night
that still lingers in the chambers of memory.
It is the new chorus of our forgotten comrades
and the halleluyahs of our second selves.

Notes

lines 1–4   These first four lines suggest a sense of ending and of irreparable
loss through their enumeration and the falling cadence which comes to a
dead halt in line 6.
lines 7–8   The shared sense of sorrow and bereavement.
line 7   *the eternal gateman*   Both a real and a legendary figure; the caretaker
who keeps the local cemetery tidy and shuts the gate after each burial

ceremony. This is what he exists for and does perpetually. He seems eternal in comparison to those whose burial he brings to an end. Thus his presence, while implying the last act of separating the dead from the living, suggests permanence and continuity.

line 10 The music of the hymns and the drums at the wake-keeping ceremony on the night that precedes the burial of the dead.

lines 12–13 The most difficult lines but obviously the ones toward which the whole poem moves. Their importance lies in the fact that they affirm as present (line 12 begins with *It is*) what has been referred to as the future in lines 5, 8 and 9.

Questions

1 Comment on the three tenses used in the poem and show their function in unfolding the attitude of the speaker.
2 Explain the connection between the events mentioned in the first four lines of the poem.
3 Explain the significance of the distinction between the music heard that night (line 10) and the new chorus (line 12).
4 How would you illustrate the fact that the poem is meant to be intoned as a chant? (See especially lines 2–4, 5–7 and 8–10.)

Commentary

This is an early poem of Awoonor's – the title poem of the collection brought out in 1964 by Mbari Publications of Ibadan, Nigeria. With its dirge-like rhythm, as well as the local colour of its setting on the shores of South-Eastern Ghana, it is a characteristic Awoonor poem. The evocation of Keta (the main town of this region perpetually subject to sea erosion and written about by both Awoonor and Kwesi Brew) with its prominently located cemeteries and its frequent burial ceremonies and wake-keeping, is strong in the poem. But the use of local colour enables the poet to suggest the universal elements of the experience he is dealing with. For example, the "shore" of the first line of the poem suggests the limits of life, the beginning of the boundless sea upon which the dead sail away from the land of the living – the material of so many myths.

The evocation of the particular rites surrounding the burial of the dead in a closely-knit community also enables the poet to affirm a sense of continuity here and now, and a communion of the dead and the living which is unique. Celebrating these elements the poet gives a new chorus to the otherwise forgotten friends and rediscovers himself in his song and in his vocation as a poet (as if it were a second self, transcending that which is in constant danger of dying with his comrades).

We have found a new land

The smart professionals in three piece
Sweating away their humanity in dribblets
And wiping the blood from their brow

We have found a new land
5   This side of eternity
Where our blackness does not matter
And our songs are dying on our lips.
Standing at hell-gate you watch those who seek admission
Still the familiar faces that watched and gave you up
10 As the one who had let the side down,
"Come on, old boy, you cannot dress like that"
And tears well in my eyes for them
Those who want to be seen in the best company
Have abjured the magic of being themselves
15 And in the new land we have found
The water is drying from the towel
Our songs are dead and we sell them dead to the other side
Reaching for the Stars we stop at the house of the Moon
And pause to relearn the wisdom of our fathers.

Notes

line 1   three piece   A man's suit, made of three pieces (a pair of trousers, a
   coat and a vest), suitable for temperate and cold climates, but particularly
   uncomfortable for tropical wear.
line 2   in dribblets   Slowly, piece by piece.
line 3   A variation on wiping the sweat from the brow.
lines 4–7   These are lines attributed to the professionals in an attempt to
   justify their behaviour.
line 8   You here refers to the speaker who is also *the one* in line 10.
   admission   To the land of the dead through hell-gate. By imitating
   others they cease to be their unique selves and give up the mystery of
   their individuality.
line 16   Symbolic of a season of drought: in other words, we have become
   sterile and unproductive.
line 17   the other side   Foreigners, possibly Europeans; we sell our sterile art
   forms to others, as if they represented fine creativity.
lines 18–19   The stars are further off than the moon; hence the line could
   be an indirect reference to the Black Star of Ghama for which spurious
   achievements have been claimed.

Questions

1 Comment on the meaning and appropriateness of the description in line 2.
2 Write a brief account in your own words of the kind of person the speaker
   describes in lines 8–12.
3 Would you say that the poet's attitude to his theme is ambivalent?

Commentary

Written in the early 1960s, the poem's intentions are clear. It starts off as a
powerful and stinging satire on the misguided attempt by some members of the

professional elite of the newly independent African states to copy the manners of speech and dress of their former colonial masters. The poet sees as an unpardonable crime the desire to pursue a so-called common humanity – *a new land where one's blackness does not matter* – shared with the erstwhile colonial rulers, and in so doing to lose personal and national identity. The guilty are considered dead and the poet pitifully watches them enter the hell of their own creation.

From line 13 the detached attitude of the satirist gives way to the guilt of a participant and a solidarity with the guilty. The *they* of the previous lines is absorbed by a *me* who finally undertake the praiseworthy task of relearning *the wisdom of our fathers* and presumably recovering the true self.

More messages

I can go placing faggots on those fires
fanning the innerwards: I can sneak
along like the crawling beetles
seeking through dust and dirt
5 the lonely miracle of redemption
I will sit by the roadside, breaking
the palm kernel, eating of the white
with the visiting mice
throwing the chaff to the easternly wind
10 But will they let me go?

to nowhere where I can see
the sunlight fall on the green waters
and the ferrymen hurrying home
across with their heavy cargoes
15 of man flesh, child flesh and woman flesh

to sit where I can gather my thoughts
and ask what I have done so long
why could I not eat with elders
though my hands are washed clean in the salt river,
20 where they leave the paddles in the boat
to be carried by children of strangers.

Coming to that land that day
where sand strip covers childhood
and youth's memory; there was no storm
25 that did not speak to us
divining the end of our journey
promising that our palms shall prosper
and we shall not die by thirst
in the same land; where our fathers

30 lingered, ate from land and sea
   drank the sweet waters of the ancient palms.

   Will they let me go
   and pick the curing herbs behind fallen huts
   to make our cure, their cure?
35 to hoe my own fields, plant my own corn
   to wait for rain to come?

   Is the guile of the forest animal
   the lingering desire of every marksman
   returning from futile hunt
40 beaten by desert rain and thistles
   on his shoulder the limpid hare
   and empty guns?

   The sacrifice of years awaiting
   unlit fires, who to knowledge
45 prepare the feast of the resurrection
   on many rivers' shores moved
   the benevolent band, awaiting
                        that season

   The dawn second cock
50 split by the ears of rumour,
   time to wash the new corn
   ready for the grinders
   light the family fire of flimsy twigs, prepare
   the broom to sweep unto dunghills
55 Crimes that my fathers atoned for.

   Some day, by some rivers!
   We sang that song before
   in the thousand seasons of good harvest
   and full fish following our fathers' footprints
60 on the long shores.

   They heard the thunder
   from the great river's waves
   that our feet should move to make room
   for an empty empty valley.

65 What happened with cries heard under trees
   that many households are empty?
   The powder house is fallen
   So we cannot make war

For when the bulls are alive
70 could the cows perform weed.

Notes

Title   More messages   Draws attention not only to the repeated requests, but
also the urgency with which the reply is awaited and therefore the
uncertainty and anxiety this generates in the speaker. This state of
uncertainty is also conveyed by the repeated question: *'Will they let me
go?'*
line 1   faggots   Wooden logs, firewood.
line 2   innerwards   Inner parts; the half line refers to a process of self-
torture involved in attempts to save oneself. Essentially this is the
alternative open to modern man who has no belief in a god.
line 3   This particular beetle is fond of rolling cow dung into a ball which it
then pushes along.
line 4–5   Describes the second alternative way of repentance and redemptive
grace open to the Christian (*through dust and dirt*, i.e. sack cloth and
ashes). *The lonely miracle* can refer to either the claim made for the
unique and once-for-all act of redemption by Christ or to the fact that it
comes to Christians as individual lonely figures.
line 6   The third alternative way of doing penance, according to indigenous
traditions, is to lead a life of destitution, exposed to nature, sharing food
with the rodents, not daring to beg even from fellow humans.
line 11   nowhere where   The two words together generate a unique meaning.
The description which follows, although of a specific place (i.e. the
green waters of the lagoons which litter the banks of the river Volta as
it enters the sea in south-eastern Ghana, and are plied by the canoes
with an assortment of cargoes on local market days) is also mythical.
Those ferrymen are more of kutsiami (messengers and spokesmen of
death) than ordinary fishermen. This section of the poem also seems
haunted by Dylan Thomas's lines:

Never until the mankind making
Bird beast and flower
Fathering and all humbling darkness
Tells . . .

lines 18–19   These two lines are based on a well-known West African
proverb. The speaker's anguish partly stems from the fact that even
traditional wisdom no longer seems a clear guide to right conduct.
lines 19–20   salt river/where . . . There is an implicit suggestion that, though
a son of the house, the speaker has become so alienated that he is now
treated like the children of non-clansmen who are assigned menial jobs.
line 22   that day   Recalls the initial arrival and settlement of the emigrant
ancestors of the Ewes on the south-eastern littoral of Ghana.
lines 30–32   Oral tradition has it that when the emigrants first saw the
golden sand on the sea shore at the estuary of the river Volta they felt
this was the spot to stop and rest: literally, roll themselves up. This act
gave the name ANLO, to the people and the place. Afterwards, they
developed the coconut plantations referred to in line 31 as the *ancient
palms*.

line 33 fallen huts During the long period of absence, the speaker's
ancestral home seems to have been so neglected that the huts, made of
swish and thatch have fallen down.

line 41 limpid An unusual usage which combines both the idea of the small
game, lamed and possibly limping, but also "colourless" in comparison to
what big game a good marksman would have liked to come home with.

line 61 the thunder Generally regarded as the voice of the gods, hence
prophetic.

line 65 under trees The only shelter left for the orphans of the sacked
homes.

line 67 powder house The armoury where the gunpowder belonging to the
tribe is kept.

line 70 perform weed Refers to the ceremony of widowhood performed for
any woman whose husband dies. It is an elaborate and sometimes a very
painful ceremony, since tradition believes that the wife of a dead man
bears some spiritual responsibility for her husband's death. In normal
circumstances the cleansing ritual requires the sacrifice of a bull.

Questions

1 The first ten lines of this poem are a striking organisation of sounds.
Analyse them, pointing out the poetic devices used and their effect.
2 Identify some of the ways in which the speaker's anguish is presented in
the poem.
3 Often in this poem the first person singular slides into the plural. Can you
give any reasons why this is the case?
4 There is a rich bringing together of the homely and the exotic, the natural
and the supernatural, the literal and the symbolic. Pick out some examples
of these. What do you consider to be the total effect of these?
5 This poem moves at a variety of rhythmic paces. Identify some of the crucial
rhythmic changes and try to describe their effect.
6 Do you think the poet succeeds in resolving "the problem" with which he
began? If not, does this matter?

Commentary

"More Messages" is an example of a poem in the tradition of the Ewe dirge.
(Another example of this mode of poetry is Kofi Anyidoho's "Hero and Thief"
on page 305) Simply put, the Ewe dirge is a song of sorrow, lamenting changes
in the fortunes of the individual, the clan or the state. These changes, which
fate may have decreed, can also be attributed to the wrong-doing of the indi-
vidual or the group. Quite often they are the result of deserting the ways of the
ancestors who are regarded as guardian spirits. Subsequently, although appro-
priate ritual sacrifices may make some difference, the attitude is that things have
irremediably gone wrong.

With a long poem of this nature, the best approach is to try and discover the
sense-groups that go to make the total organisation of the poem. Fortunately,
the sense-groups in this poem can be easily identified, since they are made up
of parallel statements, recurrent questions and a number of alternative answers
to these questions. For example, in the first eight lines we have the parallel state-
ments which begin with (i) *I can go placing,* (ii) *I can sneak along,* (iii) *I will sit by*

the roadside. These declarations of ability and intention are followed by the question at line 10 *But will they let me go?*, repeated later at line 32. When alternative, but apparently inadequate, answers to this question have been exhausted in lines 16–32 and lines 34–36, a new question emerges in lines 37–42. This last question is both elaborate and complex, and the partial answers to it constitute the last 25 lines of the poem.

The speaker in the poem is assumed to be away from his ancestral home and a return, which is also seen as re-establishing contact with the elders in the tradition of song-making (line 18) involves a process of purification. The return is also seen as a re-enactment of the initial arrival and settlement of his emigrant ancestors.

The forty-odd lines which begin with the question at line 37 perhaps present the greatest difficulty and it may be helpful to paraphrase the question and the partial answers it receives: the speaker, who is seen as an exile (in many senses) up to line 35, is now regarded as a hunter returning home after a particularly futile trip. The question is, can he not simply admit defeat? Must he come home with, at least, a *limpid* hare, as a sacrifice to the ancestors?

Then follows the first partial answer in lines 43–55: if during his long absence, while no votive fires are lit at home (line 45) he nevertheless performed the appropriate rites even in foreign lands (line 46: *on many rivers' shores*), this will have been well received by the guardian spirits (*the benevolent band*, line 47) and therefore the return home becomes a new beginning, a cleansing, a resumption of the homely tasks ("washing the new corn", etc). Lines 56–60 confirm that this indeed had happened once (*we sang that song before*, line 57) and the clan had been the beneficiary of the ancestors' good fortune. But, true to the dirge, that good fortune cannot be repeated: for they heard the thunder that the bulls are gone and the gunpowder house is fallen.

My uncle the diviner-chieftain

Another conversation, the godlike ram of sacrifices,
the only tree of the homestead now, occupant
and regent of an ancient honour house
They all left you, the young ones,
5 the children you never had, the sons
you dreamt up filling your earth-space
Your old age and our father's name,
roaring still unquenchable flames
through our land. I recall the day
10 the dark winds rose
whirling corn-cloths
leaves and fowl feathers
into the pyramidal household dream.
Then I came home. You stood on the compound
15 of our fallen homestead
nodding. A divination proceeds
from the diviner's good stomach

older memories and fire burning
over homesteads though fallen.
20 I was the messenger of that fire
the coming of that prophecy.

Notes

line 1　*another conversation*　Two key words. The uncle does not really say
anything in this "conversation", except nod (line 16). And yet that
nodding suggests that he discerns the meaning of the storm and thus
confirms what the nephew says.
godlike ram of sacrifices　Often among the Ewe of south-eastern Ghana
the ram set aside for a sacrifice to the household gods is allowed to
fatten, age, grow a goatee, and take on the semblance of the gods
themselves.
line 6　*earth-space*　That portion of the land belonging to the family and
remaining the household's inheritance.
line 11　*corn-cloths*　The sheaths which are taken off the corn-cob.
line 13　The metaphor is both concrete and abstract:
(a) the soothsayer's official hut among the Southern Ewe of Ghana,
often thatch-roofed with a pointed apex, resembles a pyramid. The
storm then blows all kinds of rubbish into this hut, threatening the god
within.
(b) soothsaying is inherited and belongs to a family. The family's dream
that successive generations of children (the pyramid) will uphold the
name of the house is what seems momentarily threatened by the storm.
line 17　cf. Ghanaian proverb "no one prophecies on an empty belly".
lines 18–19　A burning fire in a homestead symbolises the presence of
cooking and life and is not a sign of destruction.

Question

1　List three details which indicate the solitary life of the uncle. How does
the speaker use these details to suggest the stature of the uncle?
2　What effect does the poet achieve by linking up the first eight and a half
lines and employing only one main verb in them?
3　Why is the line *Then I came home* a turning point in the development of the
poem?
4　The imagery of the poem centres round fire. What purpose does this serve?

Commentary

This poem is taken from a collection of poems, *Ride me, memory*, which gives
some indication of what the poet is attempting to do in the section, called *African
memories*, from which this particular poem comes. The section consists of a series
of six poems in which past experience is recalled and pondered. The pondering
gives the poet an assurance that family tradition calls him to his art.

　　This particular poem is made up of two sections. The first portion recalls
vividly a solitary, patriarchal figure whose dreams are powerful enough, even
when they are not fulfilled, to seem real. The second section deals with a

particular day when a wind-storm threatens to blow down the patriarch's family house, but turns out to herald the return of a son of the household. The occasion provides material for the patriarch's prophetic vision of the son's role within the household tradition. The awareness of tradition is also shown in the influence of traditional poetic techniques on this poem. For instance, the first three lines contain no verb and consist, after the opening two words, of a string of praise names – a device common in drum language and in libation texts which evoke the ancestors.

Harlem on a winter night

Huddled pavements, dark,
the lonely wail of a police-siren
moving stealthily across
grey alleys of anonymity
5 asking for food either
as plasma in hospital jars,
escaping fires in tenements
grown cold and bitter,
or seeking food in community garbage cans
10 to escape its eternal nightmare.
Harlem, the dark dirge of America
heard at evening
mean alleyways of poverty,
dispossession, early death
15 in jammed doorways and creaking elevators,
glaring defeat in the morning
of this beautiful beautiful America.

Notes

line 2   *lonely wail* Against the background of the silent wintry night, the siren of the police patrol-car stands out as if it were mourning the incidence of the crime it is tracking.

line 4   The line describes both the murky, narrow streets and the nameless crowds out of which come the victims of the frequent outbreaks of fire.

line 5   The subject of *asking* (as of *escaping* in line 7, and *seeking* in line 9) is *anonymity*, that is, the nameless crowds, whose only means of escaping the nightmare of living in Harlem is either through the blood transfusion (*plasma in hospital jars*, line 6) they receive, when admitted after burns from the frequent outbreaks of fire, or by scavenging in the neighbourhood garbage cans.

line 7   *Tenements* carries the connotation of dilapidated dwellings often in danger of catching fire. The same condition is indicated by the *creaking elevators* (lifts) in line 15.

Questions

1 Why is the police-siren described as moving *stealthily* in line 3?
2 How well does the poem convey the life of desperation in Harlem? Refer to relevant details from the poem.
3 What do you think is the poet's attitude to the situation he presents and how far is this attitude reinforced by the rhythm of the poem?

Commentary

Harlem is a slum quarter of New York City, inhabited largely by Afro-Americans or blacks, poor whites and immigrant Puerto Ricans. Like other overcrowded ghettos of large cities all over the world, it has a high crime rate, hence the constant and intimidating presence of police patrol-cars.

The first ten lines of the poem, without a main verb, constitute a series of names or appellations drummed out by the poet in the tradition of the atupan (the talking drums) before Harlem itself is first mentioned in line 11. The blot that Harlem is on the beautiful landscape of America's youthful civilisation is well captured by calling it *the dark dirge* that signals the evening overtaking America's morning. That dirge can be heard, particularly, in the last two lines of the poem. A similar judgment on America is echoed by Kofi Anyidoho's poem, "Long distance runner" which is also included in the anthology.

Titus Chukwuemeka Nwosu

Titus Chukwuemeka Nwosu was born in 1935 at Abba, Nkwerre-Isu LGA of Imo State, Nigeria. Author, poet, publisher, editorial consultant, he was educated at Stella Maris College, Port Harcourt and the University College, Ibadan where he read Classics. Between 1961 and 1970 he held many teaching positions in Port Harcourt and Lagos.

He was the first executive editor of Pilgrim Books Ltd/African Universities Press. He later set up an editorial consultancy and agency services and a full publishing concern, Cross Continent Press Limited, of which he is Managing Director. He provides editorial advisory services to many publishing houses and numerous professional societies.

T. C. Nwosu is a prolific writer. His poetry and essays have appeared in several magazines and journals. Apart from numerous educational and instructional textbooks, he has also published volumes of poetry including *And the Heavens Wept, The Blind Spots of God, Sirens of the Spirit, Poems About Love and Women, Six Dazzling Days*, a collection of poems inspired by the visit to Nigeria of Pope John Paul II and two volumes of: *Poems for the African Young.*

The call

We all dream of conquering time
so the knees may not grow sore
with earth pleading, so death may
be put to shame and into the shade.

5 But time and death are what dreams
are made of, banging at
the very doors of the day–night eye.

Dust or clay I have played
prodigal enough with such great epics
10 to feed the limbs and voices
of inspiration marking my human limits.

But not with you, distant call,
whose faith is sun to my spirit,
moon to my spear; while life
15 and love like one great staircase

grow with each climb which will end
at the top floor of the last day. . .

I remember the lures of that ancient call
when my cock-wings flapped and fluttered
20 in pursuit of your tail and I had to
pelt you with wild-olive

promising with all the somersault
to wait on this great green side
till the dark clouds have cleared.

Notes

line 1   Death sets the seal to man's life-span on earth. It is the one
inevitable end which man knows he cannot avoid and yet which he does
everything to avoid.

line 5   This line recalls Prospero's speech in Shakespeare's *The Tempest* Act
IV, Sc. I, 156–58.

> We are such stuff
> As dreams are made of; and our little life
> Is rounded with a sleep.

The poet does not consider *time* and *death* as setting any limits or
physical barriers.

lines 6–7   Refers to the function of the eye in determining day and night.

line 9   The image is from the story of the prodigal son in the Bible. "To
play prodigal" is to be reckless and wasteful, although repentant in the
end. In this context what the poet means is that he has thought
needlessly over the idea of *death* and *time*, which he refers to here as
great epics. An *epic* is a narrative which tells in grand manner the exploits
of heroes and covers a great expanse of time and space. The term *epic* is
generally used to describe a poem, play or novel which is concerned
with great themes.

lines 10–11   Limbs and voices and even inspiration are attributes of human
beings, who by their very natures are subject to time. It is man's lot to
be concerned with the *great epics* which the poet has referred to earlier.
The poet is indirectly stating the fact that his love is limitless.

line 12   *distant call*   This means love both as passion and the person loved.

line 18   *ancient call*   This refers also to love. Love and its expression are as
"old as the hills".

line 21   An olive leaf or branch is a symbol of peace. But the poet's use of
wild-olive goes beyond that and has a biblical background. The idea is
contained in the fact that Eve in the Bible is said to have covered her
nakedness with fig leaves. The image then is sexual and leads on to the
heated passion of the last two stanzas.

line 22   This line and the two that follow describe accurately a cock in
pursuit of a hen. It falls many times and often its pursuit ends without
getting to the object of its chase. It waits for another opportunity, by
which time the dark clouds would have cleared.

Questions

1 What does the poet mean by our *conquering time*?
2 Can you identify the metaphors and similes used in the fourth and fifth stanzas? How effective and relevant are the images?
3 What use does the poet make of sound patterns in this poem and how do they contribute to the effectiveness of the poem?

Commentary

This love poem falls into two clear but closely related parts; the first part defining the basis and providing the metaphor for the second part. The poet's love for the woman endures for ever and is not bound by time or space. The first three stanzas deal with the idea of limitlessness by paradoxically treating things which seem to him to be bound by time. This prepares the way for him to state the one thing which is beyond the confines of time – his love, the "distant call" of this poem. The last three stanzas deal with this idea, and his affection is conveyed by the arresting image of a cockerel chasing a hen. The intermingling of love and life in the fourth stanza introduces an interesting philosophical notion. Although life is eternal in the sense that it goes on, it terminates biologically for an individual when he is pronounced clinically dead. Similarly, although the emotion of love may endure, the means of its expression are drastically reduced when the object of love is no more. It is the finer everlasting dimension that teases the poet's thoughts.

Combat

I
The night had hung storm-bound
from a sullen wreck of a sky
like a woman in travail
Storm that wrecks hopes
5 and wrests the heart from the sword
giving the wind sturdy

arms of violence

and earthworms got the message
when the flood came with the rainstorm
10 and men cried hot tears

Because they could not speak
of the things they had seen
and heard when stars fell
and the sorrowing throng swayed

15 under the weight of loads
that bit into the small
of human feeling. . .

II
Like spearsmen filing out
with masses of dark clouds in the sky
20 in the furnace-heat of warrior drums
they sang and chanted songs
which echoed their ferocious moods
as if the earth in a death-dance
would eat their thundering feet
25 and make their skin glow and grow
with dog-barks and snake-bites
The night has heart
which men must eat
so they can scorn
30 the terrors of the night-storm
and make the eyes spurt
with flames which could
devour forests of enemies. . .

III
So out they marched
35 at beat of the tattoo
to a crossroads where they had
their first baptism of fear
under trees whose fine feathered
birds had flown in fright
40 and whose leaves lay dry
naked and lifeless
on the ghost-ground
good company with hearts of steel

They kept moving on razor-edge
45 orders broadchested crouchers
shadowed by fear of coughing
or sneezing or standing or falling
and not rising. . .

IV
Later the sun came
50 Like a cat-burglar and gave
everyone a porridge face
for it was now time
to let the knees sink
into the waiting ground

55 weary of the sound and fury
that had made night
bleed the day to death.

Suddenly everyone stared at the sun
and at the swift mercy of its coming
60 telling their wounds like beads of penance
with each sad twinge and tweak of pain
not daring to look back at fallen blood

For at sundown as everyone knows
the heat waves will once more rise
65 and leave the neighbourhood gutted with blood.

Notes

line 2   sullen wreck of a sky   Describes the dismal and destructive weather. It
seems that the troubled and tormented heavens have let loose their anger
on the earth.

line 3   travail   Labour (of child-birth).

line 5   The sword can only be wielded to achieve victory when it is backed
by a strong heart.

line 6   sturdy   Strong and dependable.

line 8   Earthworms which normally burrow in the earth are washed up during
heavy rains.

line 10   It is normally thought unmanly for a man to shed tears.

line 13   when stars fell   Falling stars traditionally foretell grave events.

lines 27–28   heart which men must eat   This is proverbial and it expresses
the idea of courage.

line 35   The *tattoo* is a drum beat used here to mean a beat for marching.

lines 47–48   falling and not rising   This is a *double entendre* or an expression
with two meanings. It is used in the sense of lying flat on the ground
after stumbling in the darkness over difficult and muddy terrain; it is
also used in the sense of dying.

line 50   A *cat-burglar* is a burglar who enters by climbing. The simile gives
the idea of the stealthy appearance of the sun.

line 51   A witty and vivid line. The mud and slime of the previous night
would have messed up their faces and bodies. At night this would be
unnoticeable, but the patterns would be conspicuous in the daytime.

line 60   As they looked over and examined the wounds they had sustained
the previous night, it seemed as if they were reciting their rosaries,
making confessions and asking for the absolution of their sins. A feeling
of satisfaction is involved.

line 61   twinge and tweak   Describe the sharp pain caused by pinching.

line 65   gutted   Here means flowing with blood. It gives the impression of
excessive bloodshed, and loss of lives.

Questions

1 Discuss the appropriateness (or inappropriateness) of the title.
2 You will notice that one of the striking features of this poem is the poet's

225

descriptive power. Discuss this aspect of the poem and comment on how the poet succeeds in building up an atmosphere of terror.

3 Why do not the soldiers dare *to look back at fallen blood* (line 62)? Identify the figure of speech used in this expression.

4 One problem that faces any writer of narrative poetry is how to sustain the poetry of the piece and the interest of the reader. Do you think that *Combat* is a successful narrative poem? What techniques does the poet use to hold our interest?

Commentary

This poem is written against the background of experiences of the Nigerian war. It is a narrative poem which tells in a vivid way the harrowing experiences of troops moving at night to take up combat positions in preparation for the bloody encounter of the following morning. In spite of the bleak and stormy weather the stout-hearted soldiers march out defiantly, chanting war songs. Dawn puts an end to their ordeal, and wearily they stop to take stock of their physical pain and human losses. The sun gives them welcome respite, only to usher in a spell of armed confrontation with their opponents during which a great deal of blood is shed. The last stanza not only gives us the impression of the magnitude of the destruction of human lives, but also gives us the feeling that this is a familiar scene.

Star dust

(For Nat)

Harvest is no blessing
When death is the crop;
He was both the crop and the harvest
The plough-man and the ploughshare
5 The bowie-knife and the handle
That cut and was cut both ways!

Full armed warrior hammered out of steel;
Muscled eye of the embattled breed.

Now no more shall your sun
10 Belch out fire-bolt
Nor mortar music mob your ears
Nor your armour outshine others!

Dust-laden star that gripped
A blazing torch in both hands
15 Whose steel-thews could

226

Smother the midday heat;
Lion with blood-light hazel eyes
Throttled by forests of fate.

As you go laurels denied
20 Your voice crushed like a wayside rose
Screams to admit
Chimney-pity and widow-feeling.

How the ululations of those cruel hours
Have so hastily passed
25 Like April showers!

What noble sieve the human memory!
O graveless one that must cling
To the harshest wings of irony
Forgive me forgive us
30 These impenitent lapses. . .

No the gods are not angry, we are;
For these dark rain-clouds
That now hang over our eyes
Will eat through to our hearts
35 And make a bitter cold of lasting sorrow.

Notes

line 4 A *plough* is a farming implement made up of a frame and a blade for
   tilling the soil, and is usually drawn by horses. The cutting blade is
   known as the *ploughshare* and the man who guides the horses as the
   plough-man. This line is a variation of the preceding line.
line 5 *bowie-knife* A long knife with a double-edged blade.
line 10 *Belch* To emit noisily. Nat is metaphorically likened to the sun,
   showing what a terror he was in his lifetime.
line 13 *Dust-laden star* This can be seen either as a play on the title of the
   poem or a variation of it. The title of the poem can be taken to mean
   the remains of a star after it has burnt itself out. The implication is
   death. But *Dust-laden star* means a star that is covered by dust which
   hides its brightness and light.
line 15 *thews* Muscles or sinews. *Steel* suggests strength and hardness.
line 17 *Lion* continues the metaphorical praise of Nat, and the description of
   his eyes as *blood-light hazel*, meaning reddish-brown or bloodshot, also
   indicates a determined and courageous man.
line 18 Choked to death by overwhelming forces of fate.
line 19 He should rightly have been decorated with *laurels* for his victorious
   exploits. But he is not so honoured because of the circumstances of his
   death.

line 20　The image of the *rose* here continues the basic idea of something precious, lovable and distinguished. Nat actually died on the road in Aba. His car which contained explosives was sprayed with gunfire and he died in the instant explosion that followed.

line 22　This line introduces local and homely colour into the poem. *Chimney* conjures up a fireplace, a warm home. Nat deserved to be mourned in the home by his wife and relations.

line 23　*ululations* Howls and screams of sadness. *Cruel hours* refer to the time of his death and the expression of sadness by those present.

line 25　*April showers* A conventional image, used to refer to things that are transient or of short duration. April rains are light and intermittent.

line 26　*sieve* A utensil with a gauze bottom used for separating finer from coarser material. It cannot be used for storing. The poet here refers to the fact that human memory is short; it cannot retain information for long.

line 28　There is irony in the manner of his death and in the fact that a "great" man could not be given the last rites which he deserved.

line 30　This means unrepented guilt. The poet here expresses guilty feelings at Nat's friends' inability to perform their last responsibility to him by way of mourning and burying him adequately.

line 31　Notice the change in tone. The impassive will of the gods ties up with the idea of fate mentioned in stanza 4, and now gives way to human anger and frustration. Also refers to the saying "whom the gods love die young".

line 32　The distinction is between the rain-clouds and the rain. The metaphor images the deep sorrow that precedes tears.

Questions

1 Comment on the play on *Harvest* and attempt an explanation of the first stanza.
2 Explain why the poet describes human memory as a sieve.
3 Why are the *we* of the last stanza angry?
4 Compare this poem to any native lamentations which you know and say whether they affect you in the same way.

Commentary

This is an elegy bewailing the death of a courageous and noble friend who died suddenly in an air-raid during the Nigerian civil war. It is an exceedingly moving poem whose effect is heightened by the poet's adoption of the three-part movement of traditional dirges. What looks like an overture is followed by a section which sings the praise of his friend through striking metaphors that record his martial and moral courage and indicate that only fate could have ended his life so abruptly. The poet next laments the ill-luck that has overtaken his friend in that his friends are not able to accord him full burial rites. The poem ends on a note of resignation and with a statement of the lingering sorrow which his friend's death causes. The poem's elegance is achieved through artistic control of the emotions expressed and appropriate variations in tone.

Yao Egblewogbe

E. Yao Egblewogbe was born in South East Ghana in 1937 and educated at the University of Ghana. After teaching in various secondary schools and teacher training colleges, in 1971 he joined the Language Centre of the University of Ghana.

The two poems anthologised here have the quality of a childlike fascination with the horrors of the adult world. Egblewogbe is a very concerned writer and, although the bulk of his poetry is lyrical and personal, his most successful poems are often social and political in comment.

The coming of day

I
They came with gift and promise
That the day had dawned
And darkness fled. Then higher and higher
The royal sun climbed, while lips cracked
5 Beneath a dying tree,
And men shaded their doubtful eyes
To see fatality in glory;
The grey dog and brown dog and the young dog,
(It had died) had ceased to bark;
10 Pastures once rich had become barren
Where fleshy cattle grazed.
And here and there the bleached skeleton
Of a goat reflects the luminous power.

Beneath the blessed silence of a glowing city
15 Children choked and mothers wept.
A woman stood agape behind the city wall;
Her song is long forgotten.
But noon was yet to come.

One tired cat, pursued by hungry mice,
20 Had seen a flameless hell
Where ghastly figures sat
Dreaming of night.

II
We were shrouded in mists of grief;
Strained hazy eyes to see
25 What the stranger had brought:

Certain uncertainties of misshaped minds
That sipped their leisure from the cup
Of human tears; pleasure boats
That sailed on the dark fluid
30 Of aching eyes till night swallowed us all.
We have seen another morrow;
We have seen other heads
Whose dark foreheads ache with thinking clear;
Men of might who wipe all tears
35 With a handkerchief of determination.
Before tomorrow they will unweave
The tapestry of deceit.
So may this mist recede
For the coming of day.

Notes

line 2 *the day* The day of independence and of freedom from colonial rule.
line 7 *fatality in glory* That which is fated, unavoidable.
line 14 Suggests the emptiness of a highly lit city whose material progress is made hollow by the starvation and suffering of its inhabitants.
line 17 *Her song* Happiness, joy.
lines 19–22 Depict a number of abnormal events. Hell, for example, usually associated with tongues of fire, is here described as flameless; its inmates, normally in perpetual darkness, here dream of night.
lines 23–26 cf. lines 7–8 above. In both cases the poet makes the point that it took people time to discern what the regime was all about; for, at first, they were doubtful whether or not they saw clearly enough.
line 25 The stranger refers back to *they* in line 1.
line 26 Certain dubious ideas from men who were themselves confused.
lines 27–30 Suggest the callousness of the political leadership.

Questions

1 Why does the poet concentrate on animal imagery in the first section?
2 What light do the abnormal events described in lines 19–22 throw on the poet's attitude to the times he is describing?
3 What is the effect of the change from the third person in the first section to the first person in the second part of the poem?

Commentary

Set in the later days of Kwame Nkrumah's regime in Ghana, the poem consists of two sections. The first section (lines 1–22) is a detached narration which vividly conveys the startling horror of the change from the bright promises of the early stages of the regime to the subsequent nightmare. Using a recurrent imagery of drought, sterility and decay, the narrator is fascinated by the image of the regime as a powerful tropical sun. As the source of light and heat, capable of both illuminating and blinding by its brightness, of warming and burning by its heat, the sun provides a mixed blessing. It is on this ambivalent nature of the regime that the narrator dwells in the first section of the poem.

In the second section the speaker has become a participant in as well as a victim of the regime. Through the imagery the grotesque regime is condemned. The poem ends on a note of hope, that a new and different day dawns.

The wizard's pride

When the story shall be told,
No matter whose death it shall report,
Then shall we, bold ones in
Black companionship,
5 Clothe ourselves in white;
The rising tomb
Shall be our lazy chair;
The place for brave men is the wilderness.

Death is everywhere;
10 So let ours come in ripe season.
One by one the fruits shall desert
The mother tree,
And the fruit tree turn firewood.

So when the story shall be told,
15 No matter whose death it shall report,
Then shall we, bold ones in
Black companionship,
Clothe us in white;
The rising tomb
20 Shall be our lazy chair;
The place for brave men is the wilderness.
Then, when at last Death finds me out
The sun will not show;
The heavy clouds will sustain their tears
25 And the hushed village shall lie
Under a canopy of ugly vultures.

Oh, do not weep; only
Send my body to the unhallowed ground.
There leave me and weep not
30 Lest you give too much in tears
To one who had so often drawn hot tears
From your sad faces.

Send me to barren spot;
I go alone that had killed so many;
35 I had lived and died a man,
So stripe my hollow face
With white chalk
And let dry leaves be my bed.
Let the drummer move the priestess to madness
40 Whose god shall claim
Honour by my death.
Only do not weep
But leave me there in solitary pride.
Lay me in with no mournful groan;
45 Rather signs of relief should stir the neighbouring grass.
The spirit-world grudges not
My well-won victory.
The souls of my victims shall bow
Before the mighty dread
50 That pushed them untimely
Into eternity.
Now leave me in this barren place
Alone.
My bold spirit shall know no fear.
55 Let no stony cross
Curse this black cemetery; instead, let
The mouldering leaves of neglected shrubs
Hide my proud bones
From the ridiculous eyes of a world
60 I never really loved.

Your tears are well preserved;
You shall need them soon;
For when the story shall be told,
No matter whose death it shall report;
65 Other men shall be dressed in white
And rest their proud heads on rising tombs
Till death
Rends them cut. Then they shall come
Here, where only bold ones
70 In black companionship
Can have a restful bed.

Notes

line 1 *the story* Usually death in the village is announced in a message
narrated by the town-crier and is preceded and concluded by the
beating of a gong.

line 5 A sign of triumph over their victims. Usually at the end of the

232

interminable law suits in Ghanaian courts the successful litigant is seen
dressed in a white headgear and strewn with powder (cf. line 37 below).

line 7 lazy chair Easy chair, so called because of the comfortable posture
its user takes.

line 8 The wilderness has the association of a battle-field and a place
studded with the skulls of dead men.

line 24 sustain their tears Withhold the rain.

line 26 canopy The vault or dome of the heavens.

line 28 Usually witches are not buried in the common village cemetery but in
an isolated patch of ground specifically reserved for them (see line 56
below).

lines 36–38 Describe a rite prepared for witches, making their death-mask a
frightful reminder of their life's activities.

lines 39–41 There is a great deal of rivalry between witches and local fetish
houses. So the death of a witch is celebrated by the priests and
priestesses of these houses as a triumph of their gods.

lines 46–47 His death is deserved because of his wicked life, and his arrival
in the spirit world is welcome to the inhabitants of the world.

lines 55–57 Instead of a sealed concrete grave with a tombstone, the bodies
of witches are casually covered with earth heaped into a mound.

line 68 Rend Renders.

Questions

1 Why is *Death* referred to as finding the speaker out in line 22 of the poem?
2 What do the circumstances surrounding the death and burial of the speaker
contribute to his stature?
3 Give examples of the process of the reversal of normal values in the poem.
4 How does the poet indicate his disapproval of the wizard's occupation?

Commentary

This poem presents one of the fascinating aspects of traditional life in rural
Africa, the person and the activities of the witch or the wizard. It is a praise-
song chanted by the wizard himself, who emerges as an impressive human type
and almost succeeds in winning our admiration for his wicked ways.

Lines 1–21 form a prologue. We are given a clear picture of the extent and
limits of the wizard's power. Because he accepts his own death as unavoidable
he can carry out his sinister activities with self-assurance and without fear. His
type of activity takes on the continuity and recurrence of a natural process.
The opening line, *When the story shall be told*, becomes a bell which tolls relent-
lessly throughout the poem drawing attention to the continuity of the wizard's
activities.

The next thirty-nine lines concentrate on the picture of the speaker's own
imagined death, which, however, in no way signals the end of his type of
activity.

The effect of the poem depends to a large extent on the shock tactics of its
imagery and bold narrative outline: black companions are dressed in white
(lines 4–5), the tomb becomes a lazy chair (lines 6–7), the fruit tree is turned
into firewood (line 13), the canopy of heaven sags with ugly vultures (line 26),
etc.

233

Michael Echeruo

Born in Okigwi, Nigeria, in 1937, Michael J. C. Echeruo was educated at Ibadan University and Cornell in the United States.

Although his work has appeared in several anthologies and he has published a slim volume of poems under the title *Mortality* in 1968, Professor Echeruo regards himself essentially as a teacher and a critic. He has taught at the University of Nigeria, Nsukka and at Ibadan, where he was Professor and Head of Department of English for several years. He is now Vice-Chancellor of Imo State University.

His poetry shows a studied craftsmanship. He virtually hoards words, using them subtly and sparingly and his poems reveal a complex, often ironic, sensibility. He is represented in this anthology by two of his "simpler" poems.

Lullaby

I
now the sun goes down
into the valley
beyond the palms;
the broods will be returning.

5 soon the last cock will crow,
the last clay-pot be stowed,
and the fifth finger licked.

sheep and dogs and kids
beside the hearth
10 sleep beyond all reproach.

II
let fireflies fly
in your eyes
by the playground sands
under a quarter of the moon.

III
15 the sun has died again
in the dark valley
beyond our loves,
beyond the high-arched roots
of the demon-tree.

234

20 then it was your afternoon
   and love was in your eyes.

   now the sun has set;
   the virgin moon is out again –
   a most maidenly quartermoon.

Notes

stanza 1 Note how the change (mentioned in the commentary that follows) is suggested by the following variations on similar statements: line 1 *the sun goes down*, line 15 *the sun has died*, line 22 *the sun has set*. In line 2 *the valley* becomes *the dark valley* in line 16. Also compare line 3 with lines 18 and 19.

line 4 broods The birds with their young.

line 10 beyond all approach In peace and innocence.

line 11 fireflies The glow-worm but, metaphorically, also the sparks of desire in the eyes.

line 14 quarter of the moon The new moon associated with a cycle of desire. If the moon is "responsible", as is often said, for this wave of desire in the female, it is the more ironical that she remains *the virgin moon* in line 23 – which of course underlines the change that man experiences in contrast to the permanence of nature. (See commentary.)

line 19 demon-tree A tropical tree with large dark-green leaves and roots which grow from the branches towards the earth, forming arches.

Questions

1 How successfully does the poet create an African setting in this poem? Identify particular elements.
2 Paying attention to the punctuation and the sounds employed in Section II, comment on the movement of this section and show how it is related to its meaning.
3 What associations do phrases like *the dark valley* and *the demon-tree* have for you? Do they throw some light on the changes suggested by lines 15 and 17?

Commentary

This is one of the most beautifully and subtly built poems, illustrating this poet's careful attention to detail and sense of irony. It centres round two separate but interlocked sequences of time: "time then" and "time now". For the sake of clarity and simplicity we can say that events in "time then" are handled in Section I of the poem, and "time now" is considered in Section III. These two sequences of time are separated by what looks at first sight as simply a period of desire (Section II of the poem), which turns out to be a period of the fulfilment or realisation of desire as well. And therefore instead of separating "time then" and "time now", it interlocks them, making "time now" an inevitable consequence of "time then". Thus, although we have said earlier that Section

235

III considers "time now", it in fact contains lines 20 and 21 which look back to "time then".

The theme of the poem is our desire for permanence in the midst of continuous change. Change is not something imposed upon us by time, although this may seem to be the case. Change is the very fulfilment of our desires. We cannot escape this consequence of our fulfilled desires. Yet we often wish we could because the things which happen outside the control of our human desires seem permanent and continuous. The sun rises in the east and sets in the west every day; its activity seems permanent and continuous.

The activities described in Section I of the poem have the continuity of habit, because they are seen from outside. They are described in the present and present future tense. Section II interposes desire and is appropriately expressed in the subjunctive tense (optative mood). Section III assumes the fulfilment of desire, expressed in the perfect and past tense, and deals with the consequences of that fulfilment. And yet, in the last two lines, this Section, which concentrates on completed action and change, is haunted by the wish for continuity and permanence. Herein lies the irony.

A lullaby is a simple song with a recurrent rhythm directed towards comforting and lulling a child to sleep. It is clearly illustrated by the second and crucial section of the poem. But it is the last two lines which underline the appropriateness of the title of the poem.

Threnody

I saw a dove.
The sky was blue.
The leaves were coming.

The spring dove sang
5 Of Earth's rebirth.
The glorious Sun was warm.

The world was blue
The trees rejoiced
The dove rejoiced with all the world.

10 The sky went cold
When I caught my dove
In the heart of spring.

And I was dead!

Notes

stanza 1 Note the punctuation of this stanza, which makes each line a separate self-contained statement of fact. Compare it, for instance with the punctuation of the third stanza, where there are two run-on lines.

line 1 Because of its use in Old Testament sacrificial rites, the *dove* has associations of innocence and purity. Something of the latter quality is certainly suggested by the dove seen on a clear sunlit day in this stanza.

stanza 4 This stanza also has run-on lines, but note the effect which the subordinate clause, in the middle, has on the movement of the stanza.

lines 10–11 Note that the change which comes follows the speaker's action in catching the dove.

Questions

1 What happens in stanza 4 and what light does this throw on the meaning of the speaker's death in the last line?

2 In view of the speaker's death, does the dove symbolise innocence or stand for something else?

Commentary

A threnody is a dirge or a song of mourning. But until the very last, surprising line this poem mentions no cause for sorrow or sadness. It is true that we get a slight suggestion of a change from the joyful events of the first three stanzas in line 10, when the sky goes cold. But even this event springs, strangely enough, from what would seem a harmless youthful adventure: i.e. bird catching – an adventure which should yield a keen sense of achievement and fulfilment. Hence it is with a shock of surprise and a sense of bafflement that the last line announces the cause for sorrow and mourning, *And I was dead!* We could understand the dove dying, arrested in the midst of its rejoicing with the rest of the world. But that in the midst of the speaker's keenly enjoyed adventure death should come upon him is a paradox. What needs to be explored is the technique by which the poet prepares for this paradoxical statement.

This is a poem in which words are sparingly used. Each stanza carefully takes or inherits material from the previous one and builds upon it. For instance, there is a world of difference between lines 2 and 7 although they seem to be saying the same thing. In line 1 we have simply *a dove*, but this becomes *the spring dove* in line 4, and finally *my dove* in the crucial line 11. *Spring* in line 4 draws together the implications of the blue sky and the coming leaves and the singing bird of the first stanza. In this manner line 9, the longest line in the poem, is a telling summary of the world of the poem before the change begins in line 10. It is exploring along these lines that brings us to the meaning or identity of the *I* in the poem and the discovery of his death in the last line.

Kalu Uka

Kalu Uka was born in 1938 in the Bende division of Imo State of Nigeria. He was educated at Hope Waddell Training Institute, Calabar, the University College, Ibadan and Toronto University in Canada. He worked for a brief period with the former Nigerian Broadcasting Corporation. Since he finished his graduate studies in Canada he has taught in the University of Leeds, England and the University of Nigeria, Nsukka and is at present Professor of Drama and Head of the department of Theatre Arts, University of Calabar, Nigeria.

Although Professor Uka is a significant and published poet and novelist, his interest is more in drama. For many years he was head of the drama section of the Department of English, University of Nigeria and was the moving spirit behind the feverish dramatic activity at Nsukka between the end of the Nigerian civil war and two years ago when he left. Playwright and actor, he acted in, directed and produced numerous plays in that period. A creative producer, his experimental techniques yield delightful insights into his productions.

His publications include: a collection of poems, *Earth to Earth* from which the poems in this anthology are taken, plays *Ikhama* and *A Harvest of Ants*, a dramatic adaptation of Achebe's *Arrow of God* and two novels, *A Consummation of Fire* and *Colonel Ben Brim*. His poems are interesting for the way in which he is concerned with the essence of poetry, used to communicate an idea, vision or feeling through imagery and sensitive interplay of words. He does not feel obliged to pay homage to his African heritage, and yet his roots are obvious.

Fear

Last night I heard – it was not in a dream
the sound of hollow drums and harsh trumpets
as if a village was marching to a graveyard,
last night, when I pasted my ear to the wind
5 and tasted the spice of eternity on my lips
I had really turned my mind away into fear.

The night grew colder and colder beneath
the blankets and I knew love is always
a thing of wounds, of hurts and smarts,
10 but fear my countrymen do not understand
and so in the sound of hollow drums and harsh flutes
we trudge on through silence to eternity.

Only the thunder will revive the drums and flutes
we travellers love so much when they arrive
15 to warn us, when they whirl from behind
that beautiful shining orphan mountain.

Oh, do not mind this song of flutes and drums
think only of the little stars strung round cradles
think only of the light whose crest we must reach
20 in the blind rage of the spark divine, think of it,
and night sounds shall be only the anger chained
within our breasts, dark like the deep grave
where souls are pasted to eternity and know not fear!

Notes

line 2   *hollow* and *harsh*   Aptly describe the sounds of the musical
        instruments they qualify, but they also carry some ominous suggestions.
        Note that in the second stanza these suggestions seem to have changed.

line 5   Thought of the graveyard immediately makes him think of not dying,
        of living long. This is part of the crux of fear.

line 9   *smarts*   Here means acute pain. The general sense of the line is that
        the poet realises that love always causes pain and anxiety.

line 13   The *thunder* is a symbol of destruction. A sense of stupor is implied
        in the preceding stanza. The *thunder* shakes this off and makes men
        think of the essence and purpose of life.

line 14   *we travellers*   Metaphorical reference to man's life in the world. We
        are all on a long journey in this world.

line 15   To *whirl* connotes swift giddy motion especially that which involves
        some type of swinging or circular movement. Picturesque and adequate
        description of thunder and lightning.

line 16   *orphan*   Here means lonely. There is something terrifying in the
        association of thunder with beauty.

line 18   The image is that of children with all the anxiety and hope which
        they cause.

line 19   Metaphorical for human ambition which drives man on to achieve the
        highest. *Crest* means the top or apex.

line 20   *the blind rage of the spark divine*   Confirms line 19, as it refers to the
        determined inspiration with which man pursues his goal.

Questions

1 What strikes you about the opening of this poem, especially the first line?
2 Why is the idea of love introduced in the second stanza. Do you think it is
   relevant?
3 The word *eternity* occurs three times. How is it used on the three different
   occasions? Can you pick out some other repetitions in the poem and say
   what you think their effects are?
4 Attempt a simple paraphrase of the last stanza and bring out the main idea
   which the poet states there. Pay particular attention to the last three lines.

This poem starts by giving the impression that the poet is going to tell us about fear in the form of the painful emotional reaction to some physical danger or violence. But we soon learn that this common-place notion is not the poet's concern, and he directs our thoughts to the type of fear that bothers him. Through the central images of the grave, drums, trumpets and flutes, we realise that the poet is directing our minds to a more fundamental and universal kind of fear: fear of the unknown and of failure, the nagging thought of life and how to preserve it, the futility of this indulgence, the hope and the anxiety which accompany it and the distracting torments of man's ambition. The musical instruments and the grave that first serve to introduce us to common "fear" soon lead us away from it. The crucial paradox is that the grave is both the image of fear and its liberation. We fear death, yet it is death that releases us from fear.

Earth to earth

As if men hung here unblown,
Their mildewed buds of love like pollen
Late caught, damp in a swollen
Drop of rain; or, like the hot
5 Tear that chills a fevered pit
After heads into bodies suckt

Like urine into parched earth
Or ancestral wine into scorched hearth,
And wear ashes and shrivelled petals,

10 Comes this season of the cassia flower,
And pent passion peers through the bower;
Comes this season, and all labour is fallen
All earthen pitcher as china broken.

Wooing was our labour then,
15 A trouble-wrapped chrysalis
Grown in the pause taken
Between that visit and this.

The ripest moment is saddest encounter
Performed without banter
20 In memory of other seasons
Of a lived love now still.

We let this one die;
We let cobwebs sweep
A skein over her face –

25 On a morning, dewdrops
Are tossed, earth to earth,
Like a veil and a shroud
Over ground imprinted by wooing feet.

Notes

lines 1–2   The metaphor and simile used here are subtle. Men are seen as
pollens of flowers (the male fertilising element in flowers) and two ideas
are immediately suggested: the idea of love that is diseased and must die
(*mildewed buds of love*) and the idea of death (because pollen is
vulnerable to dispersal by wind); men are vulnerable to emotional pangs.

lines 4–5   There seems to be some paradox here because *hot tear*(s) (the tears
of the mourners) will not normally be expected to cool down a fevered
pit.

line 6   This refers to death and the grave. Notice the finality implied in the
preferred spelling of *suckt* here. This is almost a phonetic spelling
deliberately used for effect.

line 7   parched earth   Hot and dry, thirsty earth.

line 8   scorched hearth   Fireplace that has been burnt by heat. Note its
association with ancestral. Contrast in value and quality is implied in
the use of *urine* and *wine*.

line 10   cassia   A large plant that has profuse foliage and produces beautiful
yellow or purple flowers. The metaphor of season here refers to the lady
in her bloom or youth. The second season used in this stanza refers to
her "death" in the poet's mind.

line 13   The image here is that of a large pot breaking to pieces. Again the
idea implied here is death. The use of *earthen* is symbolic when we
think of the title of the poem. All the lover's hopes and attempts to
nurture his love for the girl are dashed.

line 15   chrysalis   The pupa stage of the development of a full insect. It is
usually encased in some protective covering. This line then refers to the
adolescence of the lady. But there is an ominous note because the
chrysalis is *trouble-wrapped*. The young girl was a bundle of deceit, the
cause of much trouble and misery.

line 18   Ripeness is the point when something is fully developed and ready
to be harvested. The lady "died" when she was ripest and the last
meeting between the two lovers is this occasion of her death. cf.
Soyinka's "Abiku" line 29.

lines 22–24   Notice the tone of contempt and disregard. She only deserves to
be forgotten and discarded. Very casual attitude.

lines 25–26   This last stanza takes us to the first. The poet sees the falling
of *dewdrops* that have settled on leaves as the last rite of throwing sand
into the grave during burial. The occasion is the morning following her
"death" or the end of his love for her.

241

lines 27–28 These images describe a dewy morning. A *veil* is a light transparent material used to cover or protect a surface. It is used by women, especially during weddings. A *shroud* on the other hand is a winding-sheet or cloth used in wrapping a corpse. Like *veil* it entails covering and concealing, but it carries the suggestion of death.

There is paradox here. The dewdrops represent both veil and shroud. *Veil* for the new love she has found and *shroud* to cover her corpse because she is metaphorically dead to the poet. Notice that it is dewdrops that are tossed not earth or sand as in a real burial ceremony.

Questions

1 Up to line 18 it can be said that the poet uses end-rhymes to aid his meaning; but the effect of these rhymes seems to be most obviously felt in lines 3–6. What do you think is achieved here?
2 How does the poet indicate the idea of growth in this poem?
3 What do you think is the place of stanza 6 in this poem? (Notice the change in tone and attitude and the use of *we*.)
4 How adequate do you find the title of this poem? What has happened in the last stanza?

Commentary

The title, taken from the symbolic ceremonial utterance of the priest during a funeral, announces the dominant theme of mortality in the poem which is an elegy commemorating the early "death" of a loved one. This attitude is clearly articulated in the statement of vulnerability of the opening line. The beauty of the poem lies in the way in which the idea of "death" is insidiously suggested. The poet works through a number of images (pollens and flowers, season and dew) and employs a number of carefully worked out techniques (paradox, pun and ambivalence, sound patterns consisting of end-rhyme schemes and internal rhymes) to create an experience for the reader.

An interestingly striking feature of this poem is its structure which reinforces the meaning of the poem. The first two stanzas immediately hint at the idea of death and burial (*a fevered pit* refers to the grave), the next four stanzas take us to the time of the lady's life, her beauty and the passionate but brief love, and the final stanza take us back to the idea of death and burial and through the image of dewdrops unites this final rite with the love which the poet has for the lady.

The death which the poet writes about here is, in fact, symbolic, not real. The poet has been jilted or has had a bad experience with a young girl he adored and for him she is dead and buried. In a curious way, this is a sad love poem beautifully executed.

Taban Lo Liyong

Taban Lo Liyong is an engaging Southern Sudanese poet. Born before 1939 in Kajokaji, of the Bari–speaking group in the Kuku tribe, to Southern Sudanese and Ugandan parents, he grew up mostly in Uganda. He studied at Howard University and the University of Iowa in the United States. He has taught at the Universities of Nairobi and Papua, New Guinea where he did a lot to awaken the people to the rich heritage of their oral literature. He is at present teaching in the University of Juba, Sudan. He has a long-term interest in the traditional literature of Africa and has done much research in the oral literature of the Luo and Masaai for which he has a healthy respect. Its artistic essence is displayed in his own work in the light of contemporary experience. Much of his energy is now spent working on Sudanese oral literature and arousing the awareness of the people just as he had done in East Africa and Papua, New Guinea.

Liyong's subtle poetry has some other interesting qualities: his love of words, striking images, a liking for epigrams, a singular use of punctuation and a strong dose of cynicism and humour. He writes about society and its ills: his own, Africa's and world society. His subjects range from life to politics, sex, religion, economics, and different forms of delusions. Throughout his works, we get the impression of an alert intelligence and a strong mind that is convinced about its mission. His publications include two collections of oral literature and short stories: *Fixions* and *Eating Chiefs* and the following collections of poetry: *Franz Fanons Uneven Ribs* and *Another Nigger Dead*. Others are *East African Popular Literature, The Last Word, Thirteen Offensives* and *Meditations of Taban Lo Liyong*.

With purity hath nothing been won

with purity hath nothing been won
greece came not thru purity
christ died through the impure
only with impurity hath japan moved ahead
5 the american beast came about through things impure
purity kills creativity in the womb
impurity spreads with health
eve ate the apple for impuritys sake
my heart bless thyself
10 thou truckest not with things that are pure
impurity fills you up like angels of god

243

thou art greater than earth and hell
for impurity limiteth the child in the cradle
impurity is boundless like my soul

Notes

line 2 greece Became great through the conquest and destruction of lesser
states around it.

line 3 The betrayal and crucifixion of Christ were terrible acts but they are
now the corner-stone of the Christian religion.

line 4 Japan suffered greatly during the Second World War, particularly
with the devastation of Hiroshima. But Japan recovered to become a
leading industrial and economic power. Besides, the greatness of Japan
today is known to be based on technology which she unashamedly
"stole" and copied from others. Japan improved on what she obtained
dishonestly and is today a leading country in the world.

line 5 the american beast This refers to the American nation that was
created out of slave labour, the subjugation of races other than the
Caucasians and the dispossession of the American Indians. A big,
powerful and rich country that makes no apology for using her might
anywhere.

line 8 This is from biblical legend. The apple which Eve ate gave her
knowledge which is seen as evil, and later as disobedience. This was
what led to man's estrangement from God.

line 9 Notice the change in tone, rhythm and attitude. The emphasis now
seems to be an ironic reference to purity.

line 10 To *truck with* means to deal with in the sense of exchanging one
thing for another. To trade or bargain with.

Commentary

This poem is taken from Liyong's second volume of poetry, *Another Nigger Dead*,
a reference to the off-hand dismissal, callousness or indifference with which
white racists in America regard the news of the death of a black man. Its cynical
exploration of the opposition between purity and impurity is characteristic of
both his style and his preoccupations. He plays on the contrasting meanings of
the two words and the ironic bite of the poem is in how good, indeed, comes
out of evil and how it is that evil thrives. There is a strong sense in which this
cynical poem goes to the heart of the paradox and inscrutable outcome of events
in life. Why do the just suffer and the evil prosper? This is a riddle which
Christians have not been able to unravel. All manner of greatness has been
achieved through the exploitation and subjugation of others, through conquest
and the destruction that goes with it, through acts of terror far removed from
purity. Even creativity attempts to make order out of chaos. The negative forces
seem to be strong and the means to greatness.

It would seem, then, that the poem supports evil, since his images give weight
to the argument. But Liyong is not approving of impurity as such. He is reaching
for the irony at the heart of the world and urging that Africans should seize
it and make the best of it just as the rest of the world has done instead of being

limited and emasculated by thought of good and propriety. The rest of the poem is an exploration of the first line. But the sting is in the last two lines. This is a moralistic poem and the religious flavour of the language is compatible with the theme. Impurity is used here to refer to different types of evil, very much like the biblical usage. This poem reminds one of William Blake's *The Marriage of Heaven and Hell*.

Language is a figure of speech

IX
Never talk of right and wrong to me
Nor of left and right when I'm near.
We stand
On a facet of iceberg
5 Left is not right
Our heads pierce up
And our feet nail us down
Spectacles can't make us see
Down below is quite tartarian
10 What shall we name
What we cannot see or know?

X
The hand had five fingers
And they were equally short

But one finger out of spite
15 Decided to add an inch
To raise him above Dickenharry

The others, out of aggrandisement
Imitated likewise
The competition
20 No sooner begun
Than ever will end

One finger added more breadth
Than height and another
Shrunk out of former size
25 In order to show them
What can be achieved
With a little trying.

XI

This hunter was my neighbour
One day he went to wash in the river
30 While putting his trousers on
He failed to balance steadily
On the right foot
And his left foot muffled by the trouser leg
Stumbled into the muddy water

35 Realising that the trousers
Had not drunk water for a long time
And therefore were naturally thirsty
He told them to drink away
To their heart's content.

40 With this resolution made
My hunter friend sat down in the muddy water
Whereupon the trousers were mighty glad
And drank water to saturation.

Notes

line 9 tartarian Here means dangerous, destructive.

line 16 Dickenharry Lo Liyong is fond of coining words and this is one of them. It is a conflation or shortened form of the last two names in the expression "every Tom, Dick and Harry", referring to common or ordinary things or people.

line 17 aggrandisement Desire to increase in size and magnify power, wealth or rank.

line 33 To *muffle* something is to wrap it up to prevent it from speaking. The left foot is *muffled* because it is stuck in the trouser and cannot get through to the ground, hence the hunter stumbles.

Questions

1 In what ways would you call this poetry?
2 What influences of oral African poetry can you trace here? Discuss fully.
3 Do you think the short anecdotes here are symbolic? If so, attempt some interpretations of their symbolic natures.

Commentary

These are three movements of a long poem which treats diverse scenes dealing with man in society. There are swift changes of moods and themes, but the whole is united by the tone, the sense of concern and the patterns the poet weaves with language. Note the narrative form of the poem, its homely attitude and the speaking-voice tone and rhythm, the use of proverbs, and the parables and tales which drive home its message. Two indispensable aspects of its style are its pleasing simplicity and cynical humour.

Oswald Mbuyiseni Mtshali

Oswald Mbuyiseni Mtshali is one of the most talented black South African poets writing today. He was born in 1940 in Vryheid, Natal, where he had all his early education. Like most young people of his age he left for Johannesburg after matriculation. He was not merely drawn there by the bright lights; he had a serious purpose. He wanted to gain admission into the University of Witwatersrand. But the long arm of apartheid caught up with him. He could not be admitted and he had to content himself with earning a living. He lives in Soweto, a "Bantu location" and suburb of Johannesburg.

Mtshali's first published volume of poems with the symbolic title *Sounds of a Cowhide Drum* was issued in 1971. It was an immediate success which at once singled him out as a significant poet. He later studied in the United States where he took an M.A. He now teaches at Pace College – a model College sponsored by the United States government – in Soweto. He has published a second volume of poems, *Fire Flames*.

Mtshali writes about a people, a life and a hostile society he knows very well and has experienced. Few poets have so shrewdly and subtly hammered on the theme of survival. The great quality of Mtshali's poetry is its colloquial tone and control; the emotions are never indulged and allowed to run away with the poet when he is writing about the sufferings of his people. Rather, his theme is conveyed through distilled lyrical verse and ironic humour. And this is what gives the poetry its credibility, an engaging simplicity that enables it to make its points through cutting irony and cynicism.

Amagoduka at Glencoe Station

We travelled a long journey
through the wattle forests of Vryheid,
crossed the low-levelled Blood River
whose water flowed languidly
5   as if dispirited for the
shattered glory of my ancestors.

We passed the coalfields of Dundee –
blackheads in the wrinkled face
of Northern Zululand –
10   until our train ultimately came
to a hissing stop at Glencoe.

Many people got off
leaving the enraged train
to snort and charge at the night
15 on its way to Durban.

The time was 8 pm.

I picked up my suitcase,
sagging under the weight of a heavy overcoat
I shambled to the "non-European Males" waiting room.

20 The room was crowded
the air hung, a pall of choking odour,
rotten meat, tobacco and sour beer.

Windows were shut tight
against the sharp bite of winter.

25 Amagoduka sat on bare floor
their faces sucking the warmth
of the coal fire crackling in the corner.

They chewed dried bread
scooped corned beef with rusty knives,
30 and drank mqombothi from the plastic can
which they passed from mouth to mouth.

They spoke animatedly
and laughed in thunderous peals.

A girl peeped through the door,
35 they shuddered at the sudden cold blast,
jumped up to fondle and leer at her
"Hau! ngena Sisi! – Oh! come in sister!"

She shied like a frightened filly
banged the door and bolted.

40 They broke into a tumultuous laughter.

One of them picked up a guitar
plucked it with broken finger nails
caressed its strings with a castor oil bottle –

it sighed like a jilted girl.
45 "You play down! Phansi! Play D" he whispered.

Another joined in with a concertina,
its sound fluttered in flowery notes
like a butterfly picking pollen from flower to flower.

The two began to sing,
50 their voices crying for the mountains
and the hills of Msinga, stripped naked of
their green garment.

They crossed rivers and streams,
gouged dry by the sun rays,
55 where lowing cattle genuflected
for a blade of grass and a drop of water
on riverbeds littered with carcasses and bones.

They spoke of hollow-cheeked maidens
heaving drums of brackish water
60 from a far away fountain.

They told of big-bellied babies
sucking festering fingers
instead of their mothers' shrivelled breasts.

Two cockroaches
65 as big as my overcoat buttons
jived across the floor
snatched meat and bread crumbs
and scurried back to their hideout.

The whole group joined in unison:
70 curious eyes peered through frosted windows
"Ekhaya bafowethu! – Home brothers!"

We come from across the Tugela river,
we are going to EGoli! EGoli! EGoli!
where they'll turn us into moles
75 that eat the gold dust
and spit out blood.

We'll live in compounds
where young men are pampered
into partners for older men.

80 We'll visit shebeens
where a whore waits for a fee
to leave your balls burning
with syphilitic fire.

If the gods are with us –
85 Oh! beloved black gods of our forefathers
What have we done to you
Why have you forsaken us –
We'll return home
to find our wives nursing babies –
90 unknown to us
but only to their mothers and loafers.

Notes

line 3   *Blood River*   Named after the famous battle in which Boers defeated the Zulus in 1838.

lines 4–6   The Zulus were a great and war-like people who under Chaka strenuously resisted white incursion before they were finally conquered. That conquest was a great blow to their pride.

lines 7–9   Figurative description of the landscape dotted by black coal fields.

lines 12–14   Note the use of "intensifiers" which carry the force of images. They create a strong visual impression.

line 15   The amagoduka must change at Glencoe Station.

line 19   *shamble*   To walk awkwardly.

line 21   *pall*   Something heavy or dark which hangs over or covers.

line 25   *Amagoduka*   Mine labour recruits

line 30   *mqombothi*   A local Zulu beer

line 36   *leer*   An unpleasant smile or sideways look that expresses rudeness or sexual desire.

line 38   *filly*   Young female horse

line 40   Their mirthfulness is ironical because it only serves to portray in bold relief the agony of their suffering and endurance. The communal feeling they have here is induced by a fellowship of suffering. This picture is clearly supported by the mournful tune of the music they played.

line 46   *concertina*   Small musical wind instrument like an accordion held and played in the hands by pressing it from both ends.

lines 47–48   Striking use of alliteration.

lines 50–52   Picture of a wasted part of the country, rocky and infertile; harsh topography.
   Msinga   A town in the mountainous part of Natal Province.

line 54   *gouged*   A gouge is an instrument for cutting out hollow areas in wood. The action is performed on the river beds by drought as an agent of erosion.

lines 49–63   One of the ills and methods of apartheid is the confinement of the blacks to the geographically unproductive part of South Africa. The result is hunger, thirst, malnutrition, disease and death of both livestock and human beings. These are the features the amagoduka remember of their homes in their songs.

line 66   *jived*   Danced. Jive is a kind of dance music.

line 72   *Tugela river*   Separates Zululand from the rest of Natal Province.

line 73   *EGoli*   Means "gold". It is the popular African name for Johannesburg where South African gold is mined.

line 74   mole A small insect-eating animal with very small eyes and soft dark fur, which digs holes and passages underground and lives there.
Reference here is to the miners' work in the pits; it is dangerous to their health. Silicosis is common.
lines 77–79 Mine workers in South Africa live in dormitory-like quarters away from their homes and wives. Homosexual acts are common.
line 80   shebeens Illegal drinking places, especially where locally brewed hard alcoholic drinks are sold. Depressing picture of the life they are forced to live.
line 81   whore Woman of easy virtue who offers sex for money.
line 82   balls Testicles.
line 83   syphilitic From syphilis, a serious and deadly venereal disease which can be transmitted by sexual intercourse and inheritance.
lines 85–87 Cry of despair; expressing feeling of being abandoned by their guardian gods and the government that so mistreats them.
lines 88–90 A serious hazard of apartheid is the disruption of family life and the encouragement of casual sex.

Questions

1 What particular aspects of apartheid does Mtshali bring out in this poem?
2 Compare this poem to Jacinto's "Letter to a contract worker".
3 Discuss Mtshali's critical attitude in this poem and demonstrate the particular techniques he employs.

Commentary

Protest takes many forms. The most obvious one is that which directly inveighs against some evil practice. Another form is that which seemingly sets out to narrate experiences common to people suffering deprivation and other conditions which the critic wants to highlight without making any comments. This is more subtle. It is what Mtshali does in this narrative poem.

Ostensibly, the poem tells the story of mine workers who are on their way to Johannesburg. But right from the first stanza we are fully aware that the poem is bemoaning the humiliation and despoliation that have overtaken a once-proud people. There are two perspectives in the poem both of which are deliberately manipulated to give the impression of distance and objectivity. The first is an apparently harmless narration of the journey up to Glencoe Station and a graphic description of this miserable lot huddled in a segregated waiting room and beguiling the time. The second is the mournful duet sung by two of the group and the song the group sang in unison. The songs are particularly touching and effective. In them the singers make imaginative trips to their home-lands. The strong irony is that this is not a nostalgic longing for a place that brings happy memories but an instinctive reference to the place of their birth which they can only associate with suffering.

Through these techniques, added to vivid descriptions, powerful use of language in such a way that single words conjure the force of images, use of imagery, dark humour and a certain matter-of-fact attitude, Mtshali makes devastating criticisms of apartheid.

An abandoned bundle

The morning mist
and chimney smoke
of White City Jabavu
flowed thick yellow
5 as pus oozing
from a gigantic sore.

It smothered our little houses
like fish caught in a net.

Scavenging dogs
10 draped in red bandanas of blood
fought fiercely
for a squirming bundle.

I threw a brick;
they bared fangs
15 flicked velvet tongues of scarlet
and scurried away,
leaving a mutilated corpse –
an infant dumped on a rubbish heap –
"Oh! Baby in the Manger
20 sleep well
on human dung."

Its mother
had melted into the rays of the rising sun,
her face glittering with innocence
25 her heart as pure as untrampled dew.

Notes

line 3 Life in South Africa is highly regimented, with numerous restrictions
imposed, especially on the blacks. However, *White City Jabavu* (cf. Sun
City: a resort city in the South African black homeland of Bophota
Tswana used as a holiday centre by South African whites, a city devoted
to sensual pleasures very much like Hollywood) is an exception. Here all
racial distinctions disappear and all cats are grey. It is a fun city, like an
oasis in a desert, where there are no restrictions on social intercourse
based on colour, race, etc. By the same token it is a place of organised
moral laxity where women, especially black girls who have been so
reduced by apartheid and harsh social conditions, offer themselves for
money to live. Naturally, unwanted babies are born. Because they are an
insupportable nuisance they are dumped by their mothers whose
consciences have been destroyed by the society and the sheer struggle
for survival.

lines 4–6 Image of sickness and disease which has engulfed the country. It is a city of sin and moral degeneracy with no compunctions. This is a vivid picture of the moral disease – apartheid – that is ravaging South Africa.

line 10 *bandana* Richly coloured yellow or white spotted large handkerchief worn round the head or the neck.

line 12 *squirm* To writhe and twist.

line 15 Description of both the texture and colour of the dogs' tongues.

line 16 *scurry* To hurry with short quick steps.

line 17 *mutilate* To damage or destroy by removing parts of.

lines 19–21 There is sharp and biting irony in this disturbing comparison between Christ, the young and innocent baby in the manger, protected and worshipped by the whole world of man and nature and this equally innocent but unlucky child abandoned by a heartless woman to be devoured by dogs.

lines 22–25 The sharp contrast here between the pretended innocence of the lady and the heinous crime she has committed is well brought out by the nature imagery: *the rising sun* and *pure as untramelled dew*. These are symbols of a new day. She is ready to start her life of sin all over again as if nothing had happened.

Questions

1 Discuss the effectiveness of the imagery of the first stanza of this poem.

2 How does Mtshali manage to make his presentation of this scene so memorable?

3 Discuss the suggestion that this poem is a "metaphor of apartheid". Start by explaining what you understand by the term "metaphor of apartheid".

4 Comment on the action of the mother in the last stanza. Do you think Mtshali intends some other implications in this presentation?

Commentary

As a description of a scene, this is one of the most graphic of Mtshali's poems. But the poem goes beyond mere description. A striking feature of Mtshali's battle against apartheid and other forms of social injustice is the way he concentrates his poems on specific situations, using his irony and detached attitude to direct the attention of the reader and imply his larger concern, apartheid.

This poem demonstrates Mtshali's deft accusatory depiction of urban scenes, for it is the evil city that has bred the deviant mother in the poem. He uses the blood-chilling scene to show his outrage at the heartlessness and immorality of the city. In the particular case of South Africa, the mother in this poem is a typical victim of an unjust and sick society, while the abandoned bundle represents the cheapening of human life that is evident everywhere. On another level, the scene could also represent the savage treatment which the blacks – the abandoned bundle – receive at the hands of the whites who feel no twinge of conscience in their wild acts. It is there in the progression of the poem from the sickness and evil of the first stanza to the pretended innocence and justness of the last stanza. For Mtshali is the poet of the urban landscape of apartheid.

The birth of Shaka

His baby cry
was of a cub
tearing the neck
of the lioness
5 because he was fatherless.

The gods
boiled his blood
in a clay pot of passion
to course in his veins.

10 His heart was shaped into an ox shield
to foil every foe.

Ancestors forged
his muscles into
thongs as tough
15 as wattle bark

and nerves
as sharp as
syringa thorns.

His eyes were lanterns
20 that shone from the dark valleys of Zululand
to see white swallows
coming across the sea.
His cry to two assassin brothers:

"Lo! you can kill me
25 but you'll never rule this land!"

Notes

Title Note the spelling 'Shaka' as opposed to Senghor's 'Chaka'. 'Shaka' is
  closer to the original Zulu name.

lines 1–5 The infant Shaka is compared to a *cub*. The frightening ferocity
  which the young lion displays are signs of impatience and studied
  wildness because the controlling manly presence was absent. The cub is
  said to be *fatherless*. The parallel to Shaka whose parents separated
  when he was young and who therefore, presumably, grew up without the
  restraining influence of a father is clear. He developed an uncontrollable
  temper either because of the need to survive in a harsh environment or
  as a psychological reaction to some deprivation. It is conceivable to see
  in this metaphor a reference to the contemporary situation of many young

black children in South Africa, who having lost their fathers to the apartheid regime, grow up in anger and frustration and exhibit what may seem reckless courage.

lines 6–9 Shaka was said to possess such fierce courage, temper, leadership ability and military prowess that everything about him was larger than life. In traditional African societies and in African metaphysics it is believed great warriors and important social figures are fortified and protected by being "cooked" by the medicine-man – a process which makes them supernatural, invincible and indestructible by human agencies. That the gods themselves *boiled his blood/in a clay pot of passion* intensifies whatever passionate qualities he had and marked him as a man apart.

line 10 The martial outfit of a Zulu warrior consisted of shield and spear. This is a figurative way of expressing his bravery.

line 14 thongs Narrow strips of leather used as a fastening, sometimes plaited for use as a whiplash.

line 15 wattle Tough twigs from Australian acacia woven together to make fences, roofs, walls. The bark of the Australian and New Zealand species of the wattle plant is used for tanning leather. The general idea is to show Shaka as physically well-built and tough.

line 18 syringa thorns A syringa is a shrub that has fragrant white, pink or purplish flowers in clusters and thorns. It is also known as a mock orange.

lines 19–20 His fierce and bright eyes agree with the general image of him painted in the poem. These lines remind us of Blake's poem "The Tyger":

> Tyger! Tyger! burning bright
> In the forests of the night
> What immortal hand or eye
> Could frame thy fearful symmetry?
>
> In what distant deeps or skies
> Burnt the fire of thine eyes?
> On what wing dare he aspire?
> What the hand dare seize the fire?

line 21 Swallows are migratory birds which go to the northern hemisphere in summer. *White swallows* here refer to the Europeans (Boers) who came to colonise Zululand (South Africa). The use of *dark valleys of Zululand* (line 20) and *white swallows* has obvious racial overtones.

line 23 Shaka was treacherously assassinated by his two brothers Dingaan and Mhlangana. His death led to rivalry for kingship between the two brothers and the gradual decadence of the proud and invincible nation created by Shaka. Dingaan executed Mhlangana and was crowned king. But his kingdom was a pale shadow of that for which he committed murders. It was later annexed by the British.

line 24–25 This defiant cry that summarises Shaka's bravery and patriotism refers to both his address to his two assassin brothers and a prophetic expression of eventual defeat for the white colonisers who have taken over the people's land and subjected them to inhuman treatment. This is a cry of hope.

Questions

1 How appropriate do you find the title of this poem?
2 There is a strong background of traditional praise poetry in this poem. Compare the poem to any one praise poem of your people.
3 What particular poetic techniques does Mtshali employ in this poem and how does this piece bear out the popular theme of his poetry?

Commentary

Shaka was the most memorable and legendary Zulu warrior that lived in the nineteenth century. He came from a noble family; his father Senzangokhan was a chief and his mother wielded power and influence in the society. He served his military tutelage under Dingiswayo and succeeded his father as king of the Zulus. He was as mighty in stature as he was in war. He was notorious for his fierce temper and his ruthless and merciless execution of his wars. So extraordinary were his exploits that he was thought to possess supernatural qualities and powers and became a myth in his lifetime.

But Shaka is noted for specific great acts. He was a great leader of men and soldiers. He was the first military leader and strategist of his time to organise his soldiers into "impis" that were equivalent to the battalions of sophisticated modern armies. He was a great nation and empire builder and annexed small satellite states into a large Zulu kingdom. But, perhaps, his most meritorious act, that has lingered in the imagination of contemporary South Africans and, indeed, all black Africans, was his daring and bold resistance of the incursion of white colonisers. Shaka thus became a symbol of the greatness of the blacks and the defence of their land against white usurpers and predators. He is easily invoked as a source of inspiration and example to oppressed Africans who are fighting the forces of their destruction. Shaka was a unique historical character and the various accounts of him in oral tradition and written accounts show him as both statesman and brute and hover between fiction and reality, leaning more to larger than life figuration. Shaka's successes, naturally, brought him envy and he was betrayed by his brothers and colleagues who murdered him.

In literature epic heroes like Shaka are reputed to have mysterious ancestries and exhibit extraordinary physical and mental qualities which agree with this conceived supernatural nature. This poem, which is a celebration of both the historical and legendary Shaka, fits into this scheme and is modelled on traditional praise poetry. Indeed, in this case, there are clear evidences of Mtshali's debt to the Zulu *Izibongo* (praise-poem). The poem is a series of metaphors and similes of rage, sheer might, weaponry and fierce animals which emphasize Shaka's mysterious physical and moral strength signified in his supernaturally toughened brave heart, tough muscles and nerves. Praise is heaped upon praise right from the beginning of the poem but "the cry" that begins and ends the poem provides both thematic and structural guideposts.

Nightfall in Soweto

Nightfall comes like
a dreaded disease
seeping through the pores
of a healthy body
5 and ravaging it beyond repair.

A murderer's hand,
lurking in the shadows,
clasping the dagger,
strikes down the helpless victim.

10 I am the victim.
I am slaughtered
every night in the streets.
I am cornered by the fear
gnawing at my timid heart;
15 in my helplessness I languish.

Man has ceased to be man
Man has become beast
Man has become prey.

I am the prey;
20 I am the quarry to be run down
by the marauding beast
let loose by cruel nightfall
from his cage of death.

Where is my refuge?
25 Where am I safe?
Not in my matchbox house
Where I barricade myself against nightfall.

I tremble at his crunching footsteps,
I quake at his deafening knock at the door.
30 "Open up!" he barks like a rabid dog
thirsty for my blood.

Nightfall! Nightfall!
You are my mortal enemy.
But why were you ever created?
35 Why can't it be daytime?
Daytime forever more?

Notes

line 5 To *ravage* is to plunder or destroy. The image here is apt since disease destroys a previously healthy body. To *ravage beyond repair* is to damage permanently so that the body cannot be restored to its earlier form. Psychological damage is also implied here.

line 7 To *lurk* is to hang around in a hiding place ready to do some mischief. Petty murderers would do this.

line 14 To *gnaw* is to wear away by biting off a bit at a time. This stanza is an elaboration of the metaphor "dying by inches". Psychological death is meant here, caused by fear which discourages the heart.

line 15 To *languish* means to become feeble and ineffective because of depressing conditions.

lines 16–18 A telling transformation in the animal imagery takes place here. The savage white law officers have become beasts and the blacks less than men because they have been dehumanised.

lines 20–21 A *quarry* is an object of pursuit by a predatory animal or a hunter. A *marauding beast* is an animal that prowls about for plunder. In this context, it refers to the law-officers of South Africa.

lines 22–23 This is a striking image. Notice the personification of nightfall. The impression is that in the uncertain circumstances in which the blacks live death is always lurking around. But it is held in check in day-time; it is caged in the sense that some restraint is exercised. At night, when these officers usually hunt down their suspects, there are no restraints.

line 24 A *refuge* is a place or structure, or even a person, that provides shelter and succour to one who is either in danger or being pursued. The fragile shack which the poet lives in can ill-provide such protection. Notice that nightfall has become synonymous with horrors against which the poet barricades himself.

line 28   crunching Describes the grinding sound which the thick boots of the officer makes as he strides along. It is interesting that nowhere in the poem does the poet mention the law-officers, but we know that he is all along referring to them. In this stanza he compares them, in their blind unfeeling rage, to rabid (mad) dogs which are after his blood.

line 33   mortal enemy Means deadly enemy.

Questions

1 In what ways does the poet convey the horrors of nightfall?
2 Describe the effect of the self-identification in the poem.
3 What picture of the life of the black people in South Africa does the poet give here? How does he make it convincing?
4 Compare the imagery in the first stanza of this poem with that in the first stanza of "An abandoned bundle".
5 Compare this poem with any other in the anthology with night as theme.

Commentary

Soweto is not an African word. It is an acronym, from South West Townships, used to describe a group of townships of more than a million people, mostly black

Africans, to the south-west of Johannesburg. It is said to contain some of the largest ghettos in the world. Most of the blacks who live there, work in the city and commute to Johannesburg every day. This is a typical manifestation of the segregation of apartheid. Black Africans are forbidden to live in Johannesburg which is luxurious in contrast to the want and deprivation in Soweto. Most of the working blacks who live there minister to the domestic, social and economic needs of the white community in Johannesburg.

Life in Soweto is harsh and precarious. The inhabitants not only suffer deprivation and dehumanisation, but are also kept under constant and strict surveillance and the slightest sign of disturbance, whether real or imagined, is ruthlessly crushed. The result is that fear, violence and terror reign. The nights are particularly frightening because not only does the "law" operate mostly then, but night provides cover for other desperados to vent their frustration and anger on defenceless victims.

This poem contains an implied irony. Rather than nightfall arousing hopes of pleasant relaxation after a hard day's job, it holds terror and the possibility of death. In telling the story of his plight and almost raving against his oppressors, the poet almost lets his emotions run away with him. But the imagery succeeds in making poetry out of this agitated state: the image of wasting disease, predatory animals and their prey and the personification of night as a maleficent agent.

The first stanza images the theme of the whole poem. The second stanza contains a statement which is elaborated in the succeeding stanza. Stanzas four and five repeat the same pattern. An interesting quality to note in the poem so far is the degree of identification of the poet with the *prey* and the *victim*. The poem builds up into a crescendo in the last three stanzas, starting with *Where is my refuge* and ending in the series of rhetorical questions that emphasize the horror of nightfall. The utter helplessness of the poet is adequately conveyed through these loud cries. This poem recalls Dennis Brutus's "A troubadour, I traverse".

Just a passerby

I saw them clobber him with kieries,
I heard him scream with pain
like a victim of slaughter;
I smelt fresh blood gush
5 from his nostrils,
and flow on the street.

I walked into the church
and knelt in the pew
"Lord! I love you.
10 I also love my neighbour. Amen."

I came out
my heart as light as an angel's kiss
on the cheek of a saintly soul.

Back home I strutted
15 past a crowd of onlookers.
Then she came in –
my woman neighbour:
"Have you heard? They've killed your brother."
"O! No! I heard nothing. I've been to church."

Notes

line 1   *clobber*   To batter with a club. *Kieries* (the shortened form of
knobkieries) is a type of club with a big head usually carried about by
men in East and South Africa for defence.

line 3   *slaughter*   To kill an individual or large group of people in a
deliberate and merciless way. It is used mainly for animals, so that the
connotations of this word here are strong. Compare it with *killed* in line
18.

lines 9–10   *Love* here contrasts with the hatred that led to the *slaughter* in
the first stanza. The reference to love here is very ironical. Love for
God should be reflected in man's love for his fellow man. And the
killing is contrary to the biblical injunction, "Love thy neighbour as
thyself".

lines 11–13   The cowardly act of seeking refuge in a pious display (the
poet's feeling of unconcern could be both a criticism of his passivity and
of the system that has forced him to adopt this attitude to keep his head
on his shoulders) rids his heart of its burden of pain and guilt. Religion
here is a means of escape.

line 14   *strut*   To walk with an affected gait usually as a sign of haughtiness
or abandon. Notice the tone and attitude implied in the use of this
word. Having been to church the poet no longer feels bad.

line 19   This is a highly sarcastic line, and it sums up the attitude and
feeling in the poem. It is the type of remark which makes one either
want to cry or laugh. One ends up doing neither and merely accepts the
situation. He did not need to be told his brother had been killed. He
was a witness but was unable to intervene on behalf of his
brother. In an environment in which every black man is
cheap game (or in which life generally is precarious) the
instinct of self-preservation tends to override all other
considerations, even of blood relationship.

Questions

1 Discuss the religious imagery of this poem.
2 Write on the poet's use of similes in this poem. What does he achieve
through them?
3 What picture does the little incident recounted here paint of life in South
Africa, especially for people like the poet?

Commentary

This is a highly ironic and sarcastic poem in which the poet uses the incident of his brother being *clobbered* to death to comment on the helpless condition of blacks in South Africa. By adopting a detached attitude and using non-emotive language the poet is able to conceal a great deal of his anger and hatred, and yet make his comment pointed. The impact of the poem resides as much in the little it says, as in the much it does not say. In a poem which reminds one of the parable of the Good Samaritan in the Bible, the poet uses the incident of the killing and the evasive action of the poet going into a church to pray instead of trying to save his brother to show the violence of their society, the utter lack of love on the part of his brother's killers, the escapist nature of the religion which the poet professes and his helplessness in the system in which he lives.

If you should know me

Once concealed
Like the Devil
in the body
of a serpent –
5 as an apple of sin
in the hand
of a temptress –
I am the biter.

For all
10 I bare my heart
to see the flint
to be ignited
into a flame
shaped like three tongues
15 that tell me –
look, listen and learn
what surrounds me.

O! come search
my soul for non-existent virtues
20 outnumbered by vices
as numerous as greenflies
devouring all my righteousness.
Look upon me as a pullet crawling
from an eggshell
25 laid by a Zulu hen,
ready to fly in spirit
to all lands on earth.

Notes

line 4   *serpent*   Means snake. The poet retains the biblical term used in the Old Testament. Both serpent and apple were involved in the Fall.

lines 11   A *flint* is a hard and unyielding stone. Sparks of fire can be produced by rubbing two flints together. The discovery of fire by Stone Age man is traced to such an incident.

It is used in a metaphorical sense here, overlain by a large measure of irony. His heart (which the poet claims is soft and clear) harbours the flint which will be burnished into a flame by the harsh treatment of the whites. He is jerked out of his feeling of good-will; he realises that he has to *look, listen and learn what surrounds me.* The use of *shaped like three tongues* recalls the pentecostal fire which descended on the apostles in tongues and gave them directives about what to do after Christ's ascension.

line 21   *greenflies*   A species of flies. They usually congregate in large numbers. The use of this simile here has two significances: first it introduces a hyperbolic note emphasising how overwhelming they make their trumped up vices sound; secondly it implies dirt and sickness in contrast to *righteousness.*

line 23   *pullet*   Young chick.

line 25   *a Zulu hen*   Metaphorical for his mother. The poet is a Zulu.

Questions

1 It is possible to read the first stanza in two different ways. Identify these ways and state how each reading affects your understanding of the entire poem.

2 What do you understand by irony? Discuss its use in this poem.

3 How effective is the imagery of the last stanza? What do you think is its logical relationship with the rest of the poem?

Commentary

This poem is a subtle protest against the emotions of fear, suspicion and prejudice which stand in the way of open and meaningful human relationships. They form a barrier and make it impossible for us to know and appreciate other people for what they are. Life in South Africa, especially the relationship between the white and the black races, is dominated and polluted by these emotions.

In this poem the poet contrasts the image of him, painted by his detractors to justify their mistreatment of him, with the reality. This contrast is firmly established in the dissimilarity between the "concealment" in the first stanza and the pullet – signifying young virginal life ready to bloom to maturity and fulfilment – crawling out into freedom. The first stanza contains the familiar reference to evil in the biblical myth of how sin came into the world – through a snake which made Eve eat the forbidden apple of Paradise: Eve sealed man's damnation by tempting Adam to accept part of the fruit. Indeed, this stanza is a crisp rendering of that story, but its sting lies in the revelation by the poet that he himself is regarded as a sinner.

The poet's reaction to this denigration is an open declaration of innocence expressed ironically through the image of the flint. This cynical and sarcastic attitude is repeated in the next stanza, in which the poet invites his adversaries to search him for *non-existent virtues* – they will not bother to make anything of the virtues he possesses. He damns their whole attitude with the image of green-flies, which indicates the overwhelming nature of the vices with which he is invested. The last stanza is a plea, through the image of a hatching egg, to be seen as an innocent person whose creative spirit cherishes freedom and nurses no ill-feelings.

Atukwei Okai

Atukwei Okai (also known as John Okai) was born in 1941 in the southern part of Ghana, but was taken at an early stage to live in the north. When he returned to the south arround the age of ten he had to re-learn his native tongue, Ga, in addition to the major language of Ghana, Twi. After his secondary school education in Accra, where he was taught entirely in English, he studied at University in Moscow and London. Hence it is not surprising if his poems bear witness to this varied linguistic background.

His first volume of poems *Flowerfall* showed how influenced Okai had been by the practice of public performance of poetry in the Russia of the sixties. But since his return to Ghana Okai has sought to discover the native resources of popular and traditional oral poetry, and the result of this search is evident everywhere in his work.

Okai consciously directs his poetry, through its declamatory and dramatic nature, towards a popular audience. He does not hesitate to introduce words from the wide and varied linguistic and cultural spectrum of Ghanaian life into the same poem. This creates a particular difficulty for his readers. It is a difficulty which can be exaggerated by those who do not pay enough attention to the meaning directly communicated by the pattern of sound and rhythm, so emphatic in his poetry. For his poetry, as he has taken the trouble to demonstrate again and again, is meant for recital and performance.

In this anthology we have avoided the more extreme cases of polygot writing from Okai's pen. The two poems chosen here are, nevertheless, representative of his rhetorical, and perhaps flamboyant style. They convey his youthful and revolutionary spirit, his sense of humour and, above all, his creative control over the sounds out of which he forms his meaning.

Sunset sonata
(To Wole, with love)

   . . . let the greying day grow,
   . . . let the evening horns blow,
   . . . let the melting mountains go,
   . . . but let the sundown sow
5 In your soul
   The sky-censored seed
Of a lone
   And lonely longing

For the night
10 That, in me, must breed
Fire-desired
    For your fondling,
That I should
    Rise and crush the creed
15 That separates
    Your soil from my sapling,
And makes
    Us ride upon a horse
Whose foothold
20 On the land slackening
Echoes the cry
    That there is no heed
To the tear
    Of a fainting foundling –
25 ... O let the sundown sow,
    ... let melting mountains go,
    ... let the evening horns blow,
    ... let the greying day grow.
    ... let the greying day grow,
30 ... let the evening horns blow,
    ... let the melting mountains go,
    ... but let the sundown sow,
In your soul,
    The soul-sanctioned, bulwark-bone
35 That must steel your soul
    Against both stick and stone,
And toughen your toe
    That, to trip, is prone –
For a hundred hells
40 Hunt for the human heart
While a billion
    Blows bang upon its door,
And unpitying paws
    Pounce forth from every part
45 Till cruel cries
    Cake up at its very core;
Still stand stubborn
    To stones that strangle the dawn,
Still stand stubborn
50 To stones that maim the morn,
Still stand stubborn
    To stones that assail the sun
Still stand stubborn
    To stones that ambush man –

55 ... O let the sundown sow,
    ... let melting mountains go,
    ... let the evening horns blow,
    ... let the greying day grow.

Notes

Title   *sonata*   A basic Western European musical form consisting of three or four pieces or movements. The form usually consists of an opening statement, an exposition or development of the statement and a final recapitulation.

line 1   *greying day*   Fading day.

line 2   *evening horns*   The musical instrument, the horn, with its lowing sound, is usually associated with a winding up of the day's activities, just as the trumpet heralds the beginning of the day.

line 3   *melting mountains*   Metaphorical usage suggesting the descent of dusk, when the clear landscape of valleys and rising ground, as it were, disappear.

line 4   *sundown*   Setting sun.

line 6   *sky-censored*   That which has been checked, controlled, hence purified by the sky; that which has received the approval of the powers above (cf. *soil-sanctioned* in line 34 below).

lines 8–12, 13–16   These are difficult lines because of the elaborate and involved syntax. Perhaps a paraphrase would go like this: (8–12) the speaker hopes that the addressee's only longing will be that the coming night breeds in him (the speaker) a strong yearning for his (the addressee's) embrace. This embrace would inspire (lines 13–16) courage in the speaker to rise and fight in-built habits of thought that set them apart at the moment and prevents his spirit from receiving nourishment from the addressee's example. The lines, in short, express a yearning that Soyinka's example will inspire others like the speaker to heed the cry of the oppressed.

line 34   *soil-sanctioned*   Formed on the basis and in contrast to *sky-censored* in line 6 and suggests "fully nurtured growth and girth".
   bulwark-bone   Firm and strong bone able to stand up to pressure, cf. back-bone.

line 325   *steel*   Harden, strengthen.

line 39–40   *hundred hells/Hunt*   Countless forms of evil pursue man.

line 45–46   *cries/Cake up*   Cries that are too painful to be uttered and therefore simply freeze in the heart.

line 48   Metaphorical description of the prison walls that seek to prevent the break of the dawn of liberty.

Questions

1 Paying close attention to the first 12 lines of the poem, comment on the change in movement and meaning introduced by the word *but* in line 4.

2 This poem was dedicated to Wole Soyinka while he was in prison: how does the second part succeed in conveying the experience of imprisonment?

3 What use does the poet make of the contrasted periods of nightfall and coming day in this poem?

4 Originally a lyric was a simple verse set to music played on the string instrument (the lyre), and, generally, it is a poignant expression given in simple words to an intense feeling. For what reasons would you describe this poem as a lyric?

Commentary

This poem, written and dedicated to Wole Soyinka while he was still in prison during the Nigerian civil war, is a lyrical tribute to the spirit of protest against oppressive authority in any form. It is closely related to the longer and more rhetorical "Elavanyo Concerto" which celebrates the same spirit of defiance in the seventeenth century, of the Italian scientist Galileo Galilei. But while the longer concerto appropriately overwhelms us with a holocaust of sound, this sonata has the more subdued volume of the single voice of praise and supplication.

The opening four lines which are reversed and repeated both in the middle and at the end of the poem, with their steady rhythm and echoing moaning rhymes, create the appropriate atmosphere and tone of reverence. There is a resemblance – not to be pressed too far – between the statement, elaboration and recapitulation of these opening lines and the basic musical form of the sonata.

The poem also illustrates Okai's remarkable control over sounds, in that alliteration, assonance, end and internal rhyme all become a precise means of creating new lexical meanings from familiar words. The poem is set at the close of the day when normally the night would intensify the loneliness of the isolated prisoner. But the poet suggests a reversal of this loneliness as a result of the longing for the prisoner by those who are like-minded outside the prison walls. Thus the setting sun brings down from the sky, not the seeds of loneliness, but the god-approved seed of courage and strength. The soul of the prisoner can then stand firm against whatever threatens to strangle liberty.

Elavanyo concerto
(to Angela Davis and Wole Soyinka)

Cross.	Banner.	Swastika.	Sickle.
Dross.	Hammer.	Floodfire.	Spittle.

The sun is the centre of our system.

The leaning tower.	Two stones.	Revolution.
5 Summons to Rome.	Burning Stake.	The Inquisition.

The sun's not the centre of our system.

El Cordobes! El Cordobes!
There are some things I have to confess;
(The bulls and bulls you kill in the ring.)
10 When to the winds you all caution fling,

267

You still have things unto which to cling.
The bulls and bulls you kill in the ring
Alone have no prospects of wearing a sling.
The bulls and bulls you kill in the ring.

15 But when Galileo Galilei
Was thrown into the rot-ring of scorn,
The charging bull they hurled against him
Was armed to the horn and to the hoof
With the cudgel of hate and the spear of fear

20 And with the red-hot crowbar of anger.
Galileo Galilei in the ring
Was alone; his only weapon and friend
Was time; and time was a mere toddler then.
(And for time to mature in the marrow,

25 You certainly have to come tomorrow;
Centuries and centuries after the morrow)
And they said: Galileo Galilei,
We hear you are not at home in the mind,
We fear you must be counted with the blind.

30 You may think all your thoughts; you may,
But your ideas shan't see the light of day;
Your midday coughing hurts our midnight prayers.
And you said: two is a crowd; even the
Elements bear witness; the heavens

35 Hear evidence; the universe gives judgment.
Place no mouldy margin upon what I
Should imagine; and no single censor
In hell or heaven shall tell me censor
My sigh or sin. You retail a sick tale

40 Tailored to your taste. But toppling trees tell
Another story. When in the lap of
A man-blinded God, truth lies, lying like
The soon-to-be-unlaced lips of a hell –
Robed Iscariot the Judas jettisoned

45 Into the joyless jungle of seekers
After the truth that shall not tear apart
When torn apart, caterpillar canoes
All crawl into the highway threshold
Of a contourless anger; but the seed,

['] 50 O God, is already in the soil; the
Rains have already gone down to it.
Elavanyo! Elavanyo! better
Times cannot be too far away. I
Sit here watching the stars. Elavanyo.

55 Hei . . . Galileo Galilei . . . My eyes
are watering, their teeth are tightening, your lips
are quivering, and our solo-song slows
down to a silent stop; Hallelujah Chorus
cracks upon the shock-rock of an anti-
60 truth cataract.

O . . . Galileo Galilei . . . you fold
your face like a preying mantis pawned for
a pound of maize; and we erase all
trace, taking no chances with cheating
65 charcoal-sellers who hold the hand of hands
over the hovering hawk hankering after
human flesh.

Hei . . . Galileo Galilei . . . Time marks
time in our tears, and the rivers of truth
70 renew their roar; fire fights flesh in their
fears, and suns that shone should no more soar.

O . . . Galileo Galilei . . . truth's lip-
stick on your mind, green anger in their heart,
scorners' thick mud on your shirt, black dark-
75 ness in their hair, dry dagger in some
hand; and they crouch and come: advancing
towards you, advancing towards me,
charging against the very liver of
truth.

80 Hei . . . Galileo Galilei . . . water
walking, rainbow running, and the sky in
our song; I hear them laughing, I see you
sneezing, murderous thunder under their
tongue. Rays of knowledge pierce their eyes, smoke of
85 truth blocks their nose; and fire in the
flesh, and the rainfall on the rock, and the
myre in the mesh, and man shall not talk? amen. . .

O . . . Galileo Galilei . . .
O . . . Galileo Galilei . . .
90 Grave and grievous galley-groans all relay
The grandeur grinding of the painful play

Of rude rods on souls that forlornly pray
But whom suffering shall soon surely slay
On a particular forthdawning day.
95 They love this earth, but their bursting breath gives way,
They love this life, but their spirits won't stay.
The candlelight of knowledge and truth holds sway . . .
Inquisition fires faint-die away . . .
O, Elavanyo . . . Galileo
100 O, Elavanyo . . . Galilei.

Notes

Title Elavanyo concerto Ewe, meaning things will turn out right.
A more elaborate form of the sonata, embodying the same structural
principle but composed for a solo instrument accompanied by an
orchestra. The principle of a contest between the solo instrument and
the full orchestra is perhaps also relevant to the conflict which the poem
dramatises between Galileo and the ecclesiastical authorities of his times.
line 1 Various emblems of oppressive power. The *Cross* standing for medieval
Christendom and its antiquated scientific theories in defence of which it
persecuted people like Galileo. *Swastika*, the symbol of Nazi Germany;
and *Sickle*, the emblem of Soviet authority in the USSR.
lines 3–6 The claim of Copernicus first defended by Galileo and then
withdrawn when he was brought to trial before the papal court in Rome.
line 4 The leaning tower of Pisa, from the top of which Galileo is reputed
to have dropped two stones of differing weights which fell with the same
speed to the ground, thus disproving earlier faulty views about the laws
of motion. His views, based on scientific observation and proof, were
considered revolutionary, undermining earlier theories defended by the
fathers of the Roman Catholic Church and their learned supporters.
Hence Galileo was summoned to Rome before the papal court
responsible for investigating such heretical views. The punishment
reserved for heretics was burning at the stake. Faced with the threat of
burning, Galileo withdrew his claim.
line 7 El Cordobes is a famous Spanish bull-fighter. A *bull* also meant a papal
ban on any publication unacceptable to the Church. Galileo's struggle
against this ban is rendered concrete in stanzas 5 and 6 of the poem.
line 16 rot-ring From *rot*, which refers to the archaic theories of Galileo's
opponents, and *ring* which refers to the round of questioning Galileo
was subjected to in the papal court.
lines 18–20 A mixed metaphor describing the formidable nature of the
opposition from the authorities of the times.
line 23 A *toddler* is a child learning to walk; hence the line says roughly that
the world of scientific knowledge was still young in Galileo's day.
line 28 not at home in the mind Mad.

lines 28–32   Imagined taunts thrown at Galileo by his priestly opponents.

lines 33–41   Galileo's reply to his questioners.

line 40   Toppling trees tell   Falling trees provide evidence for a different theory.

lines 41–54   These are imagined comments by Galileo on the conditions faced by him as a result of persecution by those in authority in his time.

line 42   man-blinded God   God has, as it were, been made blind because his spokesmen uphold false views and untruths. Nevertheless the real truth lies in the lap of God himself and will burst forth in due time.

lines 43–46   One may paraphrase the lines as follows: suppressed truth is like the soon-to-be opened lips of Judas Iscariot, full of hell-like anger, because he has been rejected and compelled to join the sad company of those who seek after absolute truth. Under such conditions anger knows no limits or bursts forth in absolute chaos.

line 54   A gesture of patient waiting for better times. (The line, ending with *Elavanyo*, marks the end of the first movement of the poem. Line 55 begins a description of the long process of waiting for time to mature.)

lines 58–59   Difficult lines; possibly the meaning of the lines is that the opponents of truth celebrate their supremacy by singing hallelujah choruses. "To sing a hallelujah chorus" is a Ghanaian colloquialism meaning to celebrate a triumph.

lines 63–64   erase all/trace   All trace of truth which is considered by authority as heretical or dangerous.

lines 64–65   cheating/charcoal-sellers   Stupid gossipers.

line 68   Begins a renewal of the struggle between Galileo and his opponents. The structure of each remaining stanza gives equal attention to each side of the struggle.

line 72   truth's lipstick   As if Galileo has been kissed by truth, which has left an indelible mark on his mind.

line 75   dry dagger   Sharpened dagger.

lines 80–87   A vivid description of a number of end-of-the-world occurrences in order to give the impression of the final, almost supernatural, conflict between truth and untruth.

Questions

1 Analyse the first six lines of the poem pointing out elements of contrast and parallelism in them. Why do you think the poet uses these devices?

2 What is the effect of the internal and end rhymes employed in the second and third stanzas – lines 7–14?

3 Comment on the images used in describing the opponents of Galileo in lines 15–20.

4 What impression does the speaker give of Galileo and his opponents through their exchange in lines 27–41? What is the poet's attitude to his exchange and how does he convey this attitude to the reader?

Commentary

This long poem, dedicated to fighters against injustice and oppression, is an imaginative interpretation of the life and career of the seventeenth century Italian physicist and astronomer Galileo Galilei (1564–1642). Okai evokes, with humorous touches, the whole drama of Galileo's struggle with the ecclesiastical authority of his time and its dominant but false and archaic view of the world. Galileo's defence of Copernicus' claim that the earth moves and is not the centre of the planetary system, contrary to the belief of the Roman Catholic Church, is rendered in dramatic terms. This is a free interpretation of Galileo's career, since as a matter of history Galileo denied his views when brought before the Inquisition in 1632 and was thereafter sentenced only to life imprisonment.

The dramatic nature of the poem is indicated by its very opening: the various banners of oppressive authority in human history are put up and then immediately opposed by ironical verbal imitations – *Cross: Dross: Sickle: Spittle*. This conflict or struggle underlies the entire poem.

The poem can be divided into three sections and a conclusion: the three-part concerto movement and a final coda. Lines 1–54 (stanzas 1–12) form the first section. Lines 55–67 (stanzas 13 and 14) form the second section; lines 68–87 (stanzas 15–17) form the third section; and the last stanza, lines 88–100, draws together the themes covered.

In the first section the theme of struggle against oppressive authority is stated and elaborated in detail. Galileo is pictured in a bull-ring fighting an opponent "armed to the horn and to the hoof". There is the suggestion that suppressed truth will finally break out in a violent outburst. But this section ends on a quiet note and with a pious hope: Elavanyo, Elavanyo – things will change for the better.

The second section describes the patient waiting for better times. In temporary defeat Galileo is seen both sympathetically and yet humorously:

> *your face like a preying mantis pawned for*
> *a pound of maize...*

The third section deals with the renewal of the struggle, which has become intense and frightening. The descriptions here are awe-inspiring, almost supernatural. Yet in this almost superhuman struggle man must take a stand and speak out.

The last stanza goes over the now familiar ground of oppression suffered, but hope clung to in the belief that the "candle light of knowledge and truth holds sway and Inquisition die away".

This is a powerful poem in which the revolutionary spirit of Atukwei Okai identifies himself with kindred spirits throughout human history. The poem also shows both his strong and weak points. The poem makes its impact felt when read aloud. Its devices, like most of Okai's poems, are those of oral verse. The impossible collection of alliterative sounds is directly derived from the swearing and name-calling verse of Okai's native tongue, Ga. And read aloud, this poem is one of the best examples of African poetry drawing on native roots.

Mazisi Kunene

Mazisi Kunene is one of the most important and influential voices in modern African literature. He was born in Durban, South Africa in 1930. He studied at the University of Natal where he took an M.A. He was head of the Department of African Studies in the University College at Roma in Lesotho. He left South Africa for Britain where he became a founding member of the African Nationalist Congress. He represented the movement in Europe and America. He is at present Professor of African Languages and Literatures at the University of California, Los Angeles.

Kunene's progressive alienation from his birth place is a reflection of his opposition to the apartheid policies of South Africa. Apart from his political campaigns in the ANC, he has devoted much of his writing to a castigation of the apartheid system. Two themes tend to dominate his poetry: the theme of ancestors whom he sees as the reservoir of wisdom and moral qualities and whose presence is important for our own existence; and the theme of apartheid. His anti-apartheid poetry brims with anger and definite warning to the government about the dreadful social consequences of their policy. Two other significant facts about Kunene as an important writer are the sheer volume of his output in poetry – his two epics being monumental works – and the unique practice of writing his poetry first in his indigenous language and then translating it into English. He is known for his work on the Zulu epic entitled *Emperor Shaka the Great* and another work of epic proportions, *Anthem of the Decades*. His other published works are *Zulu Poems* and *The Ancestors and the Sacred Mountain*.

Thought on June 26

Was I wrong when I thought
All shall be avenged?
Was I wrong when I thought
The rope of iron holding the neck of young bulls
5 Shall be avenged?
Was I wrong
When I thought the orphans of sulphur
Shall rise from the ocean?
Was I depraved when I thought there need not be love.
10 There need not be forgiveness, there need not be progress,
There need not be goodness on the earth.
There need not be towns of skeletons,

Sending messages of elephants to the moon?
Was I wrong to laugh asphyxiated ecstasy
15 When the sea rose like quicklime
When the ashes on ashes were blown by the wind
When the infant sword was left alone on the hill top?
Was I wrong to erect monuments of blood?
Was I wrong to avenge the pillage of Caesar?
20 Was I wrong? Was I wrong?
Was I wrong to ignite the earth
And dance above the stars
Watching Europe burn with its civilization of fire,
Watching America disintegrate with its gods of steel,
25 Watching the persecutors of mankind turn into dust
Was I wrong? Was I wrong?

Notes

Title 26 June is South African Freedom day. First observed by both
the African National Congress and the Indian National Congress in
1950 in memory of the eighteen people killed in the May Day
demonstration of that year. In 1955 a United Congress adopted a
Freedom Charter against apartheid on that day. This poem was originally
published under the title "Poisoned Mind".

line 4 rope of Iron Means chain and *young bulls* refers to strong and healthy
young blacks in South Africa. The circumstance of the black man in
South Africa is equivalent to slavery.

line 7 sulphur A non-metallic combustible element that burns with a light-
blue flame and a stifling odour. Sulphur gases are some of the most
common and deadly gases emitted in a volcanic eruption. What the poet
is saying here is that the orphans of defiant and fiery-spirited men and
women, who had been cut down by forces that must maintain apartheid,
will rise up and revenge the death of their parents. The implied image
of a volcanic eruption is telling.

lines 9–11 There are two possible ways of reading these crucial lines. The
first is to see them as clear and forthright statements made by a mind
that has become hostile because of the enormity of the evil actions of
apartheid, a mind that is blinded by the desire for revenge and
repudiates the talk of love, forgiveness and progress. It would not
matter if the country were destroyed as long as the blacks were able to
get their revenge.
The other reading would adopt an ironic posture. If there was social
justice, there would be love in society and if some segment of society
was not gratuitously offended, then there would be nothing to forgive. If
progress means the mindless exploitation of black people, then its pursuit
is not necessary.

line 13 A possible reference to the landing of the spaceship on the moon.
The mentality that has been obsessed with progress and led to space
exploration is the same as that which tramples on blacks in South Africa.
He is certain there will be vengeance: even nature will conspire to
redress the wrong.

line 14 Suffocating laughter induced by joy and happiness. He was glad that the sea was going to avenge the wrongs the blacks have suffered.

line 15 *quicklime* A white substance obtained by the action of heat on limestone, shells and other materials that contain calcium carbonate. It is used in making mortar and cement and in neutralizing acid soil.
The metaphor of the burning acid soil here is implied and quicklime (the ocean) is needed to douse the fire and establish peace and calm.

line 16 Evil and destruction spread throughout the world. There is very often a universal dimension to Kunene's vision.

line 17 The *hill top* is the abode of the ancestors. The ancestors fully support revenge and would, in fact, fight on behalf of their wards. *Infant sword* could be a metaphor here.

line 18 To commemorate the blacks that have been killed or the large numbers that will be killed in the general bloodshed.

line 19 *Caesar* was a great historical and legendary figure. Noted for his military brilliance, political astuteness and accomplishment as a cultured man – versed in art, music, painting – he was one of the triumvirate that ruled the Roman Empire in his time. Shakespeare's *Julius Caesar* gives us a clear idea of the man's eminence. It also shows how he was assassinated, out of jealousy, by his close associates. The Zulus saw Chaka as their own Caesar. There are, indeed, many parallels in their lives, in terms of their military successes as war generals, their charisma, their ability as politicians and leaders of men, and in their end. They both became legends in their life times and have lingered in the imagination as mythical figures. Like Caesar, Chaka died at the hands of close relations – his half-brothers and his councillor. Chaka remains the symbol of resistance to white encroachment and pillage.

lines 21–26 In lines 21 and 22 the poet seems to say that Europe and America are encouraging apartheid and the poet would like to pay them back in their own coin. The poet takes sinister pleasure in causing destruction and watching in enjoyment from a safe distance. There is here another instance of the global nature of his vision.

Questions

1 What do you notice about the structure of this poem?
2 Do you think the poem gains anything because of the poet's attitude?
3 How would you defend the poet here if a critic charged him with mere ranting and not writing poetry?
4 Compare this poem with any other protest poem in this anthology.

Commentary

Most protest poems which we consider as successful art are generally distinguished by the ability of the poet to couch his anger in some subdued pattern, to mask his dislike while still expressing his objection, to avoid shrill and strident gestures. This poem is different, in that it is a direct uncompromising indictment of apartheid, almost a malediction on *the persecutors of mankind*. Yet it is good poetry.

The theme of vengeance is stated clearly and easily. It is worked through a reasoned structure of rhetorical questions which indirectly justify the poet's desire for revenge since we are made to see the injustices that the people have suffered. The constant repetition of *Was I wrong* unites the poem in the sense that it gives the impression of a call and response structure and also operates as a refrain. In between these, the poet not only expresses his anger but the kind of harm he wishes for the white oppressors. The poem starts from a specific and pungent statement of complaint in line 4 and then swells out to encompass the South African society and the whole world embodying an implied questioning of what the modern world calls civilization. The sea, ocean and fire are used as images of destruction and underscore the poet's militant call for vengeance and retribution.

This insistent questioning of what the poet thinks should be the right vengeful actions to take serves to distance him from the terrible wishes he nurses. The impression we get in the end is that he is justified and that ordinarily he is far from such ignoble thoughts that have been forced on him by circumstances. The *Was I wrong? Was I wrong?* that ends the poem lingers as an echo in the mind and we are left with the debate long after we have read the poem.

In praise of the ancestors

Even now the Forefathers still live
They are not overcome by the power of the whirlwind.
The day that sealed their eyes did not conquer them.
Even the tall boulder that stands over them
5 Casts only a humble shadow over their resting place.
They are the great voice that carries the epics.
The Ancestors have come to listen to our songs,
Overjoyed they shake their heads in ecstasy.
With us they celebrate their eternal life.
10 They climb the mountain with their children
To put the symbol of the ancient stone on its forehead.
We honour those who gave birth to us,
With them we watch the spectacle of the moving mists.
They have opened their sacred book to sing with us.
15 They are the mystery that envelops our dream.
They are the power that shall unite us.
They are the strange truth of the earth.
They came from the womb of the universe.
Restless they are, like a path of dreams,
20 Like a forest sheltering the neighbouring race of animals.
Yes, the deep eye of the universe is in our chest.
With it we stare at the centres of the sky.
We sing the anthems that celebrate their great eras,
For indeed life does not begin with us.

Notes

line 2 *whirlwind* A strong destructive wind that moves in a circle and is pipe-shaped.

line 4 *boulder* Large stone or mass of rock, in this case used to cover the graves of the ancestors.

lines 4–5 The ancestors have defied nature – day, wind, boulders, even time and death. Only their flesh died, their spirits live for ever.

line 6 In his recreation of the grandeur of the society and greatness of the ancestors, Kunene pays great attention to epics as part of the rightful product of that period. His *Anthem of the Decades* and the epic poem *Chaka* bear testimony to this.

line 23 *era* A set of years or a period of time counted from a particular point in time and known for a specific historical event or development.

Questions

1 What picture of the ancestors does the poet present here?
2 Discuss the poet's use of simile in this poem.
3 Explain line 21.
4 Compare the poet's treatment of the theme of ancestors in this poem with any other poet's treatment of the same theme. Restrict yourself to poems in this anthology.

Commentary

Certain cultural beliefs are common to many African peoples. This poem celebrates one such belief, the belief in the antiquity, the power and constant presence of ancestors. An important point of the African view of the world is that there is a strong link between the dead, especially ancestors, and the living; the ancestors are guardian angels of the living and their potency must be recognised. They are involved in all our activities and our awareness of their presence gives us assurance and confidence.

The poem is a celebration of the ancestors. In terms of the development of the ideas, we notice that it is carefully divided into five sections: lines 1–5, 6–9, 10–13, 14–18 and 19–24, each expounding different attributes and actions of the ancestors, showing our inter-relationships *For indeed life does not begin with us.*

Mukhtarr Mustapha

Mukhtarr Mustapha was born in Freetown, Sierra Leone, in 1943 of
a Muslim family. He was educated at a Western European type of school
and at University in the United States. But he has also immersed himself
in the traditional ways of his Wolof and Yoruba ancestry and travelled
widely. As a result, his familiarity with the "griot" tradition of the
Berbers of the Western Sahara has influenced his long dramatic poem
Dalabani. The short lyric *Gbassay* shows evidence of a deep under-
standing of some of his ancestral mystery cults.

Gbassay – blades in regiment

Push a porcupine quill into
My quaint eyes
Then plunge an assagai into
My fibroid face
5 Then slash my neck and stain
The tortoise back rich with my blood

Force a rug needle into my narrow
nose: force it right into my
Indigo marrow.

10 Lift my tongue and tie it
With a rope from a tethered goat
Lacerate my lips with deep sanguine
gutters splattering blood like a
Bellow in full blaze – blazing yellow

15 Disembowel my belly and feed the
Hawks that hover there hourless-
timeless black blue sky
And inside a crater bury
My ears.
20   "Is it death?"

Notes

Title   A trance-cry which became the name of a cult-group. The word itself
may have been derived from the Yoruba word *Gbase* meaning slave,
labourer, victim. *Blades in regiment* is a description of the instruments

prepared for administering the rite to the cult worshipper.

lines 1–2 Note the alliteration in these lines. The harsh consonants of *quill* and *quaint* suggest the cruelty of the action described in these lines. But *quaint* also suggests squinting eyes and, together with *fibroid face* (line 4), a picture of someone being beaten brutally so that the eyes can just peep out of a swollen face is evoked.

line 3 assagai A slender spear of hard wood often associated with the Zulu warriors of South Africa. This word goes with *porcupine quill* (line 1) and *tortoise back* (line 6) to give a ritual overtone.

line 7 rug needle A large curved needle used in sewing sacks.

line 9 indigo Colour of the marrow within the bone.

line 11 tethered goat The underlying picture of a sacrificial animal and of the ritual act comes to the surface here. The human victim becomes clearly identified with the animal.

line 12 sanguine Bloody.

lacerate Tear apart with violence.

lines 16–20 hawks Birds of prey, here used metaphorically to mean aggresive, war-loving and tyrannical men. In consigning his remains partly to the sky (*black blue sky*) and partly to the earth (*a crater*) the poet suggests the all-embracing and permanent nature of tyranny. This acceptance of the unavoidable nature of suffering prompts the triumphant question: *Is it death?*

Questions

1 By what means does the poet suggest the depth of the pain inflicted by the action described in the second section of the poem?

2 The first act of mutilation is violent, the second is deeply painful. How would you characterize the act described in section 3 of the poem? (Pay attention to the plosive sounds of this section.)

3 What is the effect of the several references to animals in this poem?

4 Why do you think the poet writes about this series of horrifying acts?

Commentary

The horrifying and disturbing imagery of this poem is related to the ritual past, as well as to the terrifying present of Africa. Firstly, it is a variation upon some of the ritual acts of age-old secret societies and cult-groups which have occasional revivals in Africa, south of the Sahara. For example, there are the rites of self-mutilation with sharp instruments which some worshippers of the Yewe or Xebieso or So cult of South-East Ghana, Togo and Dahomey undergo while in a state of trance, when not even the sharpest knives cut their bodies. A version of such cult-groups, with initiates making trance-cries of 'Krrr Gbassay Gbassay, Krrr Gbassay" when tested with sharp blades, flourished in parts of Sierra Leone in the fifties. The acts of self-mutilation, which do not harm the initiates, are seen as proof of their immunity from death.

But the poem is also a comment upon some of the horrifying experiences of some political victims of oppressive regimes in various parts of Africa, and so the poet's imagination forges links between the past and the present of Africa. And the defiant question with which the poem ends is an expression of personal courage, as well as an inspiration from the traditions of the past.

Syl Cheney-Coker

Syl Cheney-Coker was born in Freetown in 1945, where he received his early education before proceeding to the USA and studies at the Universities in Oregon and Wisconsin. He returned briefly to Sierra Leone in the early 1970s, but found President Siaka Stevens' single-party government too intolerant of free expression of dissent and criticism to remain at home for long. His life of exile, which began in the mid-1970s, has taken him through Oregon to California, down to Argentina and Chile, and the Philippines. He has taught both African and Latin American literature in universities in a number of these countries, having learnt to speak Spanish fluently and taken a keen interest in the poetry of the Chilean Pablo Neruda and the novels of Jorge Luis Borges.

Cheney-Coker's two volumes of poetry so far (*Concerto for an Exile*, 1973 and *The Graveyard also has Teeth*, 1980) can be described as a personal and passionate exploration of the experience of exile which he has known, as it were, even before his birth, as the heritage of his Creole parentage. He calls it in a revealing phrase: "the agony planted in my soul." The conflicting emotions of wanting to claim an African patrimony and yet knowing that he comes from ancestors, who were re-planted on African soil after enslavement and who then went on to attain a privileged status in Sierra Leone, often burst out as spluttering self-disgust in Cheney-Coker's poetry. At other times, however, his keen sense of identification with the down-trodden overrides this self-disgust and then his poetry embodies a revolutionary fervour and presents, through emphatic rhythms, a vision of the achievement of really free men all over the continent of Africa as through-out the world. "Freetown", anthologised here, is certainly one of his successful poems, and "Peasants" shows his revolutionary fervour and his keen sense of the injustice that those exiled from power suffer.

Freetown

Africa I have long been away from you
wandering like a Fulani cow
but every night
amidst the horrors of highway deaths
5   and the menace of neon-eyed gods
I feel the warmth of your arms
centrifugal mother reaching out to your sons
we with our different designs innumerable facets

280

but all calling you mother womb of the earth
10 liking your image but hating our differences
because we have become the shame of your race
and now on this third anniversary of my flight
my heart becomes a citadel of disgust
and I am unable to write the poem of your life

15 my creation haunts me behind the mythical dream
my river dammed by the poisonous weeds in its bed
and I think of my brothers with "black skin and white masks"
(I myself am one heh heh heh)
my sisters who plaster their skins with the white cosmetics
20 to look whiter than the snows of Europe
but listen to the sufferings of our hearts

there are those who when they come to plead
say make us Black Englishmen decorated Afro-Saxons
Creole masters leading native races
25 but we African wandering urchins
who will return one day
say oh listen Africa
the tomtoms of the revolution
beat in our hearts at night

30 make us the seven hundred parts of your race
stretching from the east to the west
but united inside your womb
because I have dreamt in the shadows of Freetown
crashing under the yoke of its ferocious civilization!

Notes

line 2 Fulani A nomadic tribe who move along the Sahel region with their
cattle.
lines 4–5 The theme of travelling around and being on the move is taken up
in these lines. The speaker seems to be on the highways of Europe or
America, with their fast moving vehicles, which are often the cause of
accidents and death. *Neon-eyed gods* refers to the headlamps of these
vehicles which throw out yellowish beams.
line 7 centrifugal Spreading outwards from one central point.
line 10 In spite of so much talk of African unity, the differences and
divisions of its people and their conflicts abound.
line 11 the shame of your race As *womb of the earth* (line 9), Africa is seen
as the origin of all the human race, among whom Africans bear the
shame of poverty, deprivation and underdevelopment.
line 15 I am tormented by the dream of what I could create, but am unable
to. (Presumably, overwhelmed by the shame of being African.)
line 16 my river My imagination or source of inspiration.

line 17 "*black skins and white masks*" A famous remark of Franz Fanon, about educated Africans who imitate Europeans. In line 19, Cheney-Coker extends the irony of the remark by suggesting that educated African women, in contrast to the men, imitate the white skin of Europeans.

line 24 The line refers specifically to the situation in Freetown, where the half-caste descendants of the slaves freed and settled on the land, look down on the original inhabitants of the country and refer to them in derogatory terms as "the natives".

line 34 This is a very ambiguous line, particularly the phrase *ferocious civilization*. Perhaps a line from another of his poems may throw some light on the ending of "Freetown": in "On Being a Poet Alone in Sierra Leone", the poet calls Sierra Leone, "a colossus strangled by fratricidal parasites". *Ferocious civilization* may mean that Freetown has the potential of a great civilization. To crash under the yoke of that civilization will therefore release the latent energies, making it realize its destiny as the city of the truly liberated.

Questions

1 Attempt a complete punctuation of the poem, introducing commas, full stops, quotation marks, where you think they are required. What do you consider the effect of these sense-group markers on the poem?
2 The poet speaks of being "a wandering cow" and "a wandering urchin". Find one word which describes his manner of life.
3 If the poet were to write the poem of Africa's life what do you think it would reveal? You may wish to read lines 14–16 carefully.
4 From line 22 onwards, the poet speaks of two types of Africans and their dreams. Describe in your own words the two types and their dreams.
5 The poet may be genuinely moved by the plight of contemporary Africa, but his hopes for the continent remain vague. Would you agree? Refer to portions of the poem to support your view.

Commentary

This poem comes from Cheney-Coker's collection *Concerto for an Exile* and belongs to a poetic genre now familiar to students of modern African poetry: the poem of longing and dreaming about Africa written by someone away from his home. Examples abound in Senghor's collection *Chants d'Ombre* and two of his poems in this anthology – "In memoriam" and "Nuit de Sine" – illustrate the genre. The image of Africa as a mother with warm nurturing arms was also made familiar through Senghor's poetry.

An interesting feature of Cheney-Coker's variation on the now familiar theme is the fact that, although the title of the poem is "Freetown", there is no reference to the city until the last but one line. Then the city's symbolic significance, based on the history of its founding, is used. The poem is mainly on Africa and Freetown serves as the symbol of the hope for Africa's unity. Thus the poem belongs to that genre of writing by the African writer in exile who sees the entire continent as his home rather than the individual nation to which he belongs.

An earlier and very interesting expression of this feeling is found in Abioseh

Nicol's poem "The meaning of Africa", also included in this anthology. Nicol's poem belongs to the mood of the 1960s, while "Freetown" belongs to the late 1970s and early 1980s. For Nicol, Africa belongs to the one who tills and harvests a piece of plot in his native country. For Cheney-Coker, however, Africa is the civilization that will flower when the entire continent has been freed from "under the yoke of its ferocious subjugation".

The poet has a remarkable ease of statement and a flowing rhythm, based on the imitation of the spoken voice. The voice speaks out in elaborate and intricate periods. For example, the entire first section, consisting of 14 lines, is made up of three statements only. Similarly, the third section is one extended statement, with careful voice modulations and appropriate pauses, although the poet avoids the use of punctuation marks. The result is a passionate utterance combining self-criticism with pointed comment on contemporary Africa.

Peasants

The agony: I say their agony!

the agony of imagining their squalor but never knowing it
the agony of cramping them in roach infected shacks
the agony of treating them like chattel slaves
5 the agony of feeding them abstract theories they do not understand
the agony of their lugubrious eyes and bartered souls
the agony of giving them party cards but never party support
the agony of marshalling them on election day but never on banquet
    nights
the agony of giving them melliferous words but mildewed bread
0 the agony of their cooking hearths dampened with unuse
the agony of their naked feet on the hot burning tarmac
the agony of their children with projectile bellies
the agony of long miserable nights
the agony of their thatched houses with too many holes
5 the agony of erecting hotels but being barred from them
the agony of watching the cavalcade of limousines
the agony of grand state balls for God knows who
the agony of those who study meaningless 'isms in incomprehensible
    languages
the agony of intolerable fees for schools but with no jobs in sight
0 the agony of it all I say the agony of it all
but above all the damn agony of appealing to their patience
Africa beware! their patience is running out!

Notes

line 1 This is a significant line and a clue to the varied meanings of the
    word *agony*, which emerge from the poem. First of all, the word refers

here to the sufferings of the exploited and deprived peasant farmers of most independent African countries. Often, however, the word refers to the crimes of the exploiters and, indirectly, the anguish these crimes arouse in the speaker. The very first usage of the word, then, is abstract and generalised. The second usage in the line insists on drawing attention to the concrete suffering of the victims of exploitation.

line 3   *roach*   Shortened form of cockroach.

line 4   *chattel*   Animal or beast meant for sale.

line 6   *lugubrious*   Sad, full of sorrow, full of darkness and despair.

line 8   *marshall*   To gather together and urge towards a particular action.

line 9   *melliferous*   Honey bearing, hence sweet-sounding promises; *mildewed* means mouldy, hence unedible.

line 12   *projectile bellies*   Protruding stomachs, the result of malnutrition; the sign of kwashiokor.

line 16   *cavalcade of limousines*   A fleet of huge luxury cars.

line 18   *'isms*   Generally, an abbreviation for words that describe political beliefs. Example, marxism, socialism, capitalism.

Questions

1 In which lines does the word *agony* refer specifically to the feelings of the speaker, and in which does it refer to those with whom he sympathises?

2 Identify the lines in which the word refers to the "evil" represented by the exploiters of the peasants and put in your own words what the word means in these lines.

3 In what ways does the speaker suggest that he is also guilty?

4 Apart from the first and the last line, the poet does not use any punctuation marks. Why do you think he uses them in these two lines?

5 How does the movement of the poem convey the speaker's feelings?

Commentary

This poem opens with two contrasted uses of the key word *agony*, which recurs like a litany throughout, except in the last line. In the first line, the poet deals firmly with the temptation to talk in a general way about the suffering and exploitation of the peasants. Although the sympathy of men like him may be admirable, the first line insists that it is the sufferings of the peasants that the poem is concerned with.

The feeling of outrage from which the poem seems to originate is enacted in the dramatic changes of the voice we hear speaking. It is also enacted by the variety of rhythmic units which is the result of the contrast between long and short lines. We also sense the poet's anger through the antithetical statements which emphasise the hypocrisy and the cynicism of those in power in Africa: e.g. lines 7 and 8. By means of these devices the poem builds to a climax in lines 18 to 22. Lines 18 and 19, through which the angry voice of the speaker sputters elaborate phrases, are contrasted to the clipped emphatic shout: *The agony of it all I say the agony of it all.*

Then finally the voice explodes in the last two lines.

Stephen Lubega

Stephen Lubega was born in 1945 in Masaka, Uganda. He received his secondary education at Bukalasa Seminary. He later went to the National Teacher's College, Kyambogo and then Makerere University. He has been teaching in secondary schools since then.

Lubega's poetic ability showed itself quite early. He was the first editor of *Student Lines*, a literary magazine of the National Teacher's College; his poetry has been published in *Zuka* and *Flamingo* and also broadcast by the BBC. Lubega is a sensitive poet who is inspired by nature and who observes it keenly.

Evening

Never has the death of a poet
Been tolled by all the world.
God's work on earth, though
Has its universal funeral in the west,
5 Recurrent grave of day's almighty soul.

Never was victory so trumpeted
As that of the sun scorching his fiery way
And then in gorgeous colours falling,
Trailing stars.
10 Life, death, water and aridity
Bow to his morning ray.

With his passing, death stirs in the thicket.
In church the bell is tolled,
In barracks at the last bugle note
15 Soldiers like ants file,
The busy woman scolds her child,
Drunkards like sick dogs retch homewards.
The night voice is a harsh guitar

But on a hill among musizi trees
20 Sweet nuns sing the litanies
Of the virgin whose Son we know.
Priests like lamp posts in a graveyard
Stoop over the breviary.

There's a piping of crickets in the bush
25 And a bellowing of frogs –
All sing the ancient elegy
For the sun that has died in the west.

Notes

line 1   Opening tribute to the sun. The sun is personified and eulogised in
martial and regal terms. The sun is called a *poet* not only to show its
power of creativity because many things in the world depend on it for
their existence but also because it is the light of the sun that enables us
to see the beauty of creation. When the sun sets (the death of a poet)
its light is cut off and with it the variegated splendour of the earth as
the latter is covered by one grey or dark sheet of night.

line 2   *toll*   To ring a bell slowly and repeatedly especially to announce the
death of someone. The sun rules over the whole world and so news of
its death must spread throughout the world. The experience is universal.

line 4   The earth dies when the sun sets in the west.

line 5   *Recurrent*   Means to happen again and again; *grave* means the west
where the sun sets; *day's almighty soul* refers to the sun which provides
the light that forms the day.

line 6   *trumpeted*   Loudly announced. The fierce rays of the sun subdue all
and proclaim its might. This power is complemented by its colourful
setting in the evening.

lines 8–9   The setting sun is often a breath-taking sight. Stars appear at
night after the sun's departure. The sun reigns and departs in style.

line 12   Death is also personified here. *Stir* means to move about and *thicket*
means thick growth of bushes and small trees.

line 17   *retch*   To try unsuccessfully to vomit.

line 18   It is quiet everywhere at night so the slightest sounds seem to be
exaggerated, hence the image of *a harsh guitar*.

line 20   A *litany* is a type of prayer in the Christian church in which the
priest calls out and the congregation replies in the same words.

line 21   Refers to the Virgin Mary and her son Jesus Christ.

line 23   *breviary*   A prayer book used in the Roman Catholic Church which
contains prayers to be said by the priests each day.

lines 24–26   *elegy*   An elegy is a poem or song written to mourn or lament
the death or loss of something. The chirping of the *crickets* and the
croaking of the *frogs* all proclaim the death of day. This has been from
the beginning of time and could be referred to as "the ancient elegy".
The poet might also be referring to the familiar evening hymn "Now the
day is over".

Questions

1 In what ways would you describe this poem as a nature poem?
2 Although the title of the poem is "Evening" the poet spends much time
writing about the sun. Do you think this enhances or detracts from his
theme and how?

3 Discuss the organisation of the imagery of this poem. How relevant do you find the imagery of death?

Commentary

Using conventional metaphors of the sun or day representing light and life and evening or darkness representing death, the poet writes about evening as the result of the absence of the sun. Because the sun's departure brings darkness to the world, the whole world is seen as mourning it. Metaphorically, the world dies at night, since human beings and nature go to sleep and most activities cease. The poet deliberately talks about the sun in glowing terms, extolling its power and almighty influence which touches every aspect of life. This is in sharp contrast to the picture when the sun disappears.

The first two stanzas are concerned with the universal sway of the sun and its inevitable setting every day. The third and fourth stanzas are concerned with evening scenes which result from the sun going away. Whereas the third stanza gives a general but homely picture, starting with the insecurity of life which darkness portends to the various activities that characterise the evening – church bells calling people to evening prayers, the bugle in the barracks, drunks wending their ways home – the last stanza concentrates on a scene of prayer by nuns and priests. Here man and nature unite in their acknowledgement, through their songs, that it is evening. Perhaps, the nuns and priests are not only glorifying the hand that guides the sun (the sun is after all "God's work on earth") they are also preparing for their own ends. The quiet and peaceful atmosphere worked out through the alliterative and onomatopoeic sounds contrasts with the activity of the third stanza.

Bai Tamiah Moore

Bai Tamiah Moore is probably the most popular and best known of Liberia's contemporary writers. Born near Monrovia about 1920, Moore had his early education in the United States where he took a degree in biology. After a period as head of the Bureau of Agriculture in the Liberian Ministry of Interior, he was appointed Assistant Minister of Culture in the Ministry of Information, Tourism and Culture. He gave up that position and lived as a private citizen until his death in January 1988.

Moore was seriously interested in the folk tales, legends and oral poetry of his people, and travelled widely in his country, collecting and translating these tales. Some are now taught in schools. This interest in the countryside and culture of his people went with a keen observation of contemporary social scenes. The result is that these two strands meet in his works and make them very representative of Liberia. He was in the forefront of the efforts to promote Liberian indigenous culture through literature and writing. He wrote and published stories, poems and novels. Indeed, he started writing poetry when he was in high school, after realising that the only way he could invoke his own inner spring was by drawing on traditional imagery and locale and not by aping American and other foreign writers. The influence of Gola folk songs is evident in his poetry.

His published works include *Ebony Dust, Grassroots*, collections of poems, and *Murder in the Cassava Patch*, a short novel, based on a sensational incident. He was still actively writing until his death and not only had a number of unpublished manuscripts in English, but also wrote in *vai*, one of the indigenous languages of Liberia. The poems included in this anthology are taken from *Ebony Dust*.

Harvest moon

Of all the moons the gods bestowed
Glato is the farmer's dream.
She brings the golden paddy fields
And drives the hungry moons away.
5 All the fields, like a thousand incense burning
Fill the air with fragrance,
Of golden heads of rice
Of okra, corn and condiments
With which the farmer's spouse
10 Can keep aglow her hearth.

Along the winding village trails
Melodious harvest songs in glee
From lips of carefree maidens,
Welcome love and merriment.
15 When the harvest sun is setting
Over the hills, the trees and fields,
The family moving to the town
Are silhouetted against the sky
With all their home utensils
20 Gently balanced on the head.
Glato is the planning moon
For feast to those who long have gone
To the fertile farming lands
Where all the tribes must some day meet;
25 It might have been the village doctor,
Gifted in the arts of cures,
Or the midwife of the village
Who rescued innocent maidens
Beset with fears of nature.
30 Or perhaps a lowly sire,
Who was sought in every council
And envied by some tyrant chief,
Or the jovial village smithy
Whose communal place of duty
35 Called the farmers from afar;
Or a village belle or lad
On whom the tribe bestowed
The secret of their mores.
For these perhaps there'll be no cow,
40 But the farmer's only goat or sheep
Will grace the palate of the friends
Who come to share in mirth
The memory of the ones departed
To the fertile farming lands.
45 In harvest moon when tom-toms and the singing
Of the young entune the jungle
With a gripping syncopation,
And the moonbeams turn to silver
A hundred million silent leaves,
50 The surging urge of dancing feet
Along the winding village trails
Beat up a rhythmic tempo.

Notes

line 1 moons The moon is an important symbol in traditional society. Apart
from the influence which it is said to exert on human beings, it is an

important measure of time. Each moon that indicates the duration of a lunar month has a definite name and signifies some specific activity in the lives of the people. *Moon* is used in this poem not only in the sense of the heavenly body, but also in the sense of "Month".

line 2 *Glato* Dewoin word for October, which is the month for harvesting.

line 3 *paddy fields* Rice fields. Rice is the staple food of the people.

lines 5–20 Harvest time is important in the yearly cycle of rural people. Harvest is a communal and social activity which involves the whole community irrespective of sex, age or rank.

lines 21 ff. Do you think a note of sadness and reflection is introduced into the poem by the reference to the dead? In African society there is the belief that a strong link exists between the dead and the living. A number of ceremonies including second burials are performed regularly not only to remember and honour the dead and emphasise the fact of their constant presence but also sometimes to appease them. Indeed, the dead are generally offered the first morsels of food or drops of drink to show that they are remembered and to invoke their blessing and guidance. So, in the season of plenty, the living ensure that they put something away with which to celebrate the memory of the dead. Notice that the "fertile farming lands" which yield the plenteous harvest also serve as the insatiable grave for the departed; there is a certain cycle of nourishment which ensures the survival of the species. At another level, death is indeed, the ultimate harvest.

line 34 *communal place of duty* The blacksmith's workshop is one of the spots in rural communities where people congregate to gossip and regale themselves with stories.

line 46 *entune* The spirited singing of the young people and the echo of their music spreads in such a way as to give the impression that the forests were tuned, (given or had a good tune) and joined in the singing. The forest becomes part of the joyful celebration.

line 47 *syncopation* Musical term used to describe the variation in rhythm achieved by shifting the accent on low notes and extending this over many notes.

Questions

1 How does the poet convey to the reader the sense of ripeness and plenty of the harvest season? (Look at the images of sight, colour, smell, mood, taste, sound.)

2 This poem tells us a lot about African society and not just harvesting. By close reference to the poem and specific devices used, show how the poet subtly brings out features and characteristics of a typical African society.

Commentary

The harvest festival is one of the most remarkable occasions in rural African communities or in any community for that matter. This poem describes a typical scene during the harvesting period in Liberia. It is a period of ripeness, festivity and plenty, of joy and communal celebrations in which the people rejoice in the fruits of their labour and are thankful for the full barns which will ensure that life will go on, after the scarcity of "the hungry moons". The poet carefully describes the farmlands and presents a vivid picture of the busyness and joy which are evident on the rural paths leading from the farms to the villages and in the homes.

Harvest is also the time to remember the dead. The poet uses the occasion of the realisation that death is the common end of all men irrespective of their status in life, to present a picture gallery of traditional society. So consuming is the festivity that the poem climaxes in a recreation of the music, mood and activity that engulf and unite man and nature in one moment of joy and excitement.

Dimeh in transition

Father time, forever changing
Day and night, has wrought
His magic wand, and changed
The face of Dimeh,
5 And with it, familiar faces
Of the days of my childhood.
A few tottering faces,
And the giant cottonwood trees
Towering high above the village
10 Remain the only link now
Between the old and new.
These tall and ancient guardians
Have weathered many rains and dries
Which blessed the annual harvests
15 Since the village had its birth.
Only they, though mute, have harboured
In their boughs, the history of the village.
The new faces who come and go,
Some, scions of the founders,
20 Are lacking in original roots.
They scarce remember now
The final resting place
Of the founders of the village.
These restless comers also lack
25 The same deep veneration
For sacred spots about the town;
The kpakpa in the nizan
Where the medicine which
Protects the village is stored,
30 Or the black stone in the creek
Where annual sacrifices were made
To our ancestors, now resting
Under the giant cottonwood trees.

These gone ancestors serve
35 As a link between the living
And geplo, who is hidden from us.
The little friendly circles
Which shared all household chores
And which kept the village knitted
40 Into a single family web;
The old time palm wine circle
Which brought together daily
In nearby swamps or blacksmith shop
The fathers of the village
45 To share their views or gossip
Is something which is rare.
Custom so dictated, that
If a hunter bagged a game
Or the women were successful
50 With their nets in nearby streams,
Each household could be certain
Of sharing in communal luck.
The hunter's niece and nephews,
His other kins and friends,
55 The patriarch of the village
All had a claim, a portion
Of whatever game he killed.
The sisters got the pelvis
For it is they, when the hunter died
60 Who spent out theirs, to watch over his body.
In keeping with tradition
The head of every game
Is shared by niece and nephews,
Which brings to mind a custom,
65 A hunter's nephews have the right
To marry any of his daughters,
Provided they have never crossed
His wives or any of his concubines.
The old village patriarch, depending
70 On his standing in the poro,
Received what's known as jia,
Or part of the small intestines,
The privates and the navel.
So friendly were the families
75 No man could eat alone,
The standing invitations between
The households in the town
Were commonly regarded.
All mothers felt a oneness
80 For the children of the village.

As long as he was roving
With the gang about the town
Or, escorting papa on his rounds
A mother had no need to fear
85　Where junior got a stomach full.
And time was, when all the kids,
Adolescent boys and girls
And their friends from neighbouring towns
Kept the nights alive, with songs, games
90　And dances, such as "minding birds"
And "hide and seek";
Or older boys were occupied
With complicated guessing games
Acquired from the bushlore
95　They learned from crafty elders.
Rare too, are the friendly competitions
Engaged in by both old and young,
Like shooting bow and arrows, or
Pitting wits at a game of kpo, or
100　A spirited wrestling match,
Which drew together older boys
From all the neighbouring towns.
Simple village feuds, which were
Hushed in family councils
105　By dipping hands in water
Now end in court, alienating friendly ties.
Long ago, all such trivial matters
Were brought before a family head
Respected for his judgement.
110　The long awaited smell
Of the first sample of rice
Which each house wife took such pride
In preparing from her hearth
No longer comes at harvest time.
115　Father time, how long, O how long
Will these giant trees remain
With us, so they can bring
Back memories of days
Now gone forever?

Notes

line 1　Time is personified.
line 4　*Dimeh* is the poet's village.
line 7　*tottering faces*　An example of a figure of speech known as synaesthesia
　　　which basically implies the transference of sensations to a different organ
　　　or means of perception. The effect is to create the impression of simul-

taneous response which makes the image richer, fuller and more concrete. *Tottering faces* here refer to the old men who are left in the village. We normally speak of *tottering feet* to refer to the unsteady gait of the aged.

line 8　In many African traditional communities *cottonwood trees* by their sheer size, height, hardiness and longevity are symbolic and significant landmarks. They provide protection and succour (they are important economic trees) and in many cases provided the first resting place for founders of villages. Thus they are regarded as totems, closely tied to the history of the villages.

line 13　*many rains and dries*　A peculiar usage which means years and refers to the passage of time. It is also an example of synecdoche, the use of a part to signify a whole.

line 19　*scions*　Descendants, children. It is used in relation to a noble or well-known family.

line 20　These children have been born into modern times and know little of the rich culture of their parents. They visit the villages occasionally but do not settle down to continue the heritage of their forefathers. They are the "restless comers".

line 27　*kpakpa*　A medicinal plant. When squeezed, one or two drops in each nostril are effective against common cold and other ailments.

line 36　*geplo*　Coined from *ge* (to see) and *plo* (blessing). It means the all-seeing spirit or supernatural power (God) that dispenses blessing and protection.

line 43　The little huts near streams where fresh and distilled palm-wine is sold and the blacksmith's shop are two popular meeting spots for men in the village. They meet in these places to drink, talk shop, gossip and sometimes discuss serious social issues.

line 55　*The patriarch*　The oldest man in the village, usually highly respected. Age is important in African societies. The oldest man in the village commands respect and attention and is never passed over on any social occasion.

lines 55–74　The custom of assigning special parts of any animal that is killed for food to specific members of the family or community is common in Africa. There are differences in the method of sharing, however. For instance in some communities it is the first son who gets the head of any animal that is killed.

line 67　Euphemism for having sexual knowledge of a woman.

line 70　*poro*　Community, ward or compound.

line 73　*privates*　Genitals of the animal. There are a number of these peculiar usages: *kins, gone ancestors*, for example.

line 85　*junior*　Popular name (sometimes a pet name) given to or epithet used in describing a son or male child.

line 94　*bushlore*　Indigenous folklore – tales, riddles etc. The use of *bush* here is anachronistic.

line 99　*kpo*　A popular game of seeds, also known as *Ayo* (Yoruba) and *Okwe* (Igbo).

line 100　A wrestling match is one of the important cultural symbols in most African societies.

line 104　*feuds*　Quarrels, usually accompanied by violence between two people or families over a long period of time.

line 105　A binding ritual act which symbolises "burying the hatchet", forgetting and forgiving and making up quarrels in traditional communities.

Questions

1 Discuss the theme of ancestors in this poem.
2 Can you recollect life in your village? How similar is it to the life the poet presents here of his childhood?
3 Pick out the various poetic techniques which the poet uses to make what looks like an ordinary narration poetic.

Commentary

This is a narrative poem in which the poet expresses his nostalgic longing for the kind of life he lived in his childhood in the village. This enviable and exemplary life in which there was peace and security has been undermined by changes introduced by the passage of time. Using the metaphor of time the poet presents a catalogue of scenes and practices that confirm the beauty, innocence, humaneness, veneration for ancestors and the tightly knit communal nature of our traditional societies before these healthy social or ethical values were abandoned for the predatory ones introduced by modern civilized ways. Starting with the totem tree, he progresses step by step to present various aspects of village life so that what we get in the end is a deftly painted picture of a lively traditional community. Throughout the poem, there is an implied contrast between what *Dimeh* was and what it is now. The poem ends subtly with a variation of its beginning, this time employing apostrophe and rhetorical questions. This ending provides an important cyclic structure to the poem and emphasises its theme which is a lament for the glorious days that are past. The final wish is that the giant trees which bear the secret of the society and are therefore important for her continuity should remain much longer so they can continue to renew memories of past days. The lyrical quality of the poem enhances its elegiac tone.

The poem reminds us of Oliver Goldsmith's "The Deserted Village" and is a variation on the theme of the past. The poet expresses a romantic wishfulness which desperately wants to freeze time.

Khona Khasu

Khona Khasu (pronounced Kona Kaisu) is one of the more prominent young writers and promoters of arts and culture in Liberia. Born in 1942 he had his education in Liberia, Britain and the United States where he took both a B.A. (New York) and an M.F.A. (Boston). He has held many positions in the cultural life of Liberia and has directed numerous plays in his native Liberia, in Britain and America where he spent time with "The African Theatre Company of Olatunji Centre of African Culture Inc." in New York. He has also produced television plays in Liberia and held some visiting lectureships in the United States. Many of his plays are still in manuscript.

Although Khasu would seem to have done most of his work in the theatre, he has written a lot of poetry too, the bulk of it in the manuscript entitled "The Seeds of Time". The poem used in this anthology is from that collection. Khasu in his poetry is concerned to rescue the African-ness of Africans from the buffettings of Western culture; his poems are deliberate attempts to whip up awareness among Africans and celebrate the distinctive qualities and force of African culture and tradition. Often his poems are tinged by the cutting irony and sarcasm that we find in the piece used here.

Our man on Broad Street

He came down Broad Street
ninety degrees temperature
humidity eighty
he was sweating
5 sweating profusely
but
he wore a grey flannel suit
a three-piece flannel suit
vest
10 coat
and pants
all evidence of his civilization
on his head sat a hat
you could see
15 he was hot
but he could not wear
his loose
cool shirt

made of thin-out cotton
20 he could not wear the dress
suitable for his oven-hot climate
no
not at this time
this place
25 he was going for an interview
he had to wear his civilization
    on his back
    on his head
    and on his arse
30 he was civilised
his dress showed it
at the intersection of Broad and Centre Streets
he met a strangely garbed man
resplendent in his colourful robe
35 the stranger said
he was from Ashanti
the other fellow
our European-dressed friend
speaking in muffled words
40 like the talk of the drum
accused the stranger of plotting
to turn Liberia into a Jungle City
"Your costume is too bright"
he grunted
45 "Your hair too thick
not brushed
your pants
which look like
stringed together ropes
50 are like the Liberian zebra".
the stranger slowly turned
and in a polite
gentle smile
retorted in a brilliant Oxford accent:
55 "Pardon sir
could you show me where the library is
I'd like also to know where the museum is
you see
sir
60 I'm a visitor
I'd also like to spend the night
at the theatre".
and when our European-dressed friend
turned to leave
65 the stranger pleaded:

"one moment
sir
where is the city park?"
Our civilization coated friend
70 stirred in confusion
in utter amazement
he had not heard of these things before
a brief moment of thought dragged itself out
he recollected himself and said:
75 "The library you'll find
at every street corner
it has signs
they say
DO NOT ORDER YOUR DRINKS UNTIL YOU ASK THE
    PRICE
80 oh yes
the bartenders are out to cheat
as for the park each
street is a park
be careful for the traffic
85 bonds for motor accidents come quite cheaply
a dollar and fifty cents only"
after much thought
"you're in the theatre district already"
the poor stranger crunched his teeth
90 tightened his body muscles
fluids flowing instantaneously
fortified to receive the shock
"Over yonder is playing COWBOYS AND INDIANS
here
95 WHAT'S DOING PUSSYCAT?
the corner theatre has SPARTACUS' GREAT DEEDS".
"I see my friend"
the quiet stranger said
"I think I've just decided
100 I'll pass the night
in my room
reading Wole Soyinka
thanks anyway
Ol' boy".

Notes

line 1   Broad Street is the main street in Liberia. Most of the big
    departmental stores, shops, offices and cinema houses are located on it.
line 11   *pants*   Trousers.
line 29   *arse*   The use of this colloquial word meaning bottom, conveys
    contempt in the tone of the poet.

298

line 34 This is a reference to the *Kente* cloth which is the traditional attire of the Ashanti of Ghana. It is handwoven, of bright colours and striking and pleasing patterns.

line 40 Many Africans, especially those who have spent some time in Britain try to imitate the British in their speech and only end up being inaudible and incomprehensible.

line 54 *Oxford accent* Also known as "received pronunciation" is the accent associated with English men who attended Public Schools and went to Oxford and Cambridge Universities in Britain. It is something of a class identity. It was for a long time the officially approved mode of speech, symbolising the best in English speech pattern, and only people with this accent were allowed to work in the BBC and some other areas of government.

lines 56–62 The library, the museum and the theatre are important cultural symbols.

line 68 *park* A large outdoor area with well-cut grass and beautiful gardens, usually enclosed, open to the public for relaxation.

line 85 *bonds* Tickets, stipulating fines to be paid, issued by the police to motorists who infringe traffic regulations.

lines 93–96 Cheap and sensational films that appeal to low taste.

line 102 Love for literature symbolised by Soyinka's writing, is upheld as evidence of good taste and appreciation for "high art" in contradiction to the "low art" represented by the films mentioned earlier.

Questions

1 What is the effect of the repetitions the poet uses in this poem?
2 Discuss the stages in the poet's unfolding of the characters of the two people in this poem.
3 Compare this poem with Soyinka's "Telephone conversation".
4 Do you see any weaknesses in this poem? Pick out any three areas you think are weak and give reasons for your choice.

Commentary

This is a hilarious poem in which the poet satirically mocks the ludicrous outward display of civilised bearing which merely conceals an ignorant and crude inner nature. He does this by contrasting two interlocutors: one of them dressed in a three-piece suit (a familiar sight on many of our streets) clearly unsuitable for the hot African climate but which has to be endured either because our colonial mentality prescribes such outfit for formal occasions or because we want to look civilised and correctly dressed; the other dressed in convenient traditional African attire. By a subtle use of irony and humour, the poet exposes the gruff and crude character of the man in three-piece suit as opposed to the polished and cultured nature of the man in traditional clothes.

This little episode serves as a criticism of our acquisition of what we wrongly regard as civilised Western ways. What matters is not the foolish aping of the superficial and even incongruous trappings of Western civilisation but the internalisation of the finer and beautiful qualities of Western culture. This observation goes to the very root of the problem of cultural conflict, especially its moral dimensions in African states, and makes the poem serious.

Jared Angira

Jared Angira was born in Kenya in 1947, attended the University of Nairobi, where he read a degree in Commerce and edited the well-known literary and creative writing magazine, *Busara*. He began writing poetry in his early undergraduate days and has published three collections of verse so far: *Juices*, 1970, *Soft Corals*, 1974, and *The Years Go By*, 1980.

He is a subtle poet, with a talent for apt and felicitous phrasing, as the two poems included in this anthology reveal. He also has a sense of humour, often used at his own expense. Like his fellow Kenyan, Ngugi wa Thiongo, he is very critical of political and social developments in Kenya.

No coffin, no grave

He was buried without a coffin
without a grave
the scavengers performed the post-mortem
in the open mortuary
5 without sterilized knives
in front of the night club

stuttering rifles put up
the gun salute of the day
that was a state burial anyway
10 the car knelt
the red plate wept, wrapped itself in blood its master's

the diary revealed to the sea
the rain anchored there at last
isn't our flag red, black, and white?
15 so he wrapped himself well

who could signal yellow
when we had to leave politics to the experts
and brood on books
brood on hunger
20 and schoolgirls
grumble under the black pot
sleep under torn mosquito net
and let lice lick our intestines

the lord of the bar, money speaks madam
25 woman magnet, money speaks madam
we only cover the stinking darkness
of the cave of our mouths
and ask our father who is in hell to judge him
the quick and the good.

30 Well, his diary, submarine of the Third World War
showed he wished
to be buried in a gold-laden coffin
like a VIP
under the jacaranda tree beside his palace
35 a shelter for his grave
and much beer for the funeral party

anyway one noisy pupil suggested we bring
tractors and plough the land.

Notes

line 3   scavengers Possibly vultures.
line 7   stutterng rifles Onomatopeia, describing the sound of the bullets flying
    from the rifles of the assassins.
line 14 Some of the colours of the national flag of Kenya.
line 16   signal yellow A colour different from those of the national flag. In
    other words, who could contradict the politicians who alone claimed they
    knew what was good for the nation.
lines 24–25 The swaggering of the politician at his favourite night club.
line 30   submarine of the Third World War (Layers upon layers of irony) (i)
    Literally, his diary is submarine, having been discovered in the sea; (ii)
    the diary's contents constitute the destructive weapons (submarines)
    responsible for the war of deprivation raging in the Third World; (iii)
    such acts of exploitation and irresponsibility as this politician's might
    eventually plunge the world into a third global war.

Questions

1 Identify the various details by means of which the ostentatious life style of
    the politician is suggested in the poem.
2 Comment on the irony in the following lines: 3, 8, 15, 28. Can you identify
    some others?
3 Would you say that the poet's language is brutal and his attitude callous?

Commentary

A satirical poem about the assassination of an arrogant politician whose body
is left outside a favourite night club, apparently to be devoured by vultures.
His diary washed into the sea by rain and discovered later, reveals both his
identity and his desire for an ostentatious burial.

This is a poem on a familiar aspect of contemporary African experience: African leaders' betrayal of the hopes that the attainment of political independence raises in the hearts of the ordinary citizens of the continent. The poet's anger against this betrayal is revealed in his overt identification with the youthful protesters who are the victims of the politicians' irresponsibility. Although he tries to dissociate himself from these protesters towards the end of the poem, his satire is nevertheless undermined by his obvious showing of his hand. The success of the poem, however, lies in the consistently beautiful local ironies of phrasing it contains.

Masked

We left with the radiant rays
of the gleaming golden sun
and ascended the woody hills
past the thick green grazing lea

5 and volubly forded
the swift rolling river
that had bellied
humus and clay from the forested hills.

We heard wolves howl
10 on the massive rocks
and ferried the lake
with a deafening stony silence.
We came to the spacious arena
the wide field with myriad blossoms
15 each calling seductively for nectar
each calling cloying with beauty.

We opened our virgin palms
and received the potent juice from each
and they synthesized with
20 the beauty we had carried
and all of us went wild
with weighty rucksacks on our backs
and leather sandals
and we flew like balloons in frenzy.

25 Some broke their legs
Some broke their arms
Some went tipsy with nectar
and lost their way homewards.

302

Amid seismic snares I came home
30 and the black ram fled from me
because of my queer odour
which I brought from sojourn.

I knocked on my mother's reed door
and it smelt of burnt cowdung and goat's urine
35 she reluctantly opened
and showed me to sit on the kavirondo mat
that lay dusty and dry on the rugged floor.
I asked her to open the windows
There were NONE
40 I looked up and saw wasps and cobwebs
on the black roof

I went out to admire the meadow
and she slammed the reed door behind
and I went in my pedestal din
45 to the tingy locale from where I came.

Behind twanged the leather troubadour
and shone the black canopy
while ahead lay a giant fabric of smoke
and the only promise came

50 from the wide grassless navy blue sky.

Notes

line 19 *synthesized* Combined or blended to make a new whole.
line 29 *seismic snares* Traps like the craters left by an earthquake.
line 31 *queer odour* It is noteworthy that the change that seems to have
    taken place in the traveller is associated with the sense of smell.
line 36 *kavirondo* A straw mat made of dry reeds.
line 44 *pedestal din* Quite an obscure phrase, which could refer to the after
    effect of the frenzied experience described in section 4 of the poem.
    Pedestal literally means a base which supports or upgirds. To set up on
    a pedestal means to regard highly. So pedestal din could refer to the
    highly regarded echo or after effect of the experience presented in lines
    17–28. It is also worth noting that both *din* and *tingy*, in the next line,
    normally refer to echoed sounds.
line 46 Note that *Behind* is contrasted with *ahead* in line 48.
    twanged A nasal sound made by plucking the strings of a musical
    instrument.
    the leather troubadour A travelling minstrel or singer or poet. The phrase
    refers back to lines 22–23, where the image of the traveller as
    someone interested in beauty, begins to emerge.
line 47 *the black canopy* Possibly refers back to the black roof of line 41.

Questions

1 This poem relies on a telling use of adjectives and adverbs. Pick out the most striking of these qualifiers in the first three sections of the poem. Do they tell you anything about the nature of the journey undertaken by the speaker?

2 How would you explain the mother's attitude to her son in sections 7 and 8, especially in lines 35 to 43 of the poem?

3 Would you consider sections 4 and 5 of the poem vague about the educational experience of the travellers?

4 There seems to be a contrast between the setting and experience in sections 1–5 and the last four sections of the poem. By paying attention to the various senses emphasised in these sections of the poem, indicate the significance of the contrast.

5 How adequate is the title of the poem and what does it reveal about the poet's attitude to the experience presented in the poem?

Commentary

This poem uses the metaphor of a journey and a stay abroad which transform the traveller, so that, on his return, he is "no longer at ease in the old dispensation", to use the familiar quotation from T. S. Eliot's poem, "Journey of the Magi". At first, the journey is through a specific landscape, but later, the destination – *the spacious arena, the wide field with myriad blossoms* – suggests that the journey is a metaphor for a transforming and alienating education. The emphasis seems to be on an initiation which engages and intoxicates the senses. The poem may very well be a critical comment on the poet's discovery of his vocation as a sensitive person: the last section (lines 46–50) certainly underlines the courage in embracing a future whose only promise is a *wide grassless navy blue sky*.

Kofi Anyidoho

Kofi Anyidoho comes from Wheta, in the Volta region of Ghana, the same village as Kofi Awoonor, his cousin. Anyidoho, who now teaches literature at the University of Ghana, attended two teacher training colleges before entering the University of Ghana as a mature student. After his first degree, he took an M.A. in Folklore at Bloomington, Indiana and obtained his Ph.D. in Comparative Literature at Austin, Texas.

Since 1978 he has published three volumes of poetry: *Elegy for the Revolution* (Greenfield Review Press, 1978) *A Harvest of our Dreams* (Heinemann 1984) and *Earthchild* (Woeli, 1985). He has also edited and contributed to two volumes of critical essays on African literature. His poetry has already won a number of prizes including the Langston Hughes prize, Davidson Nichol Prize and the BBC 'Arts and Africa' Poetry Award.

Anyidoho's poetry belongs very much in the tradition of the Ewe cantor, who assumes the mantle of the seer, the spokesman or the social conscience of the ethnic group. But although his roots are drawn from Ewe traditions his clan is the entire nation of Ghana, and beyond that, the black race and the whole of humanity. His poetry memorialises, in highly crafted language, the political problems of his native Ghana as well as the global problems of the black man. The two poems anthologised here come from the collections published in 1984 and 1985.

Hero and Thief

I was counting time in the heartbeat of the storm
when Fui and Enyo came riding through whirlwinds
she with the dream beauty of new rainbows and
he in his quiet way spoke of how
5 a nervous government sits on our bankrupt stool
wearing a gown of fantasy and hope
telling tales of foreign aid and godmothers
    at Christmas time. . .

Is it enough we search the private dreams of poets
10   when our lands nighmares give birth
    to strange desires
and our children draw their wishes in quicksands
    of the Earth?

Is it enough   is it enough we probe the pampered
15   dreams of poets
while our people scratch the dunghills of this Earth
where once the flowers bloomed and poured perfume
upon the pestilence of rotten memories?
Is it enough   is it enough we dream in foreign languages
20 and drink champagne in banquet halls of a proud people
while our people crack palm kernels with their teeth?

It is not enough it isn't enough
to go in search of the lone hero
while the common thief inherits our ancient stools . . .

25 There have been thieves before in our land
when the harvest left enough surplus for the thieving hand
and the thief never reaped much more than farm owner

But the harvest dance is gone
Our harvest gatherers crawl on empty granary floors
30 picking crumbs from termite's hope
brushing tears away   gathering memories
from ashes in the sand

Our people   Oh our people
How soon again in our hive
35   Shall we swarm around our HoneyComb?

So the thieving hand has reaped much more than farm owner
and the harvest dream transforms into slow funereal hopes
the rice harvest has gone to weaverbird
the corn-on-cob has gone to grasscutter
40 the yam-in-the-mound was carried off by rat
and now we sit and watch the flowering bean
and the ripened fruit of palm being plucked
at dawn by slippery hands of night workers . . .

Tomorrow at noon we'll flock the conference hall
45 the Academy of Sciences. We will hear learned talk.
The new guru and his splendid joke   the post-mortem
expertise   the learned complex talk upon
    post-harvest perspiration of yam tubers
    the who and the what went all wrong with what with whom

50 Is it enough is it enough to dream the Moon and Stars
When this Earth we own we can't possess?

306

Notes

line 1   The line describes a state of mind indirectly related to the storm outside. Counting time suggests watching to see how the storm will turn out. But the arrival of the two friends, out of the storm, precipitates the deepest thoughts – the storm – raging in the poet's mind.

line 2   *Fui and Enyo* (Tsikata)   Two friends who bring news from Ghana.

line 3   *the dream beauty of new rainbows*   Possibly refers to the peculiar relaxed beauty of an expectant woman.

line 5   *our bankrupt stool*   As in his other poem – "Long Distance Runner" – the use of the first person plural indicates the poet's assumption of the traditional role of the cantor, the spokesman for the ethnic group or clan; in this instance, the clan is the entire nation of Ghana.

lines 6–8   Seem to refer particularly to the short-lived civil government headed by Dr Hilla Limmann in Ghana, between August 1979 and December 1981. Ghana's economy was already in tatters when Limmann came to power. But in expectation of coming to an agreement with the World Bank and the IMF, Limmann kept promising that consumer goods would arrive in the shops for Ghanaians to enjoy Christmas. Of course, they never did, and Flight Lt. Jerry Rawlings overthrew Limmann's government on 31 December 1981.

lines 9–13   The questions which recur with increasing intensity in this section could come either from one of the visiting friends or the poet himself. Whatever their source, they raise doubts about the relevance of the poet's work in a situation of horrendous material deprivation. They are indeed an indication of the storm that has been raging in the poet's mind. The elaborate verse line in this section, with its emphatic repetitions, sounds the peal of thunder as the storm breaks out.

lines 17–18   These lines would seem to suggest a recurrent pattern of poverty followed by plenitude. But, as often happens in the Ewe dirge, the occasion for the song of lament is that things have gone beyond repair. This is exactly the point that emerges in lines 25 to 27.

line 21   For a similar image of destitution and penury see line 6 of Awoonor's 'More Messages'.

lines 28–43   Constitute a sustained dirge full of powerful imagery that seems to have been triggered by the Ewe proverb, "the thief never reaped more than the farm owner". But now that a common thief inherits our ancient stools, traditional wisdom is not enough to cope with the radical situation that has arisen. Hence the transformations of traditional wisdom and the extensions of the imagery we have in lines 36 to 43.

line 44   *Tomorrow* suggests a possible change of circumstances, such as the coup which toppled Nkrumah's regime in February 1966. For, after that coup, a series of lectures on the title, "What went wrong?" were given by academics, politicians, lawyers, theologians. Obviously this poet does not believe in the effectiveness of such post-mortem exercises. The reason would seem to lie in the emphatic answer he has already given in lines 22–24: "when thievery has become a common culture, it cannot take a single hero to rescue the nation." It requires the efforts of the whole community. And throughout this poem he has assumed the communal voice calling on the group to possess the land "we own".

Questions

1 In what ways does the speaker in the poem convey his attitude to the
government of his homeland in the first section of the poem?
2 Comment on the effect of the repeated lines and phrases in section 2.
3 Do you think lines 22–24 constitute an answer to the doubts raised about
the poet's role in the preceding section? Give reasons for your view.
4 Analyse the movement of the lines 36–43, paying attention to recurrent
sentence and phrase structures and their effect?
5 Identify two sections of the poem where the poet's sense of humour is
clearly evident.

Commentary

Notice in particular the poet's use of rich and sustained imagery. In the Intro-
duction we mentioned Kofi Anyidoho as one of the younger poets who not only
draw on the rich tradition of oral poetry, but are also renewing and extending
that tradition so that it illuminates contemporary African reality. This poem
certainly bears witness to the richness and subtlety of Anyidoho's art.

Long distance runner

From Frisco once
we drove across the wide yawn of the breezy bay
to the Oakland home of Mike who fixed
a memorial dinner for his years among our people

5 They call for song and I sing the story
of our wounds: the failures and betrayals
the broken oaths of war leaders grown smooth
with ease of civil joys

They laugh they clap they call for more

10 For a change just a little change I sing
your dirge about their land's defeat in the beauty
of her dawn: the ghost of Harlem standing guard
across their bridge of mirth their launching pad of dream and myth.
I sing also your long lament for grand Geronimo
15 Amerindian chieftain who opened his heart a bit too wide
the lonely horseman who now perhaps only may be
still rides his old stallion across their dream their myth
forever riding his memory among mirages along eternities
reserved for him among snowfields spread across the breast
20 of the Earth this Earth and all his Earth.

Halfway through your songs I see the folly
and the wisdom of our choice in the cold stare
the shifting look in the eyes of our hosts our very kind hosts

Who are we to throw back at a man the image of things
25 he strove so hard to burn to ashes in history's bonfires?

We know there is an agony in waiting for the long distance runner
who breaks the finisher's line for the judges to declare he

jumped the starter's gun stepped upon some other
runner's toes threw him off balance and off the race

30 And what is a race, Cousin, without the rules
without other runners?

But leave him alone leave him alone to his
glory looming large above his olive dreams.

(Bloomington, 23 November 1978)

Notes

line 1   *Frisco*   A shortened form of San Francisco on the West coast of the
U.S.A.

line 2   *yawn of the breezy bay*   The peninsula of San Francisco is linked on
its north-eastern side by a bridge several miles long (over the bay) to the
city of Oakland.

line 3   The colloquial word *fixed* – meaning "prepared or cooked a meal" –
continues the informal tone.

line 5   *song* and *sing*   Not music as such, but the traditional role the poet
has assumed as the cantor, the man who renders history orally.

line 7   *broken oaths of war leaders*   Again a traditional context is evoked by
this phrase: the "generals" of the traditional army (literally called "war
leaders") were under oath not to turn their weapons against civilian
authority. The poet therefore sees the many coups which have brought
soldiers to power in African states as the betrayal of their oaths to the
states.

line 11   *your dirge*   The reference is to Kofi Awoonor and his poem "Harlem
on a winter night". The two poets are in fact cousins, as line 30
indicates.

line 14   *Geronimo*   An American Indian or Amerindian hero who led his
people, the Apaches, against the white European invaders and colonizers
in the late nineteenth century. He lived from 1829–1909. Eventually, he
signed treaties of peace with them, trusting that they would keep their
word. But line 15 suggests that he was unwise in trusting the white
colonizers; for most of the land originally belonging to the Amerindians
was taken from them and the few of their descendants left are isolated
and confined in reserved areas.

lines 16–17   Geronimo was very much associated in the popular mind with the powerful black horse he rode into battle. But these lines suggest that Geronimo is hardly ever remembered as a hero. He remains a lonely isolated figure from the standard history of the continent of America.

line 18   riding his memory among mirages   Suggests that, even in death, Geronimo would recall the unfulfilled expectations he had of the treaties he made: treaties that led to the life of isolation for his descendants, separated from American cities by wide snowfields.

line 20   this Earth and all his Earth   Both the physical dwelling of the living descendants and the wide expanse of eternity in which Geronimo is isolated because he is hardly remembered.

line 25   A graphic description of the human tendency to forget an unpleasant past, which otherwise brings with it a sense of guilt.

Bloomington   It is significant that Bloomington is in Indiana, a state which bears the name of the aborigines of the continent, but in which the Amerindians are kept well out of sight.

Questions

1 This poem falls into three distinct sections. How would you decribe the tone of the speaker in the three different sections?

2 Refer to Awoonor's poem, "Harlem on a winter night" on page 219, and then offer an interpretation of the lines beginning, *the ghost of Harlem . . .* and ending *pad of dream and myth.*

3 Comment on the effectiveness of the phrase *the folly and the wisdom of our choice* in lines 21 and 22.

4 Identify and comment on the poet's use of irony in the poem.

5 How does the poet's sense of humour show in spite of his strong feelings about the central theme of the poem?

Commentary

This poem is a critical indictment of white American civilization, which, the poet suggests, emerged out of the betrayal of minority races like the Amerindians and Negroes. White Americans are unwilling to admit this and would rather not be reminded of it, as happens in the poem. But, taking the view that the advance towards civilization is like an athletic competition among the various peoples of the earth – a competition with inbuilt rules and regulations – the poet suggests that those who break the rules and imagine that they will win the race, will find themselves inevitably disqualified at the end.

But the more significant aspects of the poem are the strategies which enable the poet to make this stern moral judgment without sounding self-righteous. First, there is the informal setting and tone with which the poem opens and the role which this informality enables the poet to assume: the role of the licensed entertainer as in line 9 (*They laugh they clap they call for more*). Second, there is the communal voice with which he speaks, in the tradition of the oral poet who rehearses the history, not only of his own people, but of all mankind. His reflections are offered within the context of his admission of his own folly and the folly of his people. Finally there is the ambivalence of attitude summed up by the ironical last line in which we are not even sure how to take a glory that looms large above olive dreams.

Niyi Osundare

Niyi Osundare was born in 1947 in Ikere-Ekiti, Ondo State of Nigeria. He studied at Ibadan, Leeds and Toronto and now teaches stylistics in the Department of English, University of Ibadan. Osundare who is, perhaps, the best known voice of the younger generation of Nigerian poets, has been writing poetry for some time. His poems have won several prizes both nationally and internationally, the latest being the Africa Zone of the Commonwealth Poetry Prize. He is a published poet and some of his published collections are: *I Sing of Change*, *Songs of a Marketplace*, *Village Voices*, *The Eye of the Earth* and *The Nib in the Pond*, besides his numerous poetry contributions to journals, magazines and newspapers. He is on the Editorial Board of *Opon Ifa*, an Ibadan based poetry journal and has also tried his hand at writing plays.

The titles of Osundare's collections reflect the concerns of his poetry. He aims to demystify poetry, make it accessible to the ordinary person and also use it to chastise his society and urge moral and social change. His diction is simple, with generous doses of indigenous words and phrases, his imagery and settings are for the most part rural, drawing freely on traditional proverbs and wisdom. His verse is lyrical, but his art is sophisticated, thus belying its surface simplicity.

A song for Ajegunle

You stretched out your calloused hands
Switched on your weed-infested smile
And spread your battled history
Like a tattered mat for my calling feet

5 I who like a curious bird
Have seen you sprawled out
Like an empty bag on the threshold
Of Ikoyi's bursting barns

Through roads portholed by callous rains
10 Through hovels eaves-deep in swelling pools
Through gutters heavy with burdens
Of cholera bowels
Through the feverish orchestra
Of milling musquitoes

311

15   I saw you sprawled out
      Like the daub of apprentice painter

      Here evenings are pale smokes
      Snaking out of idle kitchens
      The toothless swagger of beer parlours
20   The battering clamour of weeping wives
      The satanic rumble of supperless stomachs
      The salaaming clarion of manacling mosques

          I saw you sprawled out
          Like a sheath with an absent cutlass

25   And night, ah night, when it comes:
      The shadowy thunder of hurrying feet
      The hooded stench of nightsoil pails
      The brooding brow of startless pangs
      The sweaty stupor of crowded mats
30   The gutsy blast of angry guns

          I saw you sprawled out
          Like a stream without a bed

      Morning here is a crow without a cock
      Taps without water, tables without bread
35   Children without schools, schools without children
      And shoeless hordes drifting
      Drifting dreamily to Ikoyi chores
      Or Victoria's own Island where lawns
      Are green with sweat
40   And Senior Service brats murder the peace
      Of tired nannies

          I saw you sprawled out
          Like a cat with hidden claws

      Ajegunle
45   Oh dreg of our foaming wine
      Graveyard of our truant conscience
      Cesspool of brewing rage

          I saw you sprawled out
          Like a wounded snake

Notes

Title *Ajegunle* One of the high density areas of suburban Lagos in Nigeria where many low-income people live. Notorious for its insecurity and poor sanitation. A ghetto, contrasted with Ikoyi and Victoria Island which are fashionable and exclusive for the rich and powerful.

line 1 *calloused hands* Hands covered with hard and thick skin. Caused by poor nutrition or hard work or both.

line 2 *weeds* Wild plants which obstruct the growth of crops or flowers. Green matter on unhealthy teeth. The smile here is reluctant; wry because it conceals a troubled mind.

line 3 Life in Ajegunle has always been a fight and struggle against varied forces of destruction. Life here is like a battle.

line 5 *curious* Inquisitive, eager to know or learn.

line 6 *sprawled out* Spread out in a disorderly and formless manner.

lines 7–8 *An empty bag* is flaccid and flat. The poet condenses much meaning into these two lines. There is a sense in which Ajegunle can be seen as Ikoyi's doormat. But more significantly here, the harvest image of *bursting barns* contrasts the deprivation of Ajegunle with the over-abundance of Ikoyi.

line 9 *portholes* Small, usually circular windows or openings in a ship that let in light or air. They are also the rows of fixed windows along the side of an aircraft.

line 10 *hovels* Small, dirty places for living.

line 16 *daub* Badly painted picture, done without much skill.

line 19 *beer parlours* Small drinking places usually run by women, a bit more intimate and less expensive than standard bars and clubs. Tend to be frequented by the less privileged, and can be seedy.

line 22 *salaam* Muslim greeting meaning "peace" in Arabic, usually accompanied by a bow.
clarion Refers to both the instrument and the loud and clear sound it produces. These days the muezzin makes these calls through loud speakers when ordering Muslim faithful to prayer.
manacling Fettered, shackled and constrained. Religion: especially the fanatical form, has the ability to imprison the mind and shut out rational reasoning. Most poor and despondent people seek refuge in religion; religion becomes an opiate and this poses many problems, including the spiritual.

line 29 *stupor* A state in which one cannot think. The ill-ventilated and over-crowded hovels would induce sweat and stupor in a hot climate

line 38 *Victoria Island* Named after Queen Victoria who ruled England and the British Empire 1837–1901. An exclusive part of Lagos.

line 39 The sweat of the inhabitants of Ajegunle ensures the beauty and luxury of Ikoyi and Victoria Island. These poor people who minister to Ikoyi and Victorian Island residents tend and water the beautiful lawns.

line 40 cf. Shakespeare's *Macbeth*, Act II, scene II, line 35.

line 45 *dreg(s)* Sediment or worthless part of anything; dirty remains of drink that sink to the bottom of the glass and are thrown away. Ajegunle represents that portion of society that can exist only when the conscience of those in authority is dead and buried. These powers are selfishly (and almost irresponsibly) interested in the luxury of their class to the utter neglect of others.

line 47 *Cesspool* An underground pit or container in which sewage is gathered. A frightening image of bottled up anger and potential destructive fire.

Questions

1 Why does the poet call this poem a song? How appropiate is the title of the poem?
2 How does the poet convey the impressions of the physical environment of the evenings and nights in Ajegunle? (Take time to look at the images and the scenes they conjure up and pay attention to the choice of words.)
3 An interesting aspect of this poem is its structure. Can you attempt your own discussion of this feature?
4 Is it appropriate to describe this poem as protest poetry? Do you think it bears any resemblance to other poems in this anthology which are characterised as protest poetry?

Commentary

This poem is a song of pain, a good example of the poetry of social conscience (and protest) which draws attention to the gross inequalities that are allowed to persist in society, warns of the threat which such injustices pose to social order and the upheaval which is certain to follow when the "wounded snake" decides to strike.

The poet-persona goes out to investigate Ajegunle and the poem is a description of his impression of the place. On one level the poem is a series of intense snap-shots etched out by dense images that convey a sick and depressing environment from the point of view of the physical surroundings and inhabitants of Ajegunle. The poem presents a depressing picture of hunger, of drunks and others who take their frustrations out on their wives, and of desperate people who have turned unthinkingly to religion for solace. If the nights evoke terror and discomfort during which hordes scurry home to escape the mindless plunder and murder of robbers only to endure imprisonment in insanitary hovels, the mornings are equally cheerless for they portend long days of drudgery and exploitation. On another level, the predicament of Ajegunle is constantly sharpened by the striking contrast of it to Ikoyi and Victoria Island. This contrast is always there in the mind of the poet and it gives edge to his observations. Finally, the two-line refrains not only have an integrative structural function, they also carry the burden of meaning of the poem and the poet's intention which is to warn. Through carefully selected and graded similes which show a buildup of discontent – empty sheath without a cutlass, stream without a bed, cat with hidden claws, wounded snake – the poet draws attention to Ajegunle's potential for destructive action or vengeance.

Funso Ayejina

Like Osundare, Ayejina is one of the best known of the younger generation of Nigerian writers, especially poets. Born in 1950, he attended the Universities of Ibadan, Acadia (in Canada) and the West Indies where he specialised in the literature of that region. He now teaches in the Department of Literature in English, University of Ife. Apart from writing poetry, he has also written short stories, radio plays and critical essays. His poetry has appeared in such journals as *Okike*, *Greenfield Review* and *Opon Ifa* and some of his poems have won international prizes.

His poetry is marked by an intense exploration of indigenous idioms and images, the castigation of the lapses and failures of society, especially of the ruling class, and warning of possible upheavals. His familiarity with African and West Indian cultures and literatures gives some of his poetry the advantage of a wide spectrum from which to draw motifs and images. The bulk of his poetry is contained in the manuscript volume entitled "A Letter to Lynda and Other Poems" in the Ife Monograph series on literature and criticism.

And so it came to pass. . .

And so it came to pass
many seasons after the death of one Saviour
that a new crop of saviours, armed with party programmes
came cascading down our rivers of hope;
5 poised for the poisoning of our atlantic reservoir
they sought out the foxes in the family
to whom they gave their thirty pieces of silver
in local and foreign exchange
for the secrets of the passage—
10 way into the castle of our skins . . .

men we had taken for fearless warriors
as protectors of our secret recipes
suddenly turned crabs, carapace and all
shedding shame like water from duck-backs,
15 seeing sideways beyond the good of all
to the comfort of the selves;
and with their divination bags of tricks
slung over arrogant shoulders
they crawl over our dreams

20 under the cover of moonless nights
sidestepping traps, destroying hope
they turn our green august of rains,
of showers with which to persuade crops
towards harvest-circles
25 around whose fire we would have exchanged
happy tales of toil
into an orgy of furious flames. . .
And so it came to pass
that our saviours gave us a gift of tragedy
30 for which we are too dumb-struck to find a melody.

Notes

line 1   Biblical: many stories in the Bible begin this way.

lines 2–3   For the past twenty years, Nigeria has been ruled by different regimes of military juntas and a civilian government that made up the second Republic. Each regime that comes starts by presenting itself as the saviour of the people and raising the hopes and expectations of the citizenry, with wild promises, but ends up appearing worse than the group it succeeded. The military government headed by General Obasanjo handed over power voluntarily to a civilian government amid much jubilation and high hopes.

line 5   atlantic reservoir   Conjures up many images. Nigeria is a large country and the metaphor here may be referring to her size; the country is bound on the south by the Atlantic Ocean and the connection here is easy to see: the people are optimists and have a large reservoir of hope – reference is to their great expectations which are dashed.

line 6   foxes   Cunning and deceitful animals.

line 7   thirty pieces of silver   Judas Iscariot in the Bible betrayed Christ by accepting this amount from Christ's enemies.

line 8   local . . . exchange   Refers to the national currency, the naira; *foreign exchange* refers to hard convertible currency like the pound sterling, the American dollar, the Deutsch mark, the Japanese Yen, etc.

line 10   George Lamming wrote a novel called *In the castle of my skin*.

line 12   secret recipes   The constitution and the law hold the key to successful government, provided their provisions are firmly and fearlessly applied.

line 13   The *crab* image here is strong. A crab is a symbol of deceit; it does not crawl or walk straight, it walks sideways and crooked. Besides, *it* is protected by its hard shell (*carapace*). To say that someone does not see straight or walk straight is to say that he is dishonest.

lines 22–27   The civilian government of the second Republic in Nigeria was reputed to be the most profligate, irresponsible and corrupt in Nigerian history. They destroyed the economy of the country and brought so much hardship on the people, it will take many years for Nigeria to recover from their excesses. They were ousted by a coup d'état in 1983 and succeeded by the government of General Buhari.
Compare the warmth of fire in the hearth around which the household gathers with the fire of the guns of destruction.

Questions

1 Attempt a critical analysis of the saviour image which the poet explores in this poem.

2 What picture of the political scene does the poet present in this poem?

Commentary

This is a denunciatory poem in which the poet expresses disgust at the chicanery of politicians who came promising the people much comfort but ended up exploiting and ruining them. The strong biblical flavour in the narrative structure of the poem and the reference to Judas re-inforces the theme of deception. The crab image further enhances this point in the poem. The exploration of the unconscionable actions of politicians on whom the people had reposed much hope ends on a sad note, for the people *are too dumb-struck to find a melody*. This is a grim picture of the helpless situation in which most African societies find themselves as they are betrayed by one leadership after another. This poem is the fifth movement of a long sequence of poems entitled "The year of hope-less-hope".

Glossary

CAESURA   Pause or break in a line of poetry dictated by the rhythm. Is either initial (near the beginning), medial (in the middle) or terminal (near the end).

ENJAMBMENT   Principally used to describe the running-on of sense beyond the second line of a couplet into the first line of the next; generally used to describe run-on lines. Important for lyricism, musicality and rhythmic flow of verse.

EXTEMPORE   To perform on the spur of the moment without previous practice.

HYPERBOLE   Deliberate choice of words which give an exaggerated image of something by saying that it is like something bigger or smaller, for emphasis. Common in heroic poetry. cf. "Salute to the Elephant".

IMAGE   Verbal and imaginative representation, evoking sensations or impressions which make possible a more immediate understanding or perception of an idea or experience.

IRONY   Use of words which are clearly opposite to the professed meaning; works by awareness and exploitation of incongruity between words and their meaning, actions or results.

METAPHOR   Mode of comparison which, without using *as* or *like*, implicitly transfers quality from one thing to another by identifying them or substituting one for the other or stating that one thing is another. 'He was a tiger in the fight.'

METRE   Regular pattern of stressed and unstressed syllables in a line of poetry. The basic unit is the *foot* which is iambic, trochaic, anapaestic, dactylic, spondaic or pyrrhic depending on number of syllables and position of the stress in the foot.

OXYMORON   Juxtaposition of two words with opposite meanings to heighten effect, e.g. 'Dangerous safety', in 'In memoriam', p. 54.

PARADOX   A statement which on the surface seems self-contradictory and impossible but which has some essential truth and validity.

PARALLELISM   Placing phrases or sentences of similar construction and meaning side by side or in sequence to balance, contrast or reinforce each other. Common in oral, and satiric poetry. Important for musical and incantatory quality of verse.

PERSONIFICATION Attribution of human qualities or feelings to inanimate or abstract objects, or the representation of an abstract idea or quality by a human figure.

PROVERB Short pithy saying, hallowed by long and common usage, embodying a general truth.

RHYME Identical or similar sound patterns in poetry. They may occur within or at the end of the line (internal or end rhyme).

RHYTHM Sense of flow or regular movement communicated by the stress patterning (arrangement of stressed and unstressed syllables) in a poem. Overall rhythm is determined by the metrical variations.

SARCASM Bitter remark intended to hurt someone's feelings by using words which clearly mean the opposite of what is thought or felt.

SIMILE Explicit imaginative comparison between two things using *like* or *as* in such a way that attention is drawn to a particular quality which is thereby enhanced.

SYMBOL Object, sign, situation, shape or action which represents a person, idea or value. A symbol is elastic and dynamic and means more than its immediate referent suggests. It is a concrete image expressing an emotional or abstract idea.

SYNECDOCHE Figure of speech in which the part stands for the whole: eg 'Ten mouths' to mean 'ten people'; or 'Sine to Seine' to mean 'Senegal to France' where the rivers stand for the countries, in 'In memoriam' on p. 54.

TONE Writer's attitude toward his subject and audience reflected in the manner, mood and moral outlook implied in the work. May be serious or light, formal or intimate, scornful or sympathetic, direct or ironic.

EPIGRAM Originally a short poem of two or four rhyming lines making a telling, often humorous statement. Now any brief single line which sums up a poem is referred to as epigrammatic.

EUPHEMISM Use of a mild, vague or indirect term to avoid using a more blunt or coarse expression.

MONOLOGUE Literally, a one-person conversation. Hence an address by a single character to an assumed audience which reveals the character's own thoughts, desires and motivation. e.g. 'The Song of Malaya', p. 156.

MYTH   Originally a traditional or folk story or account of the creation. e.g. 'The Myth of the Bagre'. Now, any imaginative account of nature or experience can become a myth. e.g. 'Cactus', p. 46, and 'Three daybreaks', p. 50.

ONOMATOPEIA   Use of sounds echoing the meaning of the lines of verse in which they occur. e.g. sounds imitating the wind in 'The dry season', p. 129.

PUN   Play upon words which are either identical or similar in sound, but very different in meaning. e.g. the words *beer* and *bier* in 'Post mortem', p. 193.

RITE/RITUAL   Well-defined actions undertaken for their religious or sacred meaning and effect, e.g. the rite of initiation in 'The myth of the Bagre', p. 20. The individual activities making up the rite are the rituals. e.g. the drinking of the guinea corn beer, in the same poem.

SONNET   Poem of fourteen lines structured by means of regular rhymes into two or three units of thought, plus an epigrammatic summing-up. Three of Dennis Brutus's poems in this volume are sonnets or variations on the sonnet form.

UNDERSTATEMENT   The opposite of hyperbole; a representation which underemphasises the importance of the subject.

WITTICISM   Humorous or clever remark, striking by its brevity and aptness.